HUNTER

FROM THE COCKPIT, No 11

MAC McEWEN

PUBLICATIONS

Contents

INTRODUCTION

Air Commodore Mac McEwen AFC

THERE is an old fighter pilot saying, 'If it looks right, it'll fly right'—and if ever an aircraft bore out the truth of that saying, it was the Hawker Hunter. It had a beauty that belied its malignant purpose as a lethal war machine, and its smooth, elegant design marked it as being something that was in a class of its own. It was often described as being like a jet-engined version of the Spitfire, and it was so loved by pilots everywhere that it became something of an icon in the fighter world.

Its introduction into service, however, was fraught with problems, and it was some time—and only after a number of modifications had been incorporated—before it came to be accepted as the thoroughbred that it really was. The reasons for these early short-comings were more the result of the circumstances at the time of the aircraft's introduction rather than any lack of application by those responsible.

The Hunter was introduced in the 1950s at a time when the nation was pretty well still bankrupt after the massive effort of World War II, and most politicians were sceptical about any proposals for

new expensive armaments. They were also doubtful about the viability of supersonic flight in the light of dire warnings they had been given by the Chief Scientific Officer of the time, who once declared that man would probably be unable to cope at speeds beyond the sound barrier. The public, too, were fed up with war, and showed little interest in new military developments. So, if some of the attempts to introduce new military equipment then may now seem somewhat half-hearted, it is easy to understand why. It should also be remembered that these were the early days of jet operations, when the designers and engineers—not to mention the pilots—really were exploring the frontiers of science, and so some mistakes were inevitable.

Below: Personnel of No 257 Squadron and some of their Hunter Mk 2s at Wattisham in November 1954, all but one of which is yet to receive its yellow and green unit markings. The Squadron was the first to take delivery of the Sapphire-engined version of the aircraft, although its sister-unit at the Suffolk airfield, No 263, would be soon re-equipped too.
Right: Three Hunter Mk 4s and a two-seat Mk 7 trainer (leading) of No 4 Flying Training School—the RAF's fast-jet conversion unit, based at RAF Valley in Anglesey—overflying the Menai Bridge, in the mid-1970s.

Against that background, in March 1948 Sir Sydney Camm, the Chief Designer at Hawkers, set about satisfying the requirements of Specification 3/48, based on a design labelled P.1067, which was intended to be a replacement for the RAF Meteor. Three P.1067 prototypes were ordered, two with the new Rolls Royce AJ.65 axial jet called the Avon and producing 7,500 pounds of static thrust, and one with an Armstrong Siddeley Sapphire engine, which gave 8,000 pounds of static thrust. The idea behind this was akin to an insurance policy: by providing two choices of engine, there was an option if one of them proved to be unreliable in trials. The first P.1067 prototype, WB188, was flown from Boscombe Down on 20 July 1951 by Squadron Leader Neville Duke.

By now the P.1067 had been named 'Hunter', and, in keeping with the normal practice at that time, it was ordered into full production at Kingston and Blackpool (for the Avon-powered F.1) and at Armstrong Whitworth's plant at Coventry (for the Sapphire-engined F.2). This procedure was meant to save time and ensure a speedy introduction into

service, but the problem with that was that if the trials on the three prototypes showed that there were problems that needed to be solved before the aircraft appeared on the squadrons, it was going to be too late! With the Meteor palpably incapable of dealing with the current threat and in urgent need of replacement, and with the recent failure of the Supermarine Swift as a high-level fighter, the Government faced a further possibly embarrassing loss of face if the Hunter also failed. Thus it was decided that the risk of the P.1067 trials aircraft throwing up some major defects just had to be taken.

In the event, the Government more or less got away with it—but only just. On the face of it, the first Hunter prototype was flown in mid-1951 and the first squadrons were equipped only three years later in the case of the Mk 1s (to No 43 Squadron at Leuchars) and the Mk 2s three and a half years later, when the Wattisham wing was re-equipped. Problem solved, therefore: by 1955 the RAF had a force of supersonic fighter aircraft to meet the current Soviet threat, and the Air Ministry could congratulate itself on a job well done.

In practice, it was not quite like that. Neither of the two Hunter types could be considered operational initially because neither could satisfactorily fire its guns. In the case of the Avon-engined Mk 1, the engine tended to go out when the guns were fired, whilst in the Mk 2 the vibration caused the nosewheel to jam in the 'up' position. The early trials showed, too, that tailplane control was inadequate at high speeds and that a so-called 'all-flying' tailplane was needed. To add to these problems, the engines, particularly the Sapphire, were found to be unreliable and subject to catastrophic failures. Perhaps most crucially of all, the aircraft had insufficient fuel capacity.

COURTESY HOWARD N. TANNER Jr

But all these problems were dealt with in time, and the Hunter came to be regarded as one of the great fighters—powerful, manœuvrable, versatile, and more than a match for its peers. It was little wonder, then, that it remained in service in one form or another for over fifty years and was sold to no fewer than twenty-two other countries throughout the world, becoming one of the few worldwide successes that our aviation industry has been able to claim. In total, 1,972 Hunters were built.

Below: WN948, a Hunter Mk 2 of No 257 Squadron, immaculately presented in late 1954. The 'sister' squadron at Wattisham, No 263, was at this time still equipped with Meteor Mk 8s—two of which can be seen in the background—though would shortly also receive its new swept-wing mounts.

REQUIREMENT

Air Commodore Mac McEwen AFC

T HE introduction of jet-engined aircraft towards the end of World War II revolutionised the aviation world, of course, but few realised at the time what an astonishing rate of development would be witnessed over the next decades. As new aircraft and engines were introduced, improved replacement designs appeared seemingly overnight and new threats increasingly made air-defence aircraft obsolete almost as soon as they were declared operational.

In the immediate aftermath of the war, it may have seemed initially that Great Britain had a sound defence force in the Meteor fleet, but it soon became apparent to all that the subsonic, straight-winged Meteor would be unable to meet the emerging threat from the Soviet Union, with jet bombers such as the Il-28 coming rapidly on stream.

As early as 1944, work had begun in the United States on a swept-wing superiority fighter, which became the North American F-86 Sabre. Its design was based on a mass of data captured from Germany at the end of the war, and especially made use of the research carried out by Messerschmitt into the advantages of using swept wings to delay the onset of compressibility and allow higher Mach-number speeds than had previously been possible. The first production F-86 flew in 1948 and the aircraft entered US Air Force service in March 1949, in time for the Korean War, which broke out the following summer.

The Sabre performed spectacularly well in Korea against the Russian MiG-15, itself an excellent swept-wing fighter with a high turn of speed. Both aircraft were supersonic in a dive. Against this sort of competition, the Meteor was much inferior, and although some Meteors did take part in the Korean War, it was only in a minor rôle.

On the home front, even the RAF's bomber fleet was soon outstripping the fighter force in terms of both speed and height. The English Electric Canberra bomber flew in 1949; it had a service ceiling of

Right: The P.1067–the prototype Hunter–shows off its exceptionally clean lines for the camera during a sortie in the summer of 1951. The original paint finish was pastel green, but in due course the aircraft would be modified and resprayed–and achieve international renown as the World Air Speed record holder.

8

COURTESY PHILIP JARRETT

48,000 feet, and in 1953 set a height record of over 63,000 feet. The poor old Meteor could not match this sort of performance, and in the annual Fighter Command exercises, Canberras acting at targets had to be told to come down 10,000 feet from their normal operating altitudes to give the Meteors a chance of catching them! Anyone who doubted that the Meteor needed replacing, therefore, had only to read the conclusions of the reports into the annual exercises to be convinced otherwise. It was clear to all that the replacement had to be a swept-wing fighter that was powerful enough to be able not only to go supersonic but also to operate well at high level—somewhere in excess of 50,000 feet.

Left: The first three second-generation jet fighters to serve in the RAF. In the lead is a US-designed Sabre, a stop-gap aircraft purchased pending the arrival in service of the indigenous Swift (to port) and Hunter (to starboard)—although, in the event, the Swift demonstrated shortcomings as an interceptor and served principally in the fighter-reconnaissance rôle (as seen here). All three aircraft in the photograph are serving with the 2nd Tactical Air Force, RAF Germany, the Hunter sporting the 'sharkmouth' of No 112 Squadron.

Right: Hunter forerunners—the Hawker P.1040 (upper photograph), which was developed into the Royal Navy's Sea Hawk fighter, and the Hawker P.1081, essentially a swept-wing version of the Sea Hawk that did not go into production. Strong hints of the future Hunter are evident here, in particular in the design of the engine intakes.
Below: WB188, the first prototype Hunter, in its original configuration. The lines of the aircraft barely changed throughout the Hunter's long and distinguished career.

Above: WB202 was the Armstrong-Siddeley Sapphire-powered Hunter prototype (P.1067). It was retained by Hawker Aircraft and used for development
work, including the experimental installation of Firestreak air-to-air missiles.
Below: A glimpse of the September 1952 Farnborough Air Show, with the
second P.1067 prototype prominent. This was an exciting era in British
aviation, years before the dominance of 'shared' international aircraft
projects: a Hawker Sea Hawk is in the left foreground; a Supermarine Type
541 Swift prototype–the Hunter's great rival–and the same company's
'butterfly-tailed' Type 508 prototype (which would eventually lead to the
Royal Navy's Scimitar fighter) are parked behind; a Bristol Britannia airliner
commands the left background; a Fairey Gannet is seen with its wings folded

at far left; and a Vickers Viscount airliner and an Avro Shackleton maritime
patrol aircraft are seen on the right, with a (partially shrouded) English
Electric Canberra bomber nestling between them. In the centre background
is the unique jet-powered Short Sperrin bomber.
Opposite: The two-seat Hunter trainer was not an immediate priority in the
light of international politics in the early 1950s and the consequent need to
build as many modern fighters as quickly as possible, but it started to take
shape in 1953 with the P.1101, the prototype (XJ615) seen here. However,
development difficulties, arising principally from unacceptable airflow
patterns around the cockpit fairing, exacerbated the delay and the first
production aircraft was not delivered to the Royal Air Force until 1958.

SPECIFICATIONS
HAWKER HUNTER Mks 1–12

Manufacturer: Hawker Aircraft Ltd, Kingston-upon-Thames, Surrey. Production at Kingston, Blackpool and Dunsfold and by Sir W. G. Armstrong Whitworth Aircraft Ltd at Baginton, Coventry.

Chief Designer: Sir Sydney Camm.

Powerplant: One Rolls-Royce Avon Mk 113 developing 7,500lb (3,400kg, 33.36kN) static thrust or (Hunter Mk 4, typically) Mk 115 developing 8,000lb (3,630kg, 35.59kN) or (Hunter Mk 6) Mk 203 developing 10,000lb (4,535kg, 44.48kN) or (Hunter Mk 7, Mk 8) Mk 122 developing 7,550lb (3,425kg, 33.58kN) or (Hunter Mk 9, Mk 10) Mk 207 developing 10,150lb (4,605kg, 45.15kN) or (Hunter Mk 2, Mk 5) one Armstrong Siddeley Sapphire Mk 101 developing 8,000lb (3,630kg, 35.59kN).

Dimensions: Length overall 45ft 10in (13.97m) or (Mk 7, Mk 8) 48ft 10½in (14.92m) or (Mk 10) 46ft 1in (14.05m); wing span 33ft 8in (10.26m); height 13ft 2in (3.97m); wing area (gross) 340.0 sq ft (31.59m^2) or (Mks 6–11) 349.0 sq ft (32.42m^2).

Weights: Empty 12,128lb (5,500kg), (Mk 2) 11,973lb (5,430kg), (Mk 4, Mk 5, Mk 11) 12,543lb (5,690kg), (Mk 6) 12,760lb (5,785kg), (Mk 7, Mk 8) 13,360lb (6,060kg), (Mk 9) 13,010lb (5,900kg), (Mk 10) 13,100lb (5,940kg); loaded (clean) 16,200lb (7,350kg), (Mk 2) 16,300lb (7,395kg), (Mk 4, Mk 5, Mk 11) 17,100 (7,755kg), (Mk 6) 17,750lb (8,050kg), (Mk 7, Mk 8) 17,200lb (7,800kg), (Mk 9) 18,000lb (8,165kg), (Mk 10) 18,090lb (8,205kg); max. overload (Mk 9, Mk 10) 24,000lb (10,885kg).

Armament: Four (Mk 7, Mk 8 one) 30mm Aden cannon with 135–150rds/gun, plus (Mks 4 and later) up to 2,000lb (905kg) of underwing stores. No gun armament fitted to Mk 11.

Performance: Maximum speed (clean, at 36,000ft or 10,970m) 535kts (615mph, 990kph, Mach 0.93), (Mk 2, Mk 4, Mk 5, Mk 11) 540kts (622mph, 1,000kph, Mach 0.94), (Mk 6, Mk 9, Mk 10) 545kts (628mph, 1,010kph, Mach 0.95, (Mk 7, Mk 8) 530kts (608mph, 980kph, Mach 0.92); climb to 36,000ft (clean) 9.8min, (Mk 2, Mk 5) 8.2min, (Mk 4, Mk 11) 9.85min, (Mk 6, Mk 9, Mk 10) 7.5min, (Mk 7, Mk 8) 12.5min; service ceiling 50,000ft (15,250m) approx.

Number built: (Exc. prototype, exported and licence-built aircraft) 1,077 (139 Mk 1s, 45 Mk 2s, 349 Mk 4s, 105 Mk 5s, 384 Mk 6s, 45 Mk 7s, 10 Mk 8s); 40 ex Mk 4s converted to Mk 11, 152 ex Mk 6s to Mk 6A/Mk 9, 33 ex Mk 6s to Mk 10, one ex Mk 9 to two-seat Mk 12. One Mk 3 converted from P.1067.

So, enter the Hawker Hunter. Early design consid-erations inevitably centred around the perennial question of whether the new fighter should have two engines or one, and whether it should be a single-seater or have a crew of two. Two engines gave the obvious advantages of extra power and greater safety, but also increased the weight of the aircraft and created greater complexity, with more components that could go wrong. Many would argue that a single powerplant, properly designed, could be just as safe, and could provide a greater power-to-weight ratio and thus superior performance.

Similarly, the argument for two crewmen rather than just one seems obvious at first sight, as, in a high-workload environment, two should be able to cope better than a pilot on his own. The other side of the coin, however, is that two cockpits and ejection seats would add to the all-up weight and complexity, and, with two people involved, it could be difficult to achieve the high degree of teamwork

AD HOC COLLECTION

Above, left: WB188 in its reincarnation as the Hunter Mk 3 and the World Absolute Speed record holder. In the hands of pilot Squadron Leader Neville Duke, it reached 727.6mph on 7 September 1953. This souvenir photograph was produced to mark the event. Above: A publicity photograph of WB188 in its original state and its original pale green finish

COURTESY PHILIP JARRETT

AD HOC COLLECTION

Above and left: The red-painted Mk 3 WB188 differed from production aircraft in a number of respects, notably in being fitted with a reheat-equipped Rolls-Royce Avon R.A.7R. It also sported a new nose cone, side-mounted air brakes and, briefly, a revised windscreen. None of these modifications would be taken up by service aircraft.

needed in a high-pressure fighter combat situation. Much of a fighter pilot's performance has to be based on instinctive action and reaction, and there would be precious little time for consultation in most combat situations. Another, more cynical consideration is that to maintain an aircrew workforce of twice as many individuals would be more difficult to manage—and would cost twice as much in terms of wages and pensions and so on. Some may feel, therefore, that the Treasury's view may have held greater sway in this discussion than that of the operational planners and the engineers. In any event, when the Air Ministry finally presented its specification requirement, the decision was that the new aircraft should be a single-seat, single-engined machine.

Opposite, upper: Hunter fuselage construction at Langley, late 1954, with centre fuselage sections in the right background and mated assemblies in the left background. Amongst the forty-plus nose sections visible here are assemblies for Mk 6s and Mk 50s (Swedish export aircraft).

Opposite, lower: A view of the Hunter wing jig shop at Hawker's Kingston-upon-Thames premises. Port and starboard assemblies can be identified by reference to the undercarriage bays apparent on the lower surfaces.

Above: Rear fuselage assemblies at Langley. The temporary stencilled serial numbers identify these components as part of the second production batch of F.4s, dating the photograph at spring 1954.

Below: Mk 1 Hunters at Dunsfold. Hawker's principal facility at Kingston—the former Sopwith production plant—lacked an airfield and so the completed major components had to transported by road to Dunsfold for final assembly and flight-testing.

FROM THE COCKPIT

Air Commodore Mac McEwen AFC

THERE is a story about an Empire Test Pilots' School student who had to carry out an assessment on a Fairey Gannet, which was not everybody's favourite aircraft. Being something of a wit, he wrote his report in one sentence: 'Access to the cockpit of the Gannet is difficult; it should be made impossible.' It seems that his tutor was not amused.

There was no such problem with the Hunter. I flew my first sortie in a Hunter from RAF Wattisham (No 257 Squadron) on 2 February, 1955. It was a Mk 2, and, since there were no two-seaters available, nor a simulator, I just had to get in and fly it. As it turned out, I was flying the Hunter for three and a half years and was well on my way to getting my first 1,000 hours on type before I saw my first Mk 7 two-seater, but, like everybody else at that time,

that was no problem for me: single-seat flying was what I liked best.

Access to the Hunter's cockpit was easy via a lightweight ladder, and one felt at home straight away. The cockpit was a delight. The instrument layout was entirely conventional, with the standard blind flying panel, and the layout of the large array of switches and gauges had, clearly, been carefully thought out, so that everything came readily to hand. There was no groping for the flap lever or undercarriage button, tucked away under a coaming

Below: Major Howard N. Tanner Jr, the author's Officer Commanding on No 257 Squadron, just prior to a sortie in his Hunter Mk 2. The photograph clearly shows the position of the aircraft's four Aden cannon, and also the cine-camera mounting in the nose, which latter also housed a radar ranger. Hunter call-signs, generally appearing on the fin or aft fuselage at this time, were almost without exception also borne on the forward nosewheel door.

somewhere as one often found in cockpits of that era, and the emergency controls were well marked and easy to see.

The view from the cockpit was good, except in the rear quarter, where the ejection seat got in the way. This was catered for to some extent by a wide-angle rear-view mirror, but even when that was properly adjusted you needed to loosen the top ejection seat straps and twist round awkwardly to get a really good view behind. Since the lesson 'Beware the Hun in the sun' was still firmly ingrained in all our minds

Below: Thirty years later, in 1984, hardly anything had changed—as shown in this view of a No 1 Tactical Weapons Unit (*alias* No 79 Squadron) Hunter F.G.A.9 at Brawdy. The small number of external modifications to which the aircraft was subjected are discussed fully in the pages that follow; the renowned 'Sabrinas' over the breeches of the Aden cannon were, however, an early addition.

from the experiences of our wartime forebears, this was something of a disappointment, but we mostly flew in formations which were specifically designed to give us maximum cross cover behind anyway.

To start the engine, the low-pressure cock and battery master switch had to be on, and then the starter master bar was pulled up. The high-pressure cock, which was part of the throttle quadrant, was placed to one inch open, and then the starter button pressed. This was followed by a loud bang and a spectacular cloud of black smoke as the first cartridge fired in the starter gun (this was replaced in later marks with a lighter and more reliable Avpin chemical starter), and as the rpm rose to 2,500 and to 2,700, the throttle was closed gently to idle. The jet pipe temperature (jpt) at this time was about 560°C

Left, upper and lower: These photographs of a Hunter cockpit to the left (upper) and the right (lower) clearly show the classic instrument panel, giving the pilot a simple scan pattern to read off his speed, height, attitude, heading, rate of climb and descent, and turn. The upper photograph also shows the flap and undercarriage selectors and the emergency controls—always coloured black and yellow—for the hood jettison and for undercarriage and flap lowering. The right side of the cockpit shows the engine instruments and the fuel gauges.

Right: Two views of the Martin-Baker Type 2H ejection seat, as fitted to the single-seat Hunter. The aircraft's ejection seats were constantly improved down the years, but the 2H had a good performance and saved many lives. The Type 2H operated automatically to separate the pilot from the seat below 10,000 feet and to open his parachute.

and the oil pressure just registering at 20 pounds per square inch (psi) minimum.

Taxying was straightforward, too, with differential braking achieved by the use of rudder rather than the added complication of a steerable nosewheel. The pre-take-off checks followed the internationally accepted TAFFIOH format of trim, air brakes in/anti-icing, fuel, flaps, instruments, oxygen, and harness/hood/hydraulics. The trim and flap settings varied from type to type and with the configuration, be it 'clean' or with drop tanks or weapons stores. For this, my first flight, the trim was set to one and a half degrees nose down, and the flaps up.

Once I was lined up on the runway, the final checks were to put the power controls on and to operate the controls over their full range, and to check that the brakes held at 6,800rpm. There was an air traffic control corporal in a chequered caravan on the end of the runway, and one of his jobs was to inspect with his binoculars aircraft about to take off to see that the ejection seat pins were out and safely stowed, and that there were no safety flags showing on the aircraft to indicate that any safety locks or pins had still been left in. This didn't always work. I remember once when someone in a two-seater took off with the ladder still attached. Just how nobody

amongst the ground crew and air traffic control, let alone the pilots, didn't spot it was never really explained. Anyway, it eventually came off with a bang at about 450 knots, smashed into the port wing leading edge, and vanished into space, finally to land in a somewhat mangled condition in a farmer's field. Surprisingly, there was little damage to the aircraft, but the lesson was learned and the subsequent publicity made it clear that there is no substitute for doing your checks properly.

On another occasion a pilot got on to the runway with the aileron control locks still in position. These were quite substantial metal clamps which held the ailerons fast if the aircraft had to be parked out in the open in high winds. Each one had a prominent safety flag attached to it, and anyone doing the most cursory of pre-flight external checks could not possibly have failed to miss them. Similarly, it would have been thought that the groundcrew marshalling the aircraft from dispersal and the ATC runway controller would have been certain to see the safety flags dangling down, but somehow they failed to do so, perhaps because they were distracted at a vital moment. As it happened, the aircraft did not get airborne with the controls locked because the pilot did at least do some of his checks, and engaged the

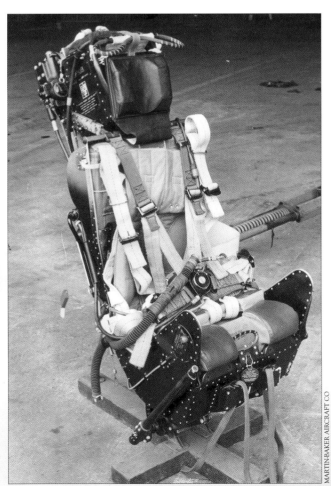

MARTIN-BAKER AIRCRAFT CO

MARTIN-BAKER AIRCRAFT CO

COURTESY TONY BUTTLER

Above: The main instrument panel of a Hunter T.7 trainer. Side-by-side accommodation for student and instructor was the preferred layout, one reason being the greater suitability of this arrangement for instrument training and weapons-aiming.

Below: A Hunter of No 66 (F) Squadron takes to the air. The aircraft is an early Mk 6—the wing lacks the leading-edge extensions that would come to characterise this and later marks—and is carrying 100-gallon drop tanks. The Squadron markings, not dissimilar to those of No 92 Squadron at first blush, were later modified, as shown elsewhere in this book.

Opposite: A smart getaway. This is a particularly interesting Hunter, a modified Mk 6—designated Mk 6A—used by BAe Dynamics at Hatfield for air-to-air missile development trials. The missile, proposed for dog-fighting, was tube-mounted with 'flip-out' stabilising fins. Normally two would be carried, but in this case the outboard tube contains instrumentation and the white 'block' on top of the tube houses a forward-looking camera. The window for the sideways-looking camera is in the port 'Sabrina'. The starboard pylon carries a full 100-gallon drop tank. George Aird is the pilot of XG210 in the photograph.

COURTESY PHILIP JARRETT

power controls prior to take-off and then went to exercise the controls over their full range to check that they had full and free movement. Unsurprisingly, there wasn't full and free movement, but 3,000 pounds of hydraulic pressure attempted to move the ailerons against the control locks and managed to twist and contort them so that they jammed with both ailerons in the up position. The control column was jammed solid too, and the aircraft was out of commission for a long time afterwards. Once again, the need to carry out checks properly was rammed home by the Flight Safety Branch. There is no record of what happened to the unhappy pilot,

but in the close world of Fighter Command everyone knew who it was.

The take-off itself was straightforward. I had never flown a machine with as powerful an engine as this before, and the initial acceleration was most noticeable—and exhilarating. In no time at all the rudder became effective, and keeping straight was easy, but there was barely time to check that the rpm were okay at 8,000 feet, that the jet pipe temperature was not above its limit of 685°C and that the oil pressure was all right and the fire warning light out, before the nose lift-off speed of 100 knots was reached. Gentle back pressure on the stick brought the nose-wheel cleanly off the ground, and by this time the acceleration was such that we seemed to be immediately at the lift-off speed of 135 knots. A further gentle back pressure on the stick, and the aircraft leapt eagerly into the air. The wheels would have been spinning like crazy by now, so the wheel brakes had to be applied as the undercarriage was raised (to reduce the risk of vibration damage in the wheel well). Then all that remained was to select the cabin pressurization 'on' and await the arrival of the climbing speed of 430 knots—which seemed to take no time at all. In fact, the time from brakes-off to 430 knots was one minute fifteen seconds, although it seemed much less than that at the time. Thus was completed the first of the many Hunter take-offs I was to carry out down the years. We were airborne.

* * *

It quickly became obvious that the Hunter was something special. On the occasion of my first solo, the aircraft configuration was clean, because it was fresh from the factory at the beginning of the delivery to service stage, and there were no external fuel tanks or weapons available at that time to hinder the aerodynamic flow. It handled superbly.

The briefing had warned against being taken by surprise by the initial nose-up change of trim, which was very pronounced as the undercarriage folded away and the aircraft picked up speed. I was also warned against over-controlling on the ailerons, which in power control mode were far more sensitive than any of us had experienced before. The briefing from the older hands was, 'Get airborne and then keep saying to yourself, "I will not rock my wings. I will not climb like a bastard. And by the time you've got that bit hacked you'll be passing 15,000 feet and you'll have time to look up and see the rear-view mirror for the first time—and glance at the two most frightened eyes you've ever seen in your life staring straight back at you!" ' I was forewarned, therefore, and did manage not to climb too steeply away as I had seen others do, and neither did I rock my wings too much, but I did see those two eyes staring straight back at me as they'd said I would, and they did look a bit frightened!

All the controls were crisp and light and it was just too easy to put the aircraft exactly where I wanted it. Clearly it was a beautiful platform for flying on instruments, with none of the inertia and control heaviness I had experienced on my previous aircraft types. If it was a steady instrument platform, then I had no doubts at all that it would also be a marvellous weapons-aiming platform, which it certainly did turn out to be. Unfortunately, a clean aircraft meant that there was very little fuel aboard, because there was simply nowhere to put it. The wings were thin, so the integral tanks were unable to carry much, and the fuselage was just about fully taken up with the engine and jetpipe. Small fuel tanks were even put in the flaps at one stage, although that did not materially help. So a clean Hunter only carried a little less than 350 gallons of fuel—enough for only fifteen minutes or so at high speed and low level, or for a 30-35 minute sortie if you climbed to the tropopause and stayed there.

Above: Two Mk 2s from the author's squadron, No 257, make a departure from RAF Wattisham early in 1955. The wheels are almost fully retracted, despite the fact that the aircraft are a mere thirty feet off the runway.
Below: Another rapid retraction, this time by the pilot of a Hunter Mk 6 of No 4 Flying Training Squadron. This particular aircraft, XF509, had a exceptionally varied career, serving in a number of front-line squadrons and also serving briefly as a chase-plane for the BAC 221 (the former Fairey F.D.2 World Absolute Speed Record holder) in connection with the Concorde airliner programme. Following its withdrawal from service it was utilised as an instructional airframe and was later purchased by Humbrol Ltd and displayed at that company's premises at Marfleet, Hull.

Later, when all the squadron aircraft had been delivered and the support supplies began to arrive, 100-gallon drop tanks were fitted on pylons under the wings to add to the range and endurance of the Hunter, and these undoubtedly made life easier for the pilot, enabling sorties of an hour's duration to become commonplace and providing greater reserves of fuel to cater for bad weather landings. With the

100-gallon tanks fitted, however, the Hunter lost some of that crispness that had so impressed everyone who flew it 'clean'. It was still a country mile better than many of its contemporaries, however, and it remained a joy to fly up to the end of its days.

For the moment, though, on that first solo, I revelled in flying one of the most precise flying machines ever produced. Not that the lack of fuel didn't register. I had barely become established in the full-powered climb before I noticed that the needles on the gauges had moved off full and were sliding across the dials at a rather rapid rate. The climb itself was breathtaking in those days. The initial rate of climb was 11,000 feet a minute. That, however, did not register on the rate-of-climb-and-descent indicator (RCDI) as it was way off the scale and the needle was jammed firmly to the instrument's 'up' limit. The rate of climb fell away as height was gained and the air became thinner, of course, but a Sapphire-engined Mk 2 still reached 40,000 feet in eight minutes and forty seconds, which was pretty impressive and certainly satisfied the Hunter's requirement to be a quick-reaction, high-level fighter. When the definitive version of the Hunter, the Mk 6, eventually came along, with the big 200-series Avon engine, it could get to 40,000 feet in just six minutes, but in 1953 the Mk 2's performance was considered admirable. The service ceiling of 52,000 feet could be reached quite easily, and that was as high as a fighter needed to go against the current threat.

Handling generally was consistently good, and no one could criticise the effectiveness of the ailerons. Rates of roll were excellent throughout the speed range from the stall (about 100 knots indicated air speed) right up to the limiting IAS of 620 knots. The faster you went, the more rapidly the Hunter would roll, of course, until at very high IAS, when it was possible to jack-stall the ailerons. This was a safety design feature that ensured that the hydraulic jacks came to a limit to prevent the ailerons being over-stressed. At low speeds, during scissors manœuvres (rapid reversals of turn used in combat, either by rolling through the upright or through the inverted to gain an advantage on an adversary), there was all the control you needed and few, if any, fighters of the day would have cared to take on a Hunter in close combat. The rate of turn could be increased significantly by the judicious use of a small amount of flap, and the technique was to fly the turn at full power with your throttle hand resting on the flap lever, raising and lowering the flap as dictated by the

Above and below: Two views of Mk 1 WT626, emphasising the purity of line of the original design, as yet unencumbered by 'add-ons'. This particular aircraft, shown here in September 1954, was issued to the Hunter conversion unit, No 229 OCU, at Chivenor. The presentation of the underwing serial numbers would later be revised, because with this arrangement the introduction of underwing paraphernalia tended to obscure the aircraft's identity; see, for example, the photograph on page 31 for a comparison.

speed. In combat, too, it was possible suddenly to drop full flap to decelerate, thereby causing the opponent to overshoot or forcing him to fly-through, but the speed had to be watched carefully as the flaps were limited to 250 knots above 38 degrees. The roll rate could be speeded up with bootfuls of rudder in tight situations, but flick rolls were prohibited officially, and the hierarchy discouraged overuse of the rudder anyway, fearing that it would lead to loss of control.

In fact, pilots quickly found that the Hunter was a most forgiving aeroplane. Aerobatics were a pleasure, whether you were doing low-level display aerobatics or more elegant classic aerobatics at higher altitudes. Spinning was prohibited, although the Pilot's Notes gave a detailed description of the various recovery procedures for upright and inverted spins, and laid great stress on the need to keep the ailerons neutral during the recovery, as only a little in-spin or out-spin aileron could prevent recovery altogether. However, most of us had watched Hawker test pilot Bill Bedford performing his remarkable thirteen-turn spins over the crowds at the Farnborough Air Show often enough to know that spins were nothing to be afraid of if you knew what you were doing. Fortunately, in squadron service spins were not really a

Above and right: Photographed by a Meteor chase-plane, the silver-finished third prototype Hunter is put through its paces. The impact made by the aircraft on its unveiling is difficult to overstate: jets, swept-back wings, world records and 'the sound barrier' were hot topics of conversation, and the Hunter amply fulfilled the requirements of all four. Truly was it an exciting time—and the Royal Air Force was regaining its rightful place as the envy of the world.

problem. To begin with, it was not that easy to induce a Hunter to spin unless you were very determined to do so by putting on full rudder and holding full back stick. Most people found, therefore, that if you were in a difficult position during aerobatics or combat, with the nose too high, the speed too low, and no more engine power available, the best technique was simply to centralise the controls and let the aircraft sort it out itself. On every occasion that happened to me—which was often in the early days—the aircraft would just gently recover to controlled flight and the only problem was that sometimes it took a lot of height to facilitate this recovery. Since we only did aerobatics and combat above 7,000 feet as a norm, however, height loss was very seldom a consideration.

When the Hunter first entered service, the elevator control came in for some criticism. It was perfect for most of the flight envelope, but in a supersonic dive it became very heavy beyond Mach

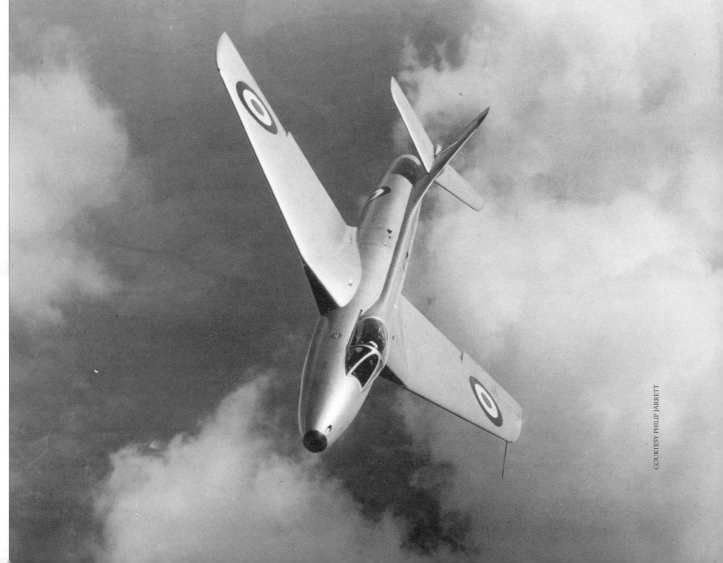

0.96, and at speeds of Mach 1.05 and beyond the variable-incidence tail plane trimmer had to be used in the recovery. Care had then to be taken to anticipate the strong nose-up trim reversal which occurred as the speed reduced to subsonic. The aircraft was also prone to 'pitch-up' in high-speed high-'g' turns, when the nose would rear up alarmingly despite full forward pressure on the stick and the speed would drop off rapidly. A pilot had to pull through some very heavy buffet to reach this stage, and some said it was ham-fisted flying rather than a design defect. However, Royal Air Force fighter pilots have always cherished a reputation for being brave and daring, and the training they received went out of its way to encourage such a spirit, so to ask pilots to be more gentle on the controls would have gone against the grain and been contrary to the ethos of the Service.

The problem really was that in some circumstances the variable-incidence tailplane trimmer was too slow. What the aircraft really needed was a slab tailplane as fitted to the F-86 Sabre, and all those who had flown that great aircraft called for it loud and long. What it actually got in the end was an electric follow-up tailplane, and a modified wing with the leading edge extended on the outer portion. This was known as the 'sawtooth' leading-edge wing and had the benefit of moving the mean centre of pressure (CP) forward so that, when the wing tip did eventually stall, forward movement of the CP was less marked and the degree of pitch-up therefore was also less. The combination of these two improvements largely did away with the problems with the elevator, but all aircraft have a foible of some sort, and most experienced Hunter pilots always remained aware of it.

Finally, from a handling point of view, the vexed question of manual controls will always arise. Without the benefit of the power controls, which provided 3,000psi of hydraulic pressure to power the controls, the Hunter was transformed and flew like a heavy bomber. So to have a hydraulic failure could be something of a shock. The controls initially felt as if they had seized, and the break-out force needed to initiate a turn was considerable, and often took two hands. It was vital to keep the aircraft trimmed, as holding an out-of-trim force for any length of time would tax even the strongest, and the most obvious step to take right at the beginning was to get the speed down to reduce the control forces—and then to keep it down. The Pilot's Notes give the limiting speeds for manual as Mach 0.75 below 15,000 feet,

but anybody in his right mind would get the speed back to somewhere below 250 knots straightaway unless he had a special reason for not doing so.

Once the speed has been reduced, however, flying the Hunter in manual was not a great problem. The circuit was flown wider than usual for comfort, and the approach longer and straighter than usual to allow for final adjustments, but otherwise it was not much different from a normal circuit, and, as long as the aircraft was trimmed well, the touch-down presented no difficulties. We had to switch the power controls off and practise manual landings each month just to keep our hands in, and I do not recall a single accident arising from that.

Having said that, there was one incident that was complicated by the 'manual issue', if not actually caused by it. A No 257 Squadron pilot from Wattisham, Flying Officer Reg Young, was cruising slowly back to base having switched off his power controls to do his monthly practice manual let-down and landing when he was 'bounced' by a USAF F-84F Thunderstreak from Bentwaters. It was an established procedure in the 1950s that if you were on your way home and you saw another fighter aircraft, especially one from another air force, you engaged it and tried to take cine film through the gun sight to prove that you could have shot him down had it been wartime. If he saw you coming—as he should have done—he would take evasive action and a dogfight would ensue. This was strictly forbidden, of course, but everybody turned a blind eye to it as it encouraged a spirit of competition and, incidentally, taught pilots to keep a good look-out. One of the lessons from past air combat is that most people who are killed never see their adversaries, and the first they know of being attacked is when cannon shells begin smashing into their cockpits. The RAF pilot saw the Thunderstreak diving in on him, but he could not do much about it as by the time he had initiated a turn in manual it would have been all over. He tried to reselect power controls, but on the earlier systems they did not always re-engage properly in the air, and that was the case this time. He was stuck in manual, therefore, and would have to just sit there and take his medicine. The accepted practice was that if an attacked aircraft did not react, the attacker (assuming that his approach had not been

Right: The Hunter Mk 2 was rapidly superseded by the Mk 5, also Sapphire-powered but with greater fuel capacity and hardpoints for underwing stores. This example is from No 56 Squadron, based at Waterbeach. The Squadron had briefly operated Supermarine Swifts, but the shortcomings of the latter led to their quickly being supplanted by Hunters.

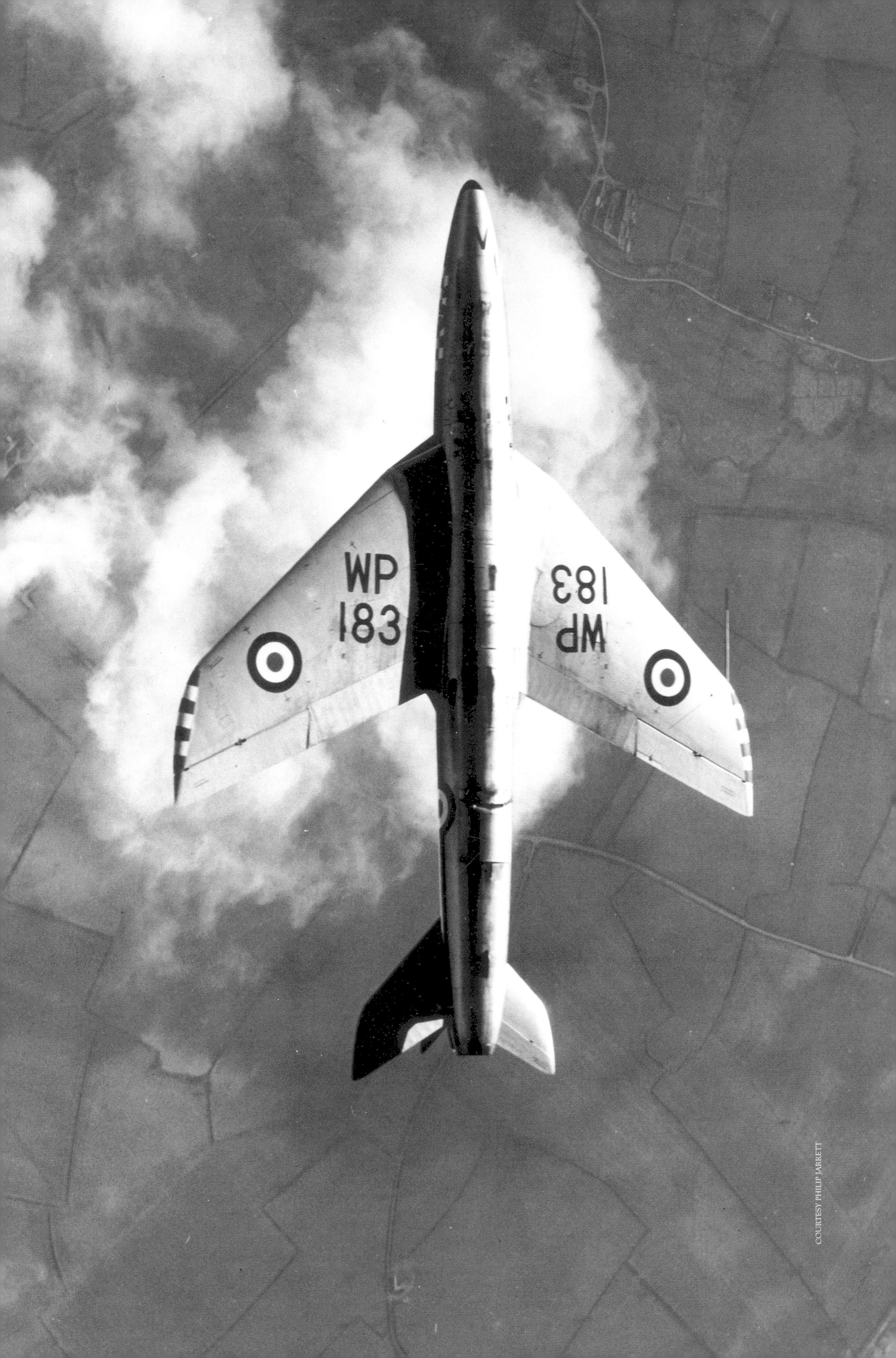

COURTESY PHILIP JARRETT

Above: A Hunter F.R.10 fighter-reconnaissance aircraft serving with No 1417 Flight in the Aden Protectorate banks away displaying its undercarriage. Based on the upgraded Mk 9 (itself a development of the Mk 6), the F.R.10 retained the four Aden cannon but was fitted with F.95 camera equipment in the nose. Large, 230-gallon drop tanks could be carried inboard, as here.

spotted) would fly directly underneath the target, as close as he dared, and then pull up violently in front of him, hoping to tip him upside down in the slipstream. To the attacked pilot, if the attack really had not been seen coming in, the sudden roar of the other jet passing close underneath him, followed by the sight of a bright red (and very close) jetpipe filling his windscreen as the attacker reared up in front, could be quite frightening, especially if the slipstream really did have the desired effect of turning him upside down. Unfortunately, in this instance there was more of a jolt than usual, because the fin of the Thunderstreak struck the nose cone of the Hunter a violent blow as the USAF pilot pulled up just a shade too early. A mid-air collision! Miraculously, little damage was done; the fin-tip aerial of the Thunderstreak and the radar-ranging nose cone on the Hunter had to be changed, and a bit of paintwork repair was necessary, but otherwise all was well. The two commanders got together on the telephone afterwards to discuss it, as both pilots, in the shock of the moment, had reported the collision to their respective Air Traffic Centres, but the incident was pretty well hushed up and the upshot was that No 257 Squadron was invited over to Bentwaters, just up the road, to a full dining-in night at the weekend.

Bonds were established, friendships made, and the two air forces indulged in some worthwhile and thoroughly enjoyable liaison work. Moreover, if it did nothing else, the incident showed how vulnerable a Hunter would be in wartime with a hydraulic and power control failure.

I have never in any way been brawny of arm, but I never found flying in manual as much of a struggle as some made it out to be. I was once practising low-level aerobatics over a disused airfield in Devon and had just gone over the top of a pretty tight loop at about 3,500 feet above ground level and was pointing vertically at the ground, when I had a turret drive failure—which caused the immediate and total loss of all electrics and hydraulics. The Emergency Flight Reference Cards, which all pilots carry in their trouser pockets and which should always be referred to in an emergency (had I had time to take them out of my pocket), would have droned on about reducing speed, switching the tailplane trim interconnection off, switching off the booster pumps, etc., etc., but I

Top: Hunter Mk 2s and Mk 5s of the Wattisham Wing (Nos 257 and 263 Squadrons) prepare for take off from their Suffolk base, late 1955 or early 1956. WP189, leading, is the Wing Commander's aircraft; assigned to neither squadron (though featuring the yellow nose wheel door for No 257), it carries the appropriate rank pennant and a large, unidentified crest.
Above: Another Wing Commander's Hunter—that of No 122 Wing in RAF Germany—was this F.4, flown by Wing Commander C. S. West and carrying miniature emblems of the four component units, Nos 4, 93, 98 and 118 Squadrons, based at Jever in the mid-1950s.
Below: A pair of Royal Navy Hunter Mk 11s. The story of the somewhat fortuitous acquisition of these aircraft by the Fleet Air Arm is described on pages 144–150.

BRIAN SHARMAN, COURTESY TONY BUTTLER/ROGER LINDSAY

Above: Squadron Leader Norman Buddin, OC No 118 Squadron in 1955, pulls his Hunter Mk 4 WT751 alongside the Meteor photo 'plane for an intimate portrait.

Right: A Hunter Mk 6 of No 74 (F) Squadron banks away from the camera to reveal its undersurfaces and plenty of staining on the belly.

Below: A No 65 Squadron Hunter Mk 6 being readied for flight at Duxford, showing the unit markings to advantage and also a freshly repainted nose cone and the Aden blast deflectors that were introduced in the late 1950s. The name above the unit emblem reads 'Flt. Lt. T. J. G. Hooper'.

Opposite, top: The Hunter's cleanliness of line, exemplified by a Mk 2 of No 257 Squadron.

Opposite, bottom: First regeneration: a Hunter Mk 4 in the colours of No 98 Squadron, RAFG.

COURTESY TONY BUTTLER

COURTESY TONY BUTTLER

COURTESY HOWARD N. TANNER Jr

had a more pressing issue: the ground looked very close, the speed was building up rapidly, I was still pointing vertically downwards, and the power controls had clunked solidly into manual. I throttled back instinctively with my left hand, and simultaneously heaved back on the stick with my right hand. Such is the extra power that terror invokes that I felt no control heaviness of any sort. The Hunter pulled out of its dive like the thoroughbred she was and I regained level flight about 200 feet higher than I would have done had there been no emergency! I cruised home and landed, happy with my lot.

On another occasion, I was re-joining the circuit at Wattisham as the Number Two of a pair for a high-speed break into the circuit. We were doing right-hand circuits that day, and normally that would have made no difference—but it did this day. I was in

a Mk 2, with its Sapphire engine, and as I throttled back on the break and put the air brake out all hell was let loose. There was a great bang under my feet, the whole aircraft vibrated alarmingly, the rpm gauge dropped rapidly to zero, and the jpt went off the clock. I later learned that the compressor had exploded, causing the engine to seize and the compressor blades to scythe through the aircraft like shrapnel. One of these blades cut half way through the elevator control rod, but fortunately I didn't know this at the time or I'd have jumped out. I was left downwind with no engine and at only 1,000 feet, but I did still have some speed. I put the air brake in (it stayed out because the hydraulics had failed too) and pulled back on the stick to give me time to think. I ballooned out at 2,000 feet and still with 200 knots, so I called 'Mayday' to clear the other

BRIAN SHARMAN,
COURTESY ROGER LINDSAY

aircraft out of my way and headed for the airfield. With all engine, hydraulic, and electrical power gone, the undercarriage lowered with a 2,000psi emergency air bottle, as did the flaps, but I wasn't sure yet whether I would reach the airfield so I set 210 knots and decided to glide as far as I could.

I aimed at the end of the runway in a screaming right-hand turn, planning to land wheels-up on the airfield if I could reach it. Half-way round the turn I decided that I could perhaps get the undercarriage sorted out after all, so I pulled the emergency air bottle knob and immediately heard three satisfying *clunks* as the wheels came down. I was fully committed now, way below any chance of ejecting, and the rate of descent increased markedly with the under-carriage selected. If it had been a normal left-hand circuit, I could have made it to the end of the runway, but the fact that it was a right-hand circuit meant that the ATC caravan stood squarely in the way of where I wanted to go. I had 90 degrees of bank on by now and was pulling hard on the stick, hoping I might pass over the caravan and land on the runway beyond, but I was too low for that, the speed was now down to 150 knots—too low for any fancy manoeuvres—and I still hadn't had time to select flap.

So I took bank off, landed on the grass on the far side of the runway, and simultaneously booted on full right rudder and operated the flap emergency bottle. This, luckily, had the effect of lifting the aircraft off the grass momentarily and enabled me to skip fifty yards or so of thick terrain to meet the

Above: High over the cotton wool, a Hunter pilot savours the freedom of the skies. This is, again, a Hunter F.R.10—considered by many pilots to be the very best of an excellent family of variants. Introduced into service from 1960, the Mk 10 acquitted itself superbly in competition with aircraft of other NATO forces. The 'windows' for the Vinten F.95 cameras can be seen in the modified nose, and the aircraft sports a white-painted spine.
Left: A view through the starboard main intake of the author's Hunter Mk 2 after the engine explosion described in the accompanying text. Downwind and at 1,000 feet—and then this! June 1954.
Overleaf: A Hunter Mk 1 of No 43 (F) Squadron awaits its next sortie, 1955. The practice of painting call-signs on the tail cone was soon dispensed with: these fittings were interchangeable amongst aircraft, and it tended to hamper flexibility in the servicing cycle.

AUTHOR'S COLLECTION

runway about 200 yards up. I kicked the aircraft straight and stripped the left wheel in the process, but the aircraft was probably damaged beyond repair by now anyway and my only object was to stay on that precious runway. I rolled to a halt on the upwind Operational Readiness Platform (ORP) with the port tyre flailing and dragging me to a halt. Never had terra firma felt so firm!

My reason for recounting this engine-off landing story is to illustrate that the heaviness of a Hunter in manual control was never really a problem. Throughout the whole of that little incident I never once thought about how heavy the controls were.

* * *

The Hunter handled well in the circuit, and the actual landing was easy to execute, although it was not as easy to 'grease on' as its predecessors, the Meteor and the Vampire, which had soft, spongy

tyres: the Hunter's tyres were high-pressure, and the undercarriage itself felt more rigid than those of the early jets. It was getting back to the circuit that posed the real problem, however.

In the 1950s there were far more fighters buzzing around British skies than there are today, and many more airfields, so the airspace was very congested. Each airfield housed three squadrons, and having thirty or so jets in the air at any one time was commonplace during major air defence exercises. When the weather was good—marked on the weather charts as 'CAVOK' (an American term meaning ceiling and visibility unlimited)—recovering large numbers of aircraft was straightforward enough, but when the weather was bad it could become a nightmare for ATC controllers and pilots alike.

The procedure was to home aircraft to overhead base at height, and then send them on an outbound leg on the reciprocal of the in-use runway heading,

descending to half their overhead height plus 2,000 feet before turning back on to the runway heading. They would then let down in a straight line to the end of the runway, and either land straight ahead or enter the circuit if fuel allowed.

Compared with the large array of radars and beacons available today, however, airfield approach aids were very limited. Initially there was merely a manual homer, which locked on to an aircraft radio signal and gave a bearing. It was cumbersome, and somewhat akin to taking a bearing from a small yacht in a rough sea, and so the bearing was not all that accurate. Then came an automated version, the Voice Rotating Beacon (VRB). For this, the pilot tuned in to the VRB frequency and heard a voice calling out bearings in ten-degree increments. The voice got louder and louder as it reached the correct bearing and then faded away progressively as it went further away from the correct bearing, so it relied somewhat on the pilot interpreting the volume properly to get the right result. It also seemed to take ages. Fortunately, by the time the Hunter entered service the Cathode Ray Direction Finding (CRDF) system had been fitted to just about every control tower, and this was a great improvement, although there were few airfields then with their own local radar to supplement it.

The CRDF provided, as its name implies, a cath-ode ray display which, when a pilot transmitted, gave an immediate, accurate bearing or a course to steer (the reciprocal of a bearing). It was easy, therefore, for the controller to home an aircraft to overhead and then let him down into the approach procedure, and the briefest of transmissions from the aircraft enabled him to keep an accurate check on progress throughout. That was fine for a single aircraft, or even a few at a time, but when all thirty came back at once, all shouting that they were short of fuel and needed priority, it could turn nasty—especially when there were a few emergencies thrown into the mix, as was often the case. We always operated in pairs, to halve the number of units a controller had to handle, and usually landed in formation too if the weather was bad, but, even so, handling a large num-ber of fighter aircraft on an instrument recovery was a severe test for the controllers—and, on occasion, for the pilots too.

Fortunately, the controllers had great skill and were up to the task, although it needed an enormous amount of concentration. The controller would have little movement strips handed to him by an assistant, who sat beside him, and he would move these round

a 'racetrack' pattern on his desktop so that he knew where a particular call-sign was at any one moment. It was a bit like a three-dimensional board game. The strips were moved progressively round the racetrack until they reached the touchdown point, when they would be whisked off and dumped into the waste-paper basket.

I remember once watching an approach controller at Wattisham on a day when the Met forecast was wildly inaccurate and very bad weather had moved in without notice, and he recovered a horde of aircraft in such a calm and ordered way that the pilots in their cockpits would never have believed it if they could have seen what I could see—that the control-ler's blue shirt was soaked black with sweat and that his ashtray was crammed full of butts from his ener-getic chain-smoking. In the middle of this virtuoso performance, a civilian cleaner appeared with a broom and a rag and started clearing up some of the mess on the controller's console (cleaners were always given preference in the RAF because they were so few and far between, so nobody saw fit to tell him to go away). The controller stood up while the cleaner brushed the floor under his chair and then sat down again afterwards and his concentration was so complete that I doubt very much if he was ever aware that the cleaner had been anywhere near him. He just carried on talking incessantly in his calm and

Right, upper: Two Hunter Mk 6s assigned to the Air Fighting Development Squadron at RAF West Raynham, the 'sawtooth' (or 'dogtooth') extensions to the wing leading edges readily evident. This modification provided a effective final solution to the problem of pitch-up that had been a short-coming of earlier marks. The F.6 also featured the more powerful 200-series Avon engine. However, except for the leading-edge wing extensions (eventually), a minor recontouring of the tail cone, the relocation of various vents and access panels associated with the new engine and the upgrading of the various communications aerials, the new variant did not materially differ in appearance from its predecessors.
Right: Although WB188 had been experimentally fitted with air brakes on the rear fuselage flanks, the single ventral brake was retained throughout the Hunter's production run. It is seen here deployed on WT594, a Mk 1.

COURTESY PHILIP JARRETT

reassuring way, and every one of those pilots descending through thick cloud and arriving on a rain-sodden runway would have felt that he had been caring for just him and him alone, quite unaware of those torn-off strips in the waste-paper basket that represented a frantic afternoon's work. In the bar some time afterwards, I bought the controller a beer, and he looked as if he needed it.

It didn't always work smoothly, of course, and the exceptions were notable. A whole Hunter four-ship formation aerobatic team from Duxford, known as 'The Black Knights', and a Vampire two-seater which had gone off with them to take some publicity photographs, had to eject over open countryside when caught out by yet another bad weather forecast. Faced with impossible landing conditions at base, and with their intended diversions clamped and unusable too, they ran out of fuel and had to jump for it.

An even worse situation occurred in February 1956 at West Raynham when eight Hunter Mk 1s of the Day Fighter Leaders' School, which aimed to train the best fighter leaders in the country, took off to carry out a four-*versus*-four dogfight. The exercise over, they returned to overhead West Raynham at 20,000 feet in four pairs, only to be told that the weather at base was deteriorating fast, with low cloud and poor visibility. They descended anyway in tactical trail to 2,000 feet over West Raynham, but it was then decided to divert them to their primary weather diversion, which was Marham, only ten miles away to the south-west. At about this time the

Above: A Mk 9 of No 8 Squadron with two rockets on its outboard starboard pylon, activates its air brake. The photograph illustrates the later practice of raising the squadron fuselage flashes to a higher level—and one of the reasons why this was done

formation, especially those down at the back end who were running short of fuel, must have thought that a wiser decision might have been to stay at height to conserve fuel and go and land in another part of the country, but by then it was too late. Not surprisingly, the weather at Marham was not much different from the West Raynham weather just up the road, and the moment the decision to divert was made the CRDF tripped off-line. This meant that the approach controller was unable to handle the formation himself and had to hand the aircraft over to a rather more cumbersome Ground Control Approach (GCA) procedure, which required that the four pairs had to be further separated to give enough spacing for the final landing. In the end, the first pair broke out of cloud and landed at Marham, with the leader running out of fuel as he taxied back in, but the rest of the formation could not find the runway and five of them ejected. Tragically, the remaining pilot, a Royal Navy officer, crashed into the ground and was killed.

The follow-up to these sorry tales was that the weather reporting system and the criteria for diversion airfields were reviewed, and a far more sophisticated system was installed. The recovery let-down procedures were revamped so as to do away with the need to fly first to overhead the intended landing base as this wasted fuel. Instead, a dive circle was

TIM SMITH, COURTESY NIGEL WALPOLE

Above: Hunter F.G.A.9 'Y' of No 8 Squadron arrives at Beihan in the Western Aden Protectorates, 1967. The flaps are at maximum droop. The Hunter's landing speed was typically 135 knots, depending on fuel load. Below: Rubber burns as a Hunter F.R.10, XF457 of No 2 Squadron, lands at a base in RAF Germany in the mid-1960s. Like the pure fighter Mk 6, the Mk 10s were powered by the uprated Avon 200-series. By this time the 'silver' undersurfaces evident on all Hunters throughout the first years of their service had given way to Light Aircraft Grey.

established so that an approaching aircraft could descend from any angle to join the final approach radar pattern. As the years went by, too, new airfield radars were installed and all aircraft had IFF (Identification Friend or Foe) transponders fitted, and the controller was able to identify precisely which aircraft was which at a glance as well as being able to see precisely where he was.

During these numerically large recoveries to base carried out in the Hunter era, the radio had to be used sparingly because most of the time we were all on the same frequency and it quickly became overloaded. The RAF had, moreover, always prided itself on the minimal use of radio—unlike our American cousins, for example, who were invariably verbose—and it was a standard we rigidly maintained. Whenever we were in close formation, therefore, we always operated silently and used hand signals instead. If flap was to be lowered, the lead pilot raised his gloved hand and made a snapping motion with the thumb against his fingers and then nodded his head forward as the executive command. For the undercarriage, the right arm was pumped as in the motion

COURTESY NIGEL WALPOLE

DIETER SCHMIDT, COURTESY ROGER LINDSAY

of pulling a lavatory chain (where that idea came from nobody seems to know!) and, again, a nod of the head gave the command for the undercarriage-down button to be pressed.

These signals were all specified in Standard Operating Procedures (SOPs), which were common to all squadrons, the idea being that if, say, at the end of a combat sortie two aircraft ended up together, even if the pilots were complete strangers and from different units they would be able to operate efficiently and safely together. We were regularly tested on these SOPs—and woe betide anyone who got something wrong. Later, the idea was developed throughout NATO and standardised procedures quite well, enabling the different nations to work comfortably together.

In the Hunter, the let-down task from an instrument flying sortie was usually the easiest part of the flight. When the instruction to descend was given, the air brake was popped out, which induced a small but manageable change of trim, two notches of flap were lowered, and the nose was lowered if necessary in order to achieve Mach 0.9, converting to 300 knots IAS as the height reduced. The engine was throttled back to 6,500rpm, and on a perfect approach the throttle did not need to be touched again until it was time to shut the air brake and lower the undercarriage below its limiting speed of 250 knots. Then all that was required was to lower full flap at the top of the final glidepath, trim care-

Above and below: A Hunter Mk 6 of No 26 Squadron (above) and a Mk 9 of No 54 Squadron (below) approach the runway. Unlike the Mk 6, the Hunter Mks 9 and 10 could carry the elongated, 230-gallon drop tanks, significantly extending the aircraft's range. The photograph above affords a good view of the aircraft's flaps in the landing configuration.

fully so that the glidepath was maintained, and then use the throttle to control any high or low position on the glidepath and move the stick forward or back to control the speed. This last was set at 160 knots initially and allowed to taper off gradually as the height reduced to 150 knots, so that the threshold was crossed at 130–135. The pre-landing checks were the same as for a normal visual circuit, that is, air brake in, undercarriage down (three green lights), fuel enough for an overshoot (we aimed to land with a minimum of 80 gallons), flaps fully down, wheel brakes check on then off, and hydraulic pressure 2,800–3,000psi.

Off a good approach, only a shallow round-out was needed and the aircraft would settle smoothly on the runway. The brakes were very effective and needed to be applied gently at first and especially on wet runways with crosswinds up to the limit of 20 knots, but if there was little wind, or in the event of a landing on a short runway, firm braking was very effective and the anti-skid system worked well.

The after-landing checks were pretty obvious too: check brake pressure, raise the flaps to prevent them getting damaged from ground objects being thrown at them by the jetwash from other aircraft, test the fire warning light and then switch off navigation aids and the anti-'g' system. In dispersal, the power controls were switched off, as were the high-pressure and low-pressure cocks and the battery master switch. Finally, the canopy motor clutch was set to 'Free' and the Master Armament Safety Break plug was removed. The aircraft was now in a fit state to be handed over to the pilot of the next sortie, once it had been refuelled and rearmed.

The canopy switch clutch position may not seem important, but all the checks were there for a good reason and even a minor one such as this can cause trouble if not carried out properly. Flight Lieutenant 'Cherry' Kearton, one of the early Hunter flight commanders, had good cause to regret that a pilot on his first solo had not operated the clutch properly. 'Cherry'— everybody had nicknames at that time, and he got his after a famous wildlife photographer of the day—was just about to be posted overseas and one of his last duties on the Squadron was to carry out a supervised start with a new pilot. The latter got the engine started all right, but appeared not to be able to shut the canopy. Kearton knew a good bit about the Hunter, and came to the conclusion that the microswitches to the rear of the canopy switch must have tripped out. Rather than shout complicated instructions to the first solo pilot,

Kearton climbed up the ladder and reached past him to the back of the cockpit to reset the switches. He found that they had not tripped after all, however, and on pulling his hand back he must have moved the clutch to the locked position (where it should have been selected by the pilot anyway) and selected the canopy to 'closed'.

The noise of the engine drowned out the hum of the hood motor, which closed on to 'Cherry''s midriff and began to squeeze. The motor was very powerful, and a groundcrewman had been killed in a similar situation once, so he knew that he had to extract himself quickly and he squirmed backwards in some alarm. He got his torso and shoulders out successfully, but his cranium became trapped between the front windscreen strut and the canopy itself, and the canopy began to exert considerable pressure. With a desperate lunge, 'Cherry' wrenched his head free, but as he did so the leading edge of the canopy tore most of his right ear off. There was blood everywhere and the fleshy part of the ear was hanging off with only the bottom bit still attached. He looked almost comical, but it was no joke. The ambulance bore him away in double-quick time, and some ninety stitches were inserted, which saved the ear, but caused him to have a rather spectacular 'cauliflower' afterwards. But that wasn't the end of this saga.

'Cherry' reappeared with his head swathed in bandages to attend his farewell dinner night in the Officers' Mess that evening, during the course of

which he was hurt playing one of the Mess games which always followed dinner. He was accidentally kicked in the eye (the left one) and the eye slit was enlarged, causing even more blood to appear. The Station Doctor staunched the flow and did an emergency repair job on the spot, inserting further stitches to hold the wound together. Unfortunately, this happened in the early hours of the morning and the good doctor had enjoyed the evening too, with the result that one stitch passed through the lower and upper eyelid. When he got up the next day, 'Cherry' found that when he blinked his left eyelid opened and closed more slowly than the right one, because it was retarded by the rogue stitch. This was finally attended to and he went happily off to his overseas posting as planned. Legend had it that he had 100 stitches inserted altogether that day, although I doubt if anyone actually counted them.

Flying the Hunter on instruments was relatively straightforward, but it could not be done without regular practice, and pilots' standards needed to be monitored closely. In the early days this had to be done in a Vampire T.11 because there were no two-

Below: A Hunter Mk 9 of No 20 Squadron at the point of touch-down. The aircraft has the upgraded communications fit of the 1960s, which includes UHF (the dorsal aerial for which can be seen canted to starboard; the second, ventral aerial can also be made out) and the longitudinal radio compass sense aerial under the belly. Further changes would be made as the aircraft served into the 1980s.
Opposite: WB195, the second Hunter prototype, executes a textbook landing. Unlike WB188, this aircraft was cannon-armed.

seat Hunters. The two aircraft were quite different, of course, and the accurate monitoring of a pilot's instrument flying capabilities was, therefore, difficult. Some pilots may not have been quite up to scratch and had difficulty in coping with the low cloud and poor visibility in which they often found themselves. This all changed with the introduction of the Hunter two-seater, when regular checks became mandatory and a pilot's Instrument Rating became crucial. Those with White Ratings were limited to flying in only good weather, those with Green Ratings could fly down to about 500 feet and a mile's visibility (depending on the landing aid available), and only those who held a Master Green Rating were sent off when the weather was really right down to limits.

This last rating was the *crème de la crème* and much sought after by those with experience and high ability. To achieve it, the sortie pattern had to be flown within fine limits, being plus or minus no more than 50 feet in a sustained turn, for example, and with just about zero tolerance in the final stages of an approach. It had, moreover, to be flown smoothly, because it had to be remembered that most bad-weather recoveries were flown with another pilot in formation. All the ratings had oral examinations as part of the test, but the Master Green oral was by far the most comprehensive and required a deep knowledge of airmanship, meteorology, aerodynamics and aircraft instruments. Being a really good fighter pilot required not only the ability to be a good shot and to

rack the aircraft around with great daring in dog-fights, but also the ability to get back home safely afterwards in all weathers. Some pilots rather looked down their noses at instrument flying as a secondary achievement compared with getting good gunnery scores, but they were mistaken: you needed to be good at both. In the same vein, I recall famous French ace Pierre Clostermann writing that he had noticed that before combat some pilots spent their time checking out their guns and gun sights, and some spent their time checking out their parachutes and oiling the canopy runners to ensure a rapid escape. He said that all those who did that were wrong. They should have checked both their weapons and their safety equipment with equal zeal if they considered themselves proper fighter pilots.

Finally, on the subject of the approach and landing, there was great excitement at Wattisham during 1955 when we were given an Ecko approach radar to improve the airfield's bad-weather landing aids. This was a mobile radar intended for deployments to far-flung places, and we had one installed at Wattisham for an unofficial 'trial run'. Positioned half way along the runway in the middle of the airfield so that it could cope with an approach at either end, it consisted of a large mobile truck, which housed a powerful generator, and a caravan-type control room for the single controller. It had an antenna on the roof which did not rotate but could be steered in azimuth and pitch by the controller via an apparatus not dissimilar to a submarine periscope control. It was

COURTESY NIGEL WALPOLE

intended only as an approach aid, not a landing aid, and it was designed to bring an aircraft down to 500 feet above the ground, which was the official break-off height. However, we found that it could be used to land in much lower cloud bases than that—if the controller was good enough.

Our best controller was a remarkable man called Flying Officer Vic Azzaro. He had been a Lancaster tail gunner during the war and was well decorated, having survived a large number of raids over Germany. He was very quick-witted and lively, a popular member of the Mess and a regular attender most nights in the Mess bar, and he was acknowledged by all to be an excellent controller. He was also a Cockney through and through.

Above: Mission accomplished: XJ676, a Mk 6 of No 229 OCU, taxies in along the perimeter track at Chivenor.
Below: A Hunter F. Mk 1 taxying after a test flight.

For the controller, the skill with the Ecko lay in following the approach controller's CRDF bearings on an incoming aircraft closely and operating the antenna manually to 'capture' the aircraft's radar echo as early as possible, and Vic was a past master at that. The Ecko was not a precision radar and did not have a glidepath, but operated on the 'step-down' principle, that is, the controller would pass the ranges from touch-down and the height at which the aircraft should be, but could never say whether the aircraft was high or low on the intended glidepath. He would say, therefore, 'You are at four miles and

COURTESY PHILIP JARRETT

should be at 1,200 feet' (for example) and it was up to the pilot to be there. However, in azimuth Vic was precision itself, and any deviation from the centreline was picked up immediately and corrected. He never broke off at 500 feet as he was supposed to, but carried on talking, right down to the point where he would say, 'You are over touch-down now— look ahead and land', and invariably, if you followed his instructions properly, that's exactly where you were. When he had given his final instruction, Viv would leap up from his control position, fling open the top of the stable door of his caravan and look out to see if the aircraft was indeed where he had said it was.

There was an occasion on which the weather had closed in unannounced (again!) and a young pilot was trying to recover to land in conditions way below his instrument limits. He was short of fuel, too, but on his first approach, in very misty conditions, he strayed from the centreline in the later stages of the approach and, when the runway lights did eventually emerge from the gloom, he was not lined up sufficiently to land. Vic came on the radio right away and said in his uncompromising way, 'Right, you b****r— you looked up that time before I told you to. Go round again and we'll line you up again, and this time keep your b***** head down and don't look up till I give you permission to do so. Right?' A querulous voice came back from the young pilot, by now desperately low on fuel: 'Yes, sir.' He went round again, did as he was told and landed with no problem—and no doubt remained an admirer of Vic's for ever more, as we all did.

Only a slice of good luck saved us from losing our highly regarded Ecko altogether, however. Flight Lieutenant Phil Champniss was carrying out a formation Ecko approach one sunny day and, as intended, overshot at the touch-down point, leaving his Number Two to land by himself. During the overshoot, Phil turned thirty degrees left to join the circuit, but, before he had time to raise the undercarriage or climb, his Sapphire engine failed and he lost all power. He immediately pressed the engine relight button on his HP cock (which was usually most reliable), but nothing happened and he had no option but to land straight ahead on the grass. He then realised that he was pointing straight at the Ecko caravan and its generator truck only about 500 yards away—and he was still doing 130 knots. Meanwhile, Vic Azzaro had given his final instruction and then walked over to the caravan door in his usual way to see how the aircraft were getting on, and he saw to his horror a Hunter on the grass heading straight for him at a great speed. Apparently he slammed the stable door and spread himself out against it a bit like a Tom and Jerry cartoon character, in a futile effort to defend himself against the catastrophic crash that was about to happen. But time went by and nothing happened.

In the cockpit, Phil Champniss found that he had no control over his aircraft at all as, no matter what

Below: A No 92 Squadron F.6 completes a sortie. The lower profile of the tailpipe on Hunters fitted with a 200-series Avon was sharply different from that on aircraft that had the earlier 100-series engine: compare this photograph with, for example, that opposite. Uniquely, No 92's Hunters sported a chequerboard marking in the Squadron colours (red and yellow) beneath the tailplane at this time.

COURTESY PHILIP JARRETT

he did with the brakes, the tyres just skated over the grass, which had been soaked by days of rain. All he could do was brace himself for the inevitable crash. However, by some miracle, the Hunter shot through the gap between the truck and the caravan and finally came to a mud-spattered halt just before the boundary fence, leaving the pilot more shaken than somewhat, but grateful to be still alive. The gap through which the Hunter careered at 100-plus knots was measured afterwards as being 40 feet wide. The Hunter's wing span was 33 feet 8 inches, so there was just an inch or two over a yard to spare at each wing tip.

Above: With the arrival of the Hunter trainers, a braking parachute was introduced in order to help shorten landing runs, and this installation was included in subsequent marks of the aeroplane. It was of particular benefit to pilots operating in the Middle East, where runways tended to be shorter than at home.
Below: A distant view of a Hunter Mk 10 of No II (AC) Squadron with its parachute streamed.

In the years following World War II, Fighter Command's accident rates were high, and the death rate was almost scandalous. About one-third of new fighter aircraft bought by the Air Ministry—Meteor, Hunter, Lightning—were written off in accidents during the course of their lifetimes and, sadly, far too many of the accidents were fatal. Some of the

COURTESY NIGEL WALPOLE

Above: A No II (AC) Squadron Hunter T.7 with a mismatch of serial number, that on the starboard wing having been incorrectly applied. Many Hunter units favoured some sort of squadron identity colour for the forward nosewheel door in addition to the regularly applied call-sign.

Below: A Fleet Air Arm Hunter T. Mk 8 showing the vivid colour scheme in vogue for training aircraft from the early 1960s. The matt-finished black panelling immediately in front of the cockpit aided the aircrew by all but eliminating the problem of glare bouncing off the broadened nose of the two-seat Hunter; pilots of single-seaters did not encounter this problem to the same degree (and, in any case, were expected to cope!).

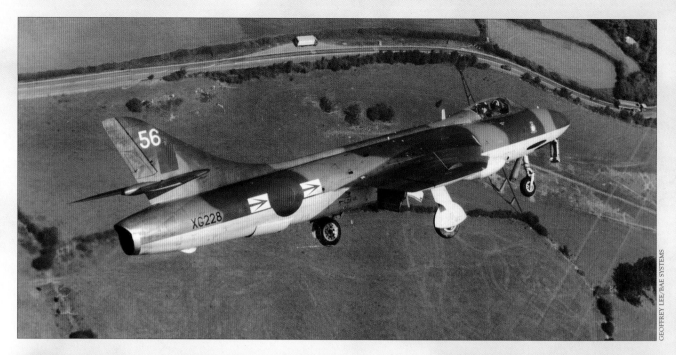

GEOFFREY LEE/BAE SYSTEMS

GEOFFREY LEE/BAE SYSTEMS

GEOFFREY LEE/BAE SYSTEMS

Top, above and left: Hunter F.G.A. Mk 9 XG228 on finals and (left) landing at Brawdy. In the first photograph, the pilot is flying downwind at 175–200 with under-carriage fully down and flaps partially deployed and in the next is seen turning crosswind, flaps fully down, at 150–170 knots on finals. At left, he touches down at about 130–135 knots, the speed varying according to his fuel load.

Right, upper and lower: Following the completion of a sortie, a Hunter might well have to be protected from the weather if parked in the open. This might mean steps to prevent rain from entering the engine vents (upper; a No 28 Squadron Mk 9) or perhaps the erection of a temporary shade to keep the cockpit cool(ish) in the baking sun (lower; a No 208 Squadron Mk 9).

deaths were caused by design faults or structural failures that could justifiably be attributed to the learning processes of designers and engineers getting to grips with the new technology and materials then becoming available in aviation. Far too many, however, were attributable to simple pilot error, brought about by carelessness or overconfidence, or lack of supervision. Part of the reason for this was that pilots were positively encouraged to be bold and dashing, keeping up the traditions of the valiant 'Few' in the Battle of Britain, and there was little concession to the fact that times were different then and that the nation was now, for the moment at least, at peace.

There appeared to be a general lack of awareness of just how inherently dangerous fighter flying could be, and pilots did not seem to respect the risks of the air in the same way that sailors had learned to respect the sea. I think it was indicative of the mindset of most of us flying Hunters that we used to say, for example. 'I hear that old so-and-so killed himself over at Tangmere yesterday', when, in fact, he hadn't killed himself at all but had met his demise as a result of circumstances beyond his control, perhaps trying to carry out a manœuvre that he had neither the skill nor the training to execute safely. The use of the well-worn phrase 'he killed himself' was probably a defence mechanism that implied that the system itself was basically sound and that the rest of us would have survived in a similar situation, so everything was all right really. Clearly, however, everything was not all right, as evidenced by the high accident rates.

To consider these and similar problems, an organisation known as Flight Safety was set up to monitor and advise on all aspects affecting aircraft accidents.

COURTESY ROGER LINDSAY

COURTESY TONY BUTTLER

I think it did a better job than was generally recognised to change attitudes to safety down the years. From the very beginning, the mainstay of its endeavours was a publication called the *Fighter Command Flight Safety Magazine*, which was published monthly, had a wide distribution and was read avidly by us all. It had articles ranging from ATC procedures to servicing safety considerations and to the safety aspects of combat exercises, and contained endless pearls of wisdom. Whether all these pearls were ingested by all its readers, however, is a matter of some debate. The major part of the magazine was devoted to a comprehensive list of every fighter accident that month, and included a brief summary of the incident, although no conclusions were given there and then. This was partly because some of the accidents were still *sub judice*, and partly because the lesson to be learnt was pretty obvious.

Each accident gave the pilot's name, his squadron and the number of hours he had flown in total and on that type. Nobody was worried in those happy days about concealing the identities or details of an individual: this was long before 'human rights' issues came to the forefront. The magazine was an excellent vehicle, therefore, for keeping tabs on one's friends.

Left: A row of T.7 tails at RAF Chivenor, showing the faired, aerodynamic parachute housings immediately over the tailpipes. The 'chute deployed through 'pop-up' doors. A point of minor interest is that XL586's fuselage serial has been applied rather further aft than was the norm for Hunters.
Below: Tragedy visited the Hunter squadrons from time to time, as on 18 August 1955 when Flying Officer William Deluce of No 14 Squadron, in WT714, lost his life following a mid-air collision near Bremen in Germany.

One could compare experience levels with one's own, and often have a good laugh at some friend's expense—for example, the pilot who flew a straightforward navigation exercise at night but put his air brake out at some stage and forgot all about it. He failed to notice the air brake indicator doll's eye showing white, or the unusually high rpm needed to maintain speed, or his excessive use of fuel. He ended up perilously short of fuel and had to divert somewhere in dodgy weather miles away from his destination. The magazine was also a means of keeping up with which of one's peers had been killed recently.

Flight Safety also used to issue some graphic posters to advertise their messages. One of the best loved was that showing the most glamorous female Wimbledon tennis star of that year. She was photographed on court partly from behind, raising the hem of her very brief skirt to reveal that she had forgotten to put her underwear on. Scrawled across the photograph was the slogan 'Don't assume—check.' Another was a picture of the remains of a Hunter strewn over a desolate hillside with the cautionary words 'Don't assume the cloud base—find out for certain. Don't assume—check.' Some wag wrote across the bottom 'So, if you don't know the cloud base, pop down through cloud to check it.' This did not go down well with Flight Safety, who did sometimes take their job too seriously.

I once had a birdstrike in a Hunter, and afterwards had to fill in a full accident report because the

COURTESY NIGEL WALPOLE

Avon engine had been damaged beyond repair. The pilot's narrative section was a bit difficult, because there had been no indication of a collision with a bird, nor any engine indication that damage had occurred. (This was not at all unusual, and speaks volumes for the robustness of the Avon engine: it could ingest all kinds of things through the air intakes and yet still perform without blemish, even though the impeller blades and perhaps the compressor blades had been damaged to the extent that a lengthy and expensive engine change became necessary.) I decided to write a brief report in just two sentences: 'I flew a perfectly normal tactics sortie in this aircraft on such-and-such a date and all engine indications were normal throughout. After landing,

the groundcrew informed me that the engine had suffered a birdstrike.' Then, as an afterthought, I added: 'Which surprised me as much as it must have surprised the bird.' I imagined that the poor old seagull, flying along without doing any harm to anyone, must have been more astonished than somewhat when a Hunter appeared from behind at 500 knots or so and swallowed him. The report went to Group HQ and came back in double-quick time with what I thought was a rather pompous note attached. It was from the Chief Engineer and said that these reports were very important as birdstrikes were proving very expensive to repair. Flippant reports such as that given by the pilot were not only unhelpful, but also in poor taste. It ended: 'Amend

J. HARMS, COURTESY ROGER LINDSAY

Above: A Hunter F.R. Mk 10 of No 8 Squadron having apparently suffered a collapse of its nosewheel or, more probably, a failure of the latter to lock on deployment. Such accidents rarely caused injury to the pilot.

Left: Engine problems were experienced too, particularly in the early days of Hunter operations (although such incidents received little publicity). An emergency of this nature, over the East Frisian Islands, involved Mk 6 XG270 of No IV Squadron in May 1957: despite a skilful landing by the pilot, Flight Lieutenant 'Ginger' Ratcliffe—who was, happily, uninjured—and valiant attempts at salvage, the aircraft was lost to the incoming tide.

Right: A Mk 10, 'S' of No II (AC) Squadron, comes to grief; for obvious reasons, the Aden ammunition has been quickly removed, the sections of the 'Sabrinas' lying alongside the fuselage.

this report.' I considered for a while, and then, in red ink, crossed out the bit saying 'as much as it must have surprised the bird' and sent it back to Group. We never heard another word.

Sometimes, however, a correcting word from one of the Flight Safety experts did not come amiss. We had a pilot at Chivenor, a squadron commander at the Operational Conversion Unit who shall remain nameless, who wrote a report once about an incident that had occurred during a practice sortie he had done in manual control in a Hunter Mk 4. He had selected manual and had found that the ailerons were a little out of trim to starboard. There was a small trimming tab on the ailerons intended to correct this very situation, so he unlocked the electric trimmer guard and gave a blip of trim to port. Unfortunately, the trimmer motor ran away to full travel to port and stuck there. The trimmer was designed to have very limited authority, and the pilot should have had little difficulty in holding the wings level in manual control, but he told Air Traffic Control that he had a problem and was coming back post-haste in an emergency. Rather dramatically, he asked for the circuit to be cleared to give him priority.

He then gave ATC a running account of his progress and of how, as he reduced speed, he was having progressively to increase the control position to starboard in order to counteract the jammed trimmer. He told ATC to stand by as he was selecting the undercarriage down on the normal system. After a bit of a pause, he came back on the air to say that he was still in control and the undercarriage was now fully down, so he was going to try a bit of flap. Another dramatic pause, and he radioed that the flap was now fully down and he was going to attempt a landing, which he duly did, still in manual control, and with the stick at half travel to starboard to maintain the wings level. In his report afterwards, he just about managed to avoid saying that anyone else would have been justified in baling out, but he made it clear that he had had to overcome insuperable odds to get the aircraft down in one piece. Wing Commander Flying said that this had been a courageous and skilful bit of flying and that the pilot deserved a Green Endorsement in his logbook to mark the achievement. The Station Commander agreed, and the report was sent off to Group Flight Safety.

The next day, Group came back to say that, since this was just a practice sortie in manual, and the aircraft hydraulic system appeared to be fully serviceable, it would be of interest to know what had happened when the pilot tried to select the power controls back on again to get 3,000psi of hydraulic pressure to work for him against the little trim tab. The question was put to the pilot, who confessed that it had never entered his head to reselect power! Group eventually ruled, therefore, that the Green Endorsement proposal was not approved, and that instead the pilot should be rebuked for having unnecessarily hazarded his aircraft. This put egg on the faces of Wing Commander Flying and the Station Commander, as well as the hapless pilot, and was cause for merriment at Chivenor for some time.

COURTESY NIGEL WALPOLE

First Flight *Flying Officer Ian Cadwallader*

Most Hunter pilots of my vintage will recall their first flight in the aircraft as a rather moving experience—very fast moving! When we pitched up to the Hunter Operational Conversion Unit, one aeroplane was very conspicuous by its absence, and that was the two-seat version of the very different aeroplane we were going to have to fly. The first part of the OCU course was some form of operational flying in Vampires—nice enough and easy to fly but, although we were not aware of it, rather underpowered.

After learning in the classroom something about the technical systems in the Hunter with which pilots were required to be familiar, and about the speeds for various manœuvres (especially landing), we sat in a cockpit to learn the positions of various controls, including the beautiful pistol grip on the stick and the large throttle lever perfectly positioned so that the left land automatically rested on it. After three or four of these 'sit in' sessions, the day dawned when it was time to don flying suit and Mae West and, having checked the Form 700 and trying to look nonchalant, walk out to the line of Hunters—all single seaters—with the instructor and then demonstrate that you remembered what to look for when doing your external check of the aircraft.

Then it was time to mount the red ladder, remove the seat pin with its large red disc, slip it into the pocket provided, and sit down. The ejection seat was as new to my course as the Hunter itself, because the Vampires on which we trained did not have them. Once you had fastened all the necessary seat connections and put on your 'bone dome' (another novelty), the instructor, standing on the ladder, watched as you went through the cockpit check.

The Hunter 1 and 4 had a separate high-pressure cock (in later marks it was incorporated in the throttle), and when starting the Avon it was essential to fire the starter cartridge as soon as possible after opening the HP cock in order to avoid a 'hot' start. Our Flight Commander instructor was a US Air Force exchange officer with a genuine southern drawl and his final instruction at the end of his pre-start briefing was, 'When you get the go from your ground man, I want for you to get that high-pressure *cawk awn*, and mash that start button! This I did—and from then on the experience was amazing.

I recall little about that first taxi out to the end of the runway, except that the Hunter seemed a big aeroplane after the Vampire, but after getting clearance to line up on the runway the next thirty minutes were, for a 20-year-old, unbelievable. The acceleration was way beyond expectation, and, once I was airborne, the undercarriage retraction button was 'mashed' as I remembered just in time to check that the gear was up before going through 250 knots. *Keep a good look-out . . .* The climb speed was 430 knots and I was already there! Trim, *keep a good look-out . . .* Pressurisation on at about 8,000 feet—that was 10,000 feet ago! *Keep a good look-out . . .* Turn out to sea, *keep a good look-out . . .* The details of the rest of that half an hour are a little blurred, but I remember doing a practice circuit at about 10,000 feet, checking the effect of flap and the undercarriage etc. and pulling back almost to the stall with full flap and gear down. I tried a couple of steep turns, then surprised myself at the rate of aileron rolls. I felt confident enough, I suppose, to return to the circuit. I got clearance to join the circuit in the approved manner with a break at 1,000 feet and I am sure that from then on the aircraft knew more about the circuit than I did, with the speed coming back nicely as I hung out the air brake, then the flap and the undercarriage, and without any help from visual glide path indicators (which are so common these days) I managed to

Few Nicer Places *Squadron Leader Roger Hymans*

It was July 1956 when I arrived at RAF Chivenor straight from my Wings course at Oakington. At the time I was very short of confidence, having gone through the (piston) Provost/Vampire course convinced every week that I would be 'chopped'; even winning the flying trophy at Oakington did not somehow lift my pessimism. Now in front of me was the mighty Hunter Mk 1. It looked huge against the Vampire: you needed a ladder to get in. There were no two-seaters, and no simulators. We did have a sort of cockpit trainer with paper instruments and wooden switches, so we had some idea where all the bits and pieces were, but that was it.

A cheerful and rather aggressive young Flying Officer helped me strap in, fired up the engine with a noisy and smelly cartridge, turned on the powered controls and, with a tap on the head, said, 'It's all yours, sunshine. Don't bloody break it!' Briefings in those days were, well, brief. High-pressure tyres and a stiff, long undercarriage, plus powerful brakes, made taxying a new experience, but eventually the end of the runway was there waiting for me. I ran through the TAFFIOH take-off checks for the fourth time before a sharp 'Get a move on!' from the duty instructor in the tower had me power up the Avon (Ah! Rolls-Royce!) against the brakes. As the aircraft started moving forward I released the brakes and went to full power. Over fifty years later I can still remember the mixture of exhilaration and fear as I set off like a startled stag towards the end of the runway. Your first experience of powered controls was just after your first take-off, and pilots would come out of the crew rooms to watch the tyro overcontrolling the ailerons as he hurtled over the Braunton Burrows waggling his wings. You felt as if you were waving goodbye—in more ways than one. The Hunter Mk 1 had very little fuel; trips lasted about 30 minutes at the most. It had a 100-series Avon which could surge at high altitude, and it also had a straight wing leading-edge, later modified on all Hunters with to incorporate a 'saw-tooth' to prevent pitch-up,

put the Hunter down in the correct place near the end of the runway and stop it without any drama on Chivenor's 2,000 yards. Elation was not a sufficiently descriptive word:

the experience was not quite the same as that I felt on my first solo in a Tiger Moth, but it was a lot more exciting— and there was more to come . . .

Top: Seconds from a mass take-off by Hunters of the Chivenor Wing. Bringing up the rear are four T.7 trainers, the dual-control variants that were unavailable to trainee Hunter pilots until the early 1960s.

Above: A Mk 6 on the No 229 Operational Conversion Unit establishment, *circa* 1965. No 229 was first tasked with Hunter training in the mid-1950s and it did not relinquish that rôle until the mid-1970s.

I experienced both of these problems at more or less the same time a few days later. I was just coming up to my fourth trip (high-level turning) when I met the young aggressive Flying Officer in the bar. He had flown on one operational tour so was of course a god. I think he felt that I was a bit wet and needed 'sharpening up', so he said that on my next trip I should get up to 40,000 feet, accelerate to .94 Mach, put on ninety degrees of bank and pull hard round the turn. It may be that he had imbibed one more Worthington than would be considered wise, but I listened avidly to the 'briefing': he was, after all, a god. The next day I did as I was told, accelerated, and pulled into a steep turn. What followed was really quite alarming. There was a loud bang from the engine as it surged and flamed out, the nose pitched up violently, and, although I had the stick hard forward against the instrument panel, the aircraft continued to rotate violently upwards. By now the air speed indicator was showing a very low figure, and then the aircraft entered a fast spin to the left.

There are few nicer places to be than a jet fighter at high altitude—it's quiet, it's smooth, and the whole world is in front of and below you—but now things had deteriorated somewhat and I had that bad feeling we all sometimes get of having made a very serious mistake. I had been shown how to enter a spin and recover in the Provost. Spinning the Vampire was a bit 'on and off' as now and then some-one would fail to recover from a practice spin and the subsequent Board of Inquiry would recommend that we gave spinning a miss until the fuss died down. I tried to remember the standard spin recovery procedure and applied the necessary control movements, but to little avail. I was descending very quickly indeed, and as the altimeter wound rapidly through 20,000 feet I was getting perturbed that I may have to use the good offices of Martin-Baker by jettisoning the aircraft. I then, for some unknown reason, put the controls into a position that would make the Hunter do what it was doing, that is, stick forward, rudder full left and aileron full left. I then moved the controls back to the centre— and, wonderfully, the spin stopped.

Many years later I spoke to the Hawker Chief Test Pilot Bill Bedford (a lovely man), and it became clear that the most important thing in the recovery from a spin was to ensure you did not have outspin aileron. By applying left aileron I had unwittingly put in the inspin necessary for recovery. Having recovered from the spin at about 12,000 feet, I re-started the engine and returned rather shakily to base. I never told anyone about the experience as it would plainly have been my fault and I would have been subjected to much abuse. There was also a fining system at Chivenor, and, as I was already in debt for calling the instructors a bunch of layabouts (£1) and then for saying it was worth it (a further 10 shillings), I just kept quiet. Later in life, when I was instructing at Chivenor and other places, I always remembered the experience of my early Hunter spin and tried not to give young pilots facetious advice in the bar. By then I might well have been, in their eyes, a 'god', and they might have been naïve enough to listen!

Right: 'I tried to remember the standard spin recovery procedure and applied the necessary control movements . . .'

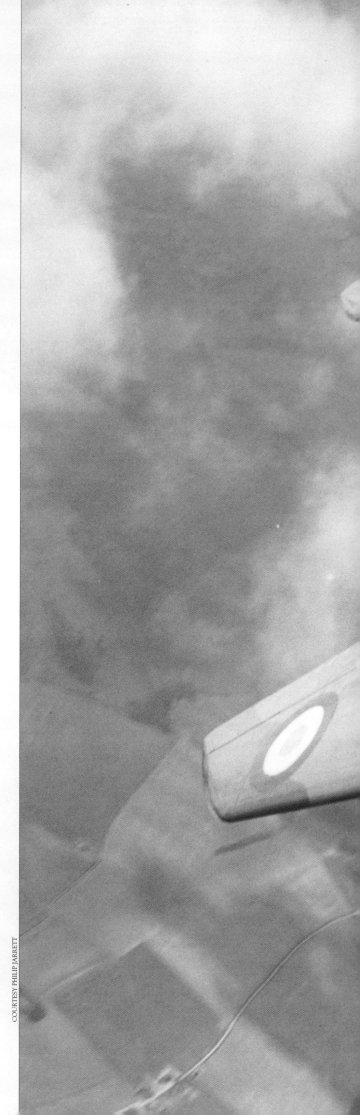

A Bit of an Adventure *Group Captain Marcus ('Oscar') Wild*

I arrived for my first operational tour rather apprehensively, just eleven days short of my twentieth birthday, but, in the event, life on 43 for a mad keen young bachelor was idyllic. We were flying the fastest aircraft in service. With two other squadrons in the Wing, the Mess was full and very lively, and at Leuchars we were on the edge of a university town. As a Pilot Officer my monthly pay of £36 was adequate, even though much of it went on my Mess bill. Rather later in my tour we got a substantial raise in flying pay, bringing my income up to £54 per month—which was rather surprising bearing in mind that a nasty redundancy programme was looming.

Our aircraft were all Mk 1s and still relatively new: the gracious lines of Sir Sydney Camm's original design had still to be marred by the gradual modifications which would turn it from a beautiful toy into an effective weapon. I was fortunate enough to meet him when the supersonic thin-wing Hunter was a sadly unfulfilled prospect. Our American exchange CO asked him if he expected any engineering problems. 'Why should I?' he replied. 'I build the best wings in the world!'

In fact the changes were already under way. At that time the only visible modification was the addition of the ventral air brake. This was to replace partial flap, originally meant as a speed brake, because of the nose-down change of trim it created at higher speeds. I was never quite convinced that this modification was necessary since later, when carrying out formation aeros on No 43 Squadron, we used to remove the air brake fuse to stop inadvertent extension and use flap instead. The authorities, in their wisdom, decided to install a 'notchier' air brake switch on the throttle. Having expressed this view, I must confess that during a fairly vigorous tail chase after a formation aerobatic session I reached for the flap lever but accidentally hit the undercarriage button. With the speed at 440 knots, twice the normal lowering speed but in tribute to the Hunter's basic structural strength, only the nosewheel door was only slightly sprained.

The ventral air brake design created its own problems because, when the guns were fired, the discarded links were rapidly caught up in the airflow and tended to scrape along the bottom of the fuselage and attack the air brake fairing. The solution to this was to install two external collection tanks under the fuselage. These were the 'Sabrinas', recalling the well-endowed shape of a starlet of that period. Rather later, when the Hunter was increasingly used for ground attack, concerns were raised about the nose-down trim change when all four cannon were fired. The solution was to put blast deflectors on the end of each barrel so that the combustion gases were deflected downwards, thereby pushing the nose back up. I believe that these ugly-looking additions reduced the range by about five per cent. Along the way the saw-toothed wing leading edge and external tanks would also change the original smooth lines.

In late 1955 to mid-1956 we were able to intercept the bomber aircraft of the period relatively easily—something embarrassingly denied to those of our fighter squadrons still equipped with Meteors. Most of the action took place above 40,000 feet, where manœuvrability was limited and overtaking speed on the newer V-bombers was low. In the autumn exercise of 1955 (appropriately called 'Beware') I remember doing my best to stay up with my leader but constantly stalling the compressor. This was a known feature of the Avon 100 series engine at high altitude, and the only solution was to throttle back and dive to clear the blockage. You were then left wondering where your leader was and struggling slowly back to his level. Another poor feature was the pressurisation, which was not up to the job. It could get quite cold at height, and if you descended rapidly into a moist atmosphere, misting or icing-up could reduce your vision at a time when fuel was low. The eventual action was to install flood flow, which vastly increased the amount of warm air entering the cockpit.

Fairly early in my tour, whilst I was pootling around off Dundee, the radar came up and asked if I would investigate a slow-moving but very high target. I set off confidently, but having got to 45,000 they said it was still 12,000 feet above me. They thought it might be a radiosonde balloon, except that it seemed to be progressing against the wind! I laboured finally to 52,800 feet, the highest I ever got in a Hunter. Eventually I overtook the target without seeing anything and then did a painfully slow, 360-degree orbit on the verge of the stall. On the second pass, with my neck craned skywards, I saw a glider-like aircraft way above me. I was just trying to describe this to the fighter controller when a rather more authoritative voice intervened and ordered me home immediately. On landing I was marshalled to the end of our ramp where the OC Flying, Wing Commander Des Sheen, was waiting. He said, 'You saw nothing,' to which I objected. He then became more emphatic, saying that if I mentioned it again he would sack me pronto. Rather puzzled, I never did mention it, but I did not understand why until Gary Powers was shot down in a U-2 in 1960. My friend Roger Hymans had a similar experience in Germany.

Sometime in 1956 No 43 Squadron was selected to undertake gun-firing trials to see how the aircraft would cope with the fairly violent dynamics of four Adens each shovelling out twenty rounds a second. We had already done some firing with low-velocity ammo, which you could see advancing about 200 yards ahead when gravity intervened and the rounds started dropping vertically. We had to fire over the sea off Leuchars at different speeds, heights and attitudes. Sadly one of our aircraft disappeared completely in this trial. On another occasion the vibration caused damage such that the nosewheels of two aircraft would not lower and we ended up with the runway blocked by two Hunters with their tails in the air.

Right: Four 'Fighting Cocks' practise formation flying over the Firth of Forth. These Hunters are Mk 4s; the Squadron had originally formed a team using the Mk 1s with which they were first issued. The aircraft's call-signs are carried on the black-painted forward nosewheel doors, and WV324 and '387 are flying *sans* 'Sabrinas'.

The avionics of the original Hunters left a lot to be desired by modern standards. For communications, it had two ten-channel VHF radios, each channel having its own crystal. If you were doing something unusual it was necessary painstakingly to re-crystallise, otherwise you had to use the crowded common frequencies. For some stupid reason—rather akin to recalling the number plate of your first motor car—I can remember that for Fighter Command Common (107.28MHz) and for Flying Training Command Common (115.56MHz). Present-day readers need to remember that there was no controlled air space above 25,000 feet in those days and you could do anything in this upper air.

In the nose there was a small radar to measure a target's range for input to the gun sight solution. I don't ever remember it working on 43, although it did on my later tours. For navigation we had a DME-like equipment which only worked spasmodically and whose beacons were infrequent outside Britain. There was a small ILS-type presentation piece of kit, Green Salad, which was meant to allow you to locate a jamming aircraft in azimuth and elevation. It worked erratically, and I once very nearly flew into the trailing aerial of a Lincoln whilst concentrating on the cross needles. To reduce drag many of the original antennæ were concealed behind dielectric skins in the fuselage and this probably reduced signal strength. I remember only the radio aerial sticking into the airflow in a Mk 1.

Travelling any distance in a Hunter Mk 1 was always a bit of an adventure, especially outside the RAF environment. The short range bestowed by a fuel load of only 2,200 pounds was a constant worry. For example, when our aerobatic team flew to Rome in June 1956 for the opening of Fiumicino Airport it took us four legs with no navig-

COURTESY MARCUS WILD

Supersonic Squitters *Air Vice-Marshal Peter Latham* CB AFC

In the mid-1950s I was on the staff of the Day Fighter Leaders' School, part of the Central Fighter Establishment and based at RAF West Raynham. The rôle of the School was to hone the dog-fighting skills of Flight Lieutenants and Squadron Leaders to ready them for becoming Flight and Squadron Commanders. We were commanded by a Wing Commander who had two Squadron Leaders and about half a dozen Flight Lieutenant instructors, of which I was one. We flew Hunter 1s, the first RAF supersonic aircraft (albeit helped by gravity). We routinely put sixteen aircraft into the air in staged, eight-*versus*-eight aerial combat. It was one of the most enjoyable jobs I ever had.

With the natural turnover of staff, a new member arrived one day who had not yet flown a Hunter. He was immediately given a rapid conversion and quickly gave himself the pleasure of a supersonic run or two over the adjacent North Sea. For totally unrelated causes he was almost immediately struck down with a bad case of diarrhœa. As a result, he was, inevitably, temporarily off flying and was relegated to permanent Ops Officer for the duration of his complaint.

This was too great an opportunity for us to forgo our favourite leisure activity of practical jokes. One fellow used his friendship with a member of the Institute of Aviation Medicine to get some Institute headed writing paper, and a letter was produced purporting to be addressed to all Fighter Command Stations for the attention of Station Medical Officers. It expressed the concern which the C-in-C had for the prevalence of diarrhœa in aircrew who exceeded the speed of sound. If this could not be halted then the efficiency of our air defence would be drastically reduced. The letter emphasised the need for total security and was accompanied by an example of a form which was to be completed by all sufferers. This would enable research into the phenomenon to begin immediately. I will spare you all the unsavoury details but in general it required the sufferer to list date and time, quantity, colour, consistency and any other information the patient thought was relevant. Our Station MO, an agreeable fellow who felt that the

Right: A Hunter F. Mk 1 being flown by a pilot assigned to the CFE at RAF West Raynham. It was here that future fighter leaders developed their skills in aerial combat—and were not averse to the odd prank!

Opposite and right: No 43 Squadron's XF997 (opposite), one of the last Mk 4s to be delivered to the RAF, following its recovery from the River Eden by a locally owned steam traction engine (right) after overshooting at Leuchars in 1956. The pilot survived the accident unhurt but the Hunter was deemed beyond economic repair and scrapped.

ational help whatsoever—and this was with some newly arrived Mk 4s, which had about 25 per cent more fuel than a Mk 1. External fuel tanks were also on the horizon but I never imagined that, five years later, I would be flying non-stop from northern Germany to Malta in the best ever Hunter, the F.R.10, with good reserves.

During my tour our runway was resurfaced and we attempted to operate off the shorter, 1,600-yard strip. It was clearly inadequate, and two of our aircraft finished up in the River Eden from which they had to be plucked by an ancient steam traction engine. Because of this, and shortly afterwards, the Powers That Be removed our newly arrived Mk 6 aircraft and my first trip was to deliver one of the shiny beasts to 'Treble One' at North Weald and bring home a rather tired Mk 4. Little did I realise that I would be flying the same Mk 6 with 'The Black Arrows' just a year later!

In autumn 1957 my tour and that of many others came to an abrupt end when the Minister of Defence decided that there was no further need for aircraft and that it would all be done by missiles. It must have taken nearly five minutes to realise what nonsense this was but, in the meanwhile, squadrons were disbanded and most of us on short-service commissions were cast to the wolves. In my end-of-tour assessment my Boss wrote the No 43 motto 'Gloria Finis'—and that is what it felt like. Rather quixotically, two of our members drove up to RNAS Lossiemouth and were in the Fleet Air Arm within a month; others were welcomed with open arms by BOAC and most seem eventually to have become 747 skippers. For my part, with the great help of my Flight Commander (a future Air Marshal), I managed to stay on in the RAF and fly the Queen of the Skies for a further six years. By 1957 most of the Hunter 1s had been withdrawn for re-engineering into other marks.

Hippocratic Oath had not pronounced unfavourably on such an activity, kept a straight face and, having shown our victim the covering letter, set him off on a regime of reporting his condition in detail. The fun lasted a few days and only ended when the victim discovered the truth. Unfortunately, this was not the end of the affair.

One Monday morning some weeks later I had my annual medical and was asked to do the usual test of climbing up and down several times on to a chair before having my blood pressure checked. Slightly concerned, the MO told me not to bother and he would repeat the test at the end of the examination. When the repeat was done he told me that my blood pressure was too high and the immediate recourse was to lose some weight as quickly as possible. I was given a 'Marriot' diet sheet and told to follow it exactly. With no alcohol, and virtually no food worth eating, my blood pressure might come down. Walking back to DFLS, seeds of doubt began to enter my mind but there was no possibility of forsaking the diet because it might be the only way of securing my flying future. However, a plan entered my head which might reveal the truth.

While following the diet to the letter, I missed no opportunity in the crew room to refer almost daily to feasts and drinks parties that I was to enjoy each evening. This heightened the hunger and the effects of sudden alcohol withdrawal. At last, on Friday evening, a voice piped up: 'But I thought you were on a diet?' As nobody but the MO and I knew about it, if it was genuine this taunt revealed the culprit. It was, of course, the victim of the diarrhœa tease. *Touché!*

Right: No 35 Day Fighter Leaders' Course, July 1956: (standing, left to right) Flight Lieutenants Clements, Harcourt-Smith, Plowman, Foulkes and Wright, Flying Officer Hampton, Flight Lieutenant Seymour, Lieutenant-Commander MacDonald, and Flight Lieutenants Wood, Buchanan, Ewan, Radice, Picking, Mansell and Hodgson; (seated, left to right) Squadron Leader Edwards, Flight Lieutenant Birnie, Squadron Leader Bushen, Wing Commander Vos (OC), Squadron Leader Downes and Flight Lieutenants Bennett and MacPherson.

Chivenor to Brüggen to Santiago *Flying Officer Mike McEvoy*

By the summer of 1956 the Sabres that comprised the interceptor force of the RAF in Germany had all been replaced with the Hunter F.4, which offered a little more endurance than the F.1 and was now able to fire its guns without affecting its engine, the early 100-series Avon. Most of the pilots on the Germany-based Hunter squadrons were ex-Sabre—many had been trained in the United States—but from early in the year the squadrons had begun to be issued with first-tourists straight out of the training system; I was the third of these on my new unit, joining No 67 Squadron at Brüggen as soon as I had finished the conversion course at No 229 OCU, Chivenor.

There were four Hunter squadrons at Brüggen: No 67 shared its hangar with the shark-mouthed No 112 Squadron, while Nos 71 (Eagle) Squadron and 130 (Punjab) Squadron—which included an elephant's head in its marking—had hangars and pans of their own. Brüggen had been purpose-built for RAF use, and in common, I believe, with all the similar bases, had a 2,800-yard runway as distinct from the 2,000 that was the norm in Fighter Command, the extra length coming in handy for me at least once.

Rivalry between the squadrons, and indeed between the flights in each squadron, was considerable; I did not find similar feelings during my subsequent period of service with Bomber Command. The competitive spirit was fostered by those in high places by the regular 'war' between No 2 Group in the north of the British area and No 83 Group, of which we were a part, further south, the notional cause of this conflict being the seizure by one side or the other of Abyssinia Beach on Sylt. This was devoted to nudists and was known universally as 'Bare-Ass Beach'. What we all knew was that we in the 2nd Tactical Air Force were of course much more 'operational' that those in RAF Fighter Command; after all, we were very close to the potential front line, whereas they were sheltering safely behind the North Sea.

Without a Hunter two-seater, my first four trips at Brüggen were in a Vampire T.11 of the Station Flight, in which I was shown the local area by day and night and had my instrument flying ability checked; and then on 26 July I was airborne for forty-five minutes in WV367 for what my log book describes as a 'famil'. There were five more flights by the end of the month, and the three on the 31st were in XF317, WV403 and XF296, all of which will reappear. Most of our flying was in two- or four-plane formations, which was expected to be the standard way in which we would go to war when the need arose.

A couple of memories of our area are still vivid. The big RAF headquarters at Rheindalen was a little to the east of us and was an excellent point from which to start the run-in to the airfield on return when landing on westerlies; the standard fighter arrival, in two or four, was *en echelon* starboard at, I think, around 250 feet, with the leader breaking to port over the threshold and the rest of us following at two-second intervals, dropping twenty degrees of flap and lowering the undercarriage when steady on the downwind leg before a curved base leg turn and straightening up not long before touch-down. The bleed valves on the F.4's Avon would emit a variable 'blue note' on the run-in, which some colleagues in the RCAF compared favourably to a bagpipe rendition of 'Annie Laurie'. And if you began at Rheindalen and got the heading slightly wrong, it wasn't difficult to find that you were breaking over the Wildenrath threshold, to the mystification of both ATCs, trying to tie up what they could see with what they had heard on the R/T (yes, I did that).

Right: Hunter XF296 in pristine condition and with the markings of the writer's squadron—No 67— presented in low-key fashion on the nose. The name 'Fg. Off. M. M. Letton' appears in small capital lettering beneath the cockpit sill. (For the story behind these markings, see overleaf.) The aircraft is in the process of having its Aden cannon pack changed, the fuselage hoisting point for this operation being tagged with a warning notice.

COURTESY SIR DAVID HARCOURT-SMITH

Our low flying was done at 250 feet in a selection of defined low-flying areas, and one of these included the Mohne Dam; the reader can, I am sure, imagine the number of times we made a low approach while whistling into our masks the theme tune from the film that had been released the year before. My other entertainment in this area was to come up behind one of the big Rhine barges, lower flaps and wheels and pull the speed back a bit for a 'carrier approach' before selecting everything up and climbing away again. We had to make our own amusement in those days.

We lost two aircraft during my time on No 67, the first resulting in a night ejection because of an engine failure just after take-off. The pilot was Lieutenant Mike Maina, RN, who, like several of his nautical brethren, was serving a tour on Hunters ahead of a posting on to Scimitars (807

ROBIN BROWN, COURTESY ROGER LINDSAY

NAS in Mike's case). With the *sang froid* expected of a dark blue pilot, he was taking a medicinal brandy and soda in the mess bar less than half an hour after banging out. There was something of a scramble to see what could be claimed as written off in the crash, especially if it had already gone AWOL from someone's inventory; with the best will in the world, however, there was no way that we could find to account for the missing eleven galvanised iron buckets that 'belonged' to Mick Letton. The second was burnt out at Sylt. The Avon 100s had a cartridge starter, which when fired turned a small turbine wheel very quickly to give the impetus to turn the engine over. To avoid accidents the standard procedure in the event of a misfire was to wait for thirty seconds before pressing the button again—which George Foulkes duly did. Unfortunately, when he made the second selection two cartridges fired at once, the small turbine burst, its little blades carved a track under the wing and the fuel in the wing tank caught fire. Fortunately, George got out promptly and safely.

Sylt was the gunnery airfield and range for all of 2 ATAF, including the other northern NATO air forces. When I was there for my one and only firing practice we shared the air with a Belgian F-84F unit and No 5 Squadron's Venoms. Although we had practised the required manœuvres at Chivenor, we had never managed any actual firing, so it was not until my dual familiarisation at Sylt that I fired Real Bullets. The 30mm shells of the Aden cannon were substantial, and comparatively lethal if they hit, but their weight meant that there was a considerable 'drop-off' with increasing range, and any attacks had, therefore, to be from close range. We fired on a banner towed by one of the resident Meteor 8 target tugs, with different coloured tipped shells for each pilot sharing the same practice session so that the results could be marked afterwards. It can now be revealed that air-to-air was not one of my talents; I remember it being said at the time that on any fighter squadron there were two who could see 'trade' at altitude and two who could shoot, and they weren't necessarily the same people. Apart from my inability to hit the flag, my abiding memories of Sylt after more than fifty years are of the accommodation, which was somewhat Gothic, and of the only time I ever consciously flew with a hangover. There was a widespread belief that the effects of this could be cured, or at least ameliorated, by 100 per cent oxygen. It didn't work for me on that flight, and having frightened myself considerably approaching to land in low cloud I did not do it again!

There were a couple of other events that I would perhaps rather have avoided. One of our regular exercises was to 'land away' at a strange (but friendly) airfield, and on 29 October, after I landed at Eindhoven following my third GCA with the Dutch controllers, XF305 needed refuelling before returning. On the Hunter there was a single pressure refuelling point in the port undercarriage well, designed, like the replaceable gun pack, to facilitate a quick turnround between operational sorties. At that time British jet engines used Avtur, and American engines Avtag—JP-1 and JP-4, I think, and I just hope I've got it right this time because fifty-two years ago I didn't. Once the mistake was realised I was advised that I would have to fly the aircraft back to Brüggen with reduced performance, and the engine and fuel system would have to be thoroughly cleaned out. It was not a popular move on my part, but though the records show that it was XF305 that self-destructed at Sylt I don't think that there is any connection.

On another occasion, the date of which is not recorded in my log book, I was taking off as Number Two in close formation with my leader when he had to abort, and, like a good wingman (I thought), I stayed with him, slowing down with some force to stay behind him (which was when the extra eight hundred yards were useful), and when he had pulled off on to the squadron pan I taxied round to the take-off point to carry out the sortie anyway. I think it must have been only on the third R/T call of 'Aircraft passing Station Flight—your brakes are on fire' that I realised they meant me. Stopping quickly, if gingerly, I think I was over the side and on to the ground without waiting for the ladder. Given that the taxiway was blocked until they could move the aircraft safely, and that all the brakes had to be changed, I wasn't popular then either.

While we were on the Hunter course at Chivenor in the hot summer of 1956, *The Aeroplane* published a two-page colour spread of RAF fighter squadron markings, in which form of heraldry I was starting to take a serious interest (thus it has remained to this day). The colour chart's appearance was timely in that when Dick Whittingham and I received our postings to Brüggen we could identify the markings of our new units, his No 67 Squadron, on which I made a slightly caustic comment, and my No 71. It was, therefore, perhaps justice that, having found on arrival that somehow our postings had become reversed, in a little while I found myself tasked with applying unit markings to No 67's Hunters. It was the practice for squadron pilots to have an aircraft allocated to them when possible, and on the return of its previous 'owner', Trevor Egginton, to Britain I inherited XF317/'U'. Up till then, while the other squadrons' aircraft had all carried their unit markings, No 67's were identified only by having their individual letters in a pale bluish-grey on the fin. When I went to see the Boss about this state of affairs I was, in the best tradition of the Service, given the task of sorting it out.

Using XF317 as a guinea pig, I adapted the red, yellow and blue markings that had been devised for the Sabre, apparently on a wet afternoon in the crewroom, by putting them either side of a simplified squadron badge. The device on this was a drongo, a small Malayan bird particularly fierce in defence of its young; this referred back to the Squadron's part in the air war in the Far East, when it was equipped with Buffalos. The Boss gave it his approval, and the Squadron started to apply it to the rest of the aircraft when opportunity arose, starting, of course, with the Boss's WV403/'J' and then Mick Letton's XF296, but only five or six had been marked up when the Squadron came to a sudden stop. The Defence White Paper of 1957 had many long-lasting effects, but one of the results of the decision that manned fighters could be replaced by missiles was the rapid disbandment of nine 2nd TAF Hunter squadrons— including the entire Brüggen Wing. No 67 had welcomed a new boss on 1 April, with the promotion of Squadron Leader Hugh Walmsley, a Griffon-Spitfire ace, to become

Above: The writer reacquaints himself with his Hunter—still with its No 67 Squadron emblem *in situ*—at RAF Halton . . .
Below: . . . and, years later, re-discovers it, now as a camera-equipped F.R. Mk 71A, in Chile.

MIKE McEVOY

Wing Commander Flying at Tangmere. His replacement, Squadron Leader G. J. Tricker, had been a flight commander on No 87 at Wahn, but with the announcement of the instant cuts on the 4th or 5th (I think) he returned rapidly to his old unit. Those of us with financial commitments in Germany—notably buying a car, for which the proud owner needed to spend a year there to avoid paying import duty—stayed a little longer on temporary attachment to other squadrons, but, having no such tie, I was on the boat train shortly after the Squadron's final fly-by of Wahn, Wildenrath and Brüggen on 16 April.

Most of the aircraft were soon redeployed as well. 'My' XF317 went to the Chivenor OCU for a short while, and then became an instructional airframe at Halton, where I found it (marked as '7773M') in the late 1960s. Like many other F.4s, it was bought back by Hawker Siddeley and remanufactured as an FR.71A for Chile, with an FR.10 nose and a 200-series Avon. It was on the Chilean Air Force's final formation of four, and I was reunited with it once more in Santiago in 2003. It now belongs to the Chilean Air and Space Museum.

My log book tells me that I flew a total of 146 hours 55 minutes on the Hunter in less than a year, neither of which periods of time seems long; even though I never became the steely-eyed fighter pilot that I, like many others of my generation, aspired to, my clear memories of that era are of how much I enjoyed flying the Hunter, if occasionally with a little trepidation. It responded quickly to the pilot's inputs, it was great fun in a long-line-astern tail-chase around the cumulus tops, and that wide-track undercarriage was very reassuring when returning to the runway. Its career was far, far longer than mine, but it played an absolutely central rôle in my early life, from which I took experiences and a view of life that have stayed with me ever since.

MIKE McEVOY

'Just a Bit of Cloud' *Flying Officer Michael Thurley*

Happy days on 'Treble-One'—mainly because of the friends I made there but also because of the foolproof Hunter. I was a four-year man, and my only squadron tour was with 'The Tremblers'. I arrived on the Squadron in April 1956 and started formation aerobatics that November. After that, my log book entries were mostly 'Form Aeros'. Off-duty highlights of the tour were the wild times in the North Weald Mess, in the local George and Dragon and in the Big Smoke. It is truly amazing how we survived those car rallies!

The Russians were coming and we did our stint on standby. One morning I was in a pair towed in thick fog to the end of the runway at dawn. The plug-in radio told us that there were no diversions, and fifteen minutes later we were scrambled to intercept yet another US aircraft. Fortunately Tangmere had just opened up, so we could land instead of ejecting. Serious business.

My landing in 1956 with a retracted right main wheel was a first time for a Hunter, and I was warned that it might swing 400 yards, which would put me into No 601 Squadron RAuxAF's hangar in the south-west corner of the airfield. I managed to keep the wing up, however, and the swing was only about twenty yards.

April 30 1957 was another memorable day for me and very nearly my last. The Standard Presentation on that afternoon was by Air Chief Marshal Sir Harry Broadhurst, a former Squadron member. In the morning we had a practice with me flying Number Five, during which my pitot head became bent 90 degrees. Not wanting, with Sir Harry listening in the tower, to announce a mid-air collision, I reported a bird strike and was instructed by Boss Topp to formate on Number Three for landing.

My memory of the afternoon is very spotty. After the parade and presentation we did our show again and, because of a strong wind, we had to land downhill on Runway 05, aiming to miss the bump at the top of the hill. I didn't, and the result was (so I am told) a very rough landing. My last memory is of seeing the rubber padding on the gun sight. The aircraft, with me still in it but unconscious, ran the length of the runway, down a drop then started knocking down lead-in light poles and breaking up. Luckily the seat fired during these impacts and delivered me away from the exploding wreck. The next thing I knew was waking up for a short period in the X-ray Department at St Margaret's Hospital in Epping, asking for, and getting, a cigarette.

Above: Michael Thurley's 'Quebec' (WT720) at rest following his skilful two-wheel landing at North Weald on 10 September 1956. Notice the Union Flag on the nose of the aircraft

Below: A quartet of Hawker Hunter Mk 4s of No 111 Squadron, showing their distinctive black and yellow unit markings, with the call-signs in the same colours. With the arrival on the Squadron of new Mk 6s in November 1956, the camouflage would go, replaced by the even more distinctive all-black finish . . .

I had two fractured vertebræ, and these were initially treated with a body cast, which quickly became 'graffitied' with rather rude messages. I then enjoyed two months at Headley Court Rehabilitation Centre in Surrey, becoming very fit with daily physiotherapy. With many thanks to a lot of string-pulling by the Boss, fighting the brass, I was back doing 'Form Aeros' again in July.

The Farnborough Air Show was the big event for 'The Black Arrows' and I was Number Five in 1957 and the lead of the left outside line in the 'Twenty-two' in 1958. The Boss was very press-on and there was never a failed show, except perhaps when I crashed on landing at the end of that Standard Presentation. In shows, the Boss's call of 'Just a bit of cloud' would warn that everything was going to go black.

During one Battle of Britain show a civilian aircraft was flying low level and passed through our nine-ship formation flying in to start the show. Someone shouted 'Break', and the effect was of the show starting with a bomb burst and leading on to a join-up and the usual pattern. The crowd liked it, little thinking that there had been a spectacular near-miss.

I am very glad I did not die on that day, as I can now, after 30 years as a Canadian GP, enjoy retirement on the shores of Ontario's Georgian Bay, reflect on memories of flying in two SBAC shows at Farnborough—Number Five in 1957 and Number Seven-One in 1958—and enjoy attending yearly Squadron reunions at RAF Leuchars with all those fine, unchanging chaps.

Below: The foam-covered remains of Michael Thurley's Hunter 6 following his 'very rough landing' on 30 April 1957 at North Weald.

Right: The crumpled nose section of the aircraft (XG203/'R'), which fortuitously broke away on the initial impact, activating the ejection seat

COURTESY MICHAEL THURLEY

Impeccable Manners *Squadron Leader Brian Weeden*

After a ground tour at HQFC, I had hoped to fly Hunter 9s. I was delighted when I got my wish and was posted to No 54 Squadron. The Boss was an old friend, Squadron Leader Dave Harcourt-Smith and I was posted to West Raynham as his 'A' Flight Commander.

A happy time: Nos 1 and 54 were based there as part of No 38 Group's 'Fire Brigade', and the squadrons could be sent anywhere in NATO or CENTO at short notice. We fired rockets, fired guns, skip-bombed, etc.—it was the dream posting. It was made perfect when, just as I arrived, the squadrons were cleared to fly low-level down to 50 feet.

One memory out of many. My deputy was Farooq Khan, on secondment from the Pakistani Air Force, a good pilot and great fun. I needed to experience a long Hunter flight (with two 230 and two 100 drop tanks) and so he arranged for us to do a direct flight to Malta. It was made more interesting because we would be pushed by a friendly jetstream and a fast time (and unofficial record) was possible. We achieved a flight time of about 2 hours 10 minutes (from overhead to overhead), but this sort of transit flying in a fighter aircraft is rather dull; even the Mystères that attempted to 'bounce' us over Marseilles were easy to shake off. Homeward bound, we dropped into Orange (to have a look at our nominated diversion airfield) and stayed over-

night. Farooq organised a taxi to take us to the town and a restaurant he knew. I was wearing my newly acquired, highly expensive No 54 Squadron tie and was impressed with his impeccable manners as he stood to one side to let me enter first. Our hostess said to me. 'I have been waiting for you'—and cut the end off my brand-new tie! 'I thought she might do that,' said Farooq and pointed to the display of squadron ties on the wall (and the gap waiting for a No 54 acquisition)! As No 54 was renowned for its practical jokers, I count myself lucky to have got away so lightly and still wear the maimed one with pride when I attend reunions. We broke no records on the flight home as the jetstream was now blowing against us.

At about this time, the Squadron was cleared to fly to 50 feet. Soon afterwards we were on a tented detachment in Scotland, an area ideal to train for this type of flying. The Boss decided that he and I would do the required check-outs using the T.7 two-seat Hunter we had. The results of the flights were much as we expected: those with plenty of experience were quickly confident and could be cleared to the lowest level, others needed an intermediary height first and the more junior ones needed to continue at 250 feet and gain more experience. Fifty feet may sound quite high, but bear in mind that, in Britain, the top of a decent-sized

COURTESY MICHAEL THURLEY

COURTESY TONY BUTTLER

tree can be higher and at 500mph (a typical routine speed for a low-level Hunter—and then without inertial navigation assistance, just a map), you need your wits about you if you are going to attack a pinpoint target. It was hard work and great fun—in fact, the most enjoyable flying I ever did.

Above: A Hunter Mk 6 of No 54 Squadron carrying 100-gallon drop tanks on its underwing pylons. With the introduction to the Squadron of the Mk 9 in 1960, the Hunters would be able to accommodate the larger, 230-gallon tank on its inboard wing pylons. The Mk 9s served until 1969, finally bringing to an end the No 54's association with the Hunter over fourteen years after it had begun.

The Uncertainty of the Jungle *Wing Commander Jak Pugh* OBE AFC

'Which was your best tour?' Without hesitation, the answer is always: 'Singapore.' Flying the Hunter anywhere in the world would take some beating, but in the vast playground of the Far East, liberally laced with unsurpassed recreation and a sparkling social life in a tropical setting, what could possibly be better? I was posted to No 20 Squadron at Tengah in 1965 during the period following the formation of the state of Malaysia—Malaya, Singapore, North Borneo (Sabah) and Sarawak—when Indonesia was perceived as posing a threat to the territories. In the context of the so-called 'Confrontation', the job of the Tengah Strike Wing, composed of No 45 Squadron (Canberra B. Mk 2), No 81 Squadron (Canberra P.R. Mk 7), Nos 60 and 64 Squadrons (Javelin F.A.W. Mk 9) and No 20 Squadron (Hunter F.G.A. Mk 9), was to deter aggression against Malaysia and, if it came to it, to mount air operations against the aggressor. No 28 Squadron (Hunter 9), based at Kai Tak, performed a similar function in Hong Kong until its disbandment in 1967, when Tengah Hunter and Javelin detachments took over.

The Hunter Mk 9 was developed for tropical duties as a successor to the Venom ground-attack fighters in the Middle East. Because of the requirement to operate from 'hot and high' runways of limited length, it was fitted with a tail parachute and, to give it a useful ferry range, provision was made for 230-gallon tanks on the inboard pylons in addition to 100-gallon tanks outboard. In this configuration the F.G.A.9 was given the extra range necessary for deployments in the Far East, for example from Singapore to Hong Kong via North Borneo and the Philippines. A radio compass was the sole navigation aid and could be comforting when outside R/T range. On the other hand, the lack of an instrument landing system definitely classed us the poor relation when staging through Clark Air Force Base in the Philippines, where unfamiliarity with USAF arrival and departure procedures could also prove embarrassing—in

particular the requirement to repeat gabbled departure instructions word for word before being given take-off clearance, the penalty for repeated failure in which was banishment to the sin bin, thus missing a take-off slot and using up precious fuel reserves.

Surprisingly, these ferry trips involving 800-mile stages rarely gave trouble, but they were not always straightforward. On one occasion I had delivered an aircraft to the Hong Kong Aircraft Engineering Company for scheduled servicing, and was due to collect another and return to Tengah. My return was delayed by a mighty cyclone which lingered over Hong Kong before trudging off towards the Philippines. I eventually timed my departure to reach Clark before the cyclone and, staying above the cloud formation, had a magnificent view of what appeared like a great slice of Swiss roll whose diameter practically spanned the entire route. The arrival at Clark was uneventful, but after taking off, bound for Borneo, things started to go wrong. The undercarriage did not retract, so I had to burn off fuel and land back at Clark. Tengah signalled instructions on how to fix what appeared to be an electrical fault. Accordingly, I changed over some fuses and set off once more, but again the undercarriage failed to retract, which meant spending a couple of days at Clark before a Javelin detachment happened to stage through on its way to Hong Kong. I had arranged to leave the sick Hunter and take a lift on the ground crew's Argosy, but one of the Javelin pilots had suffered ear trouble on the descent and the detachment commander (who shall remain nameless) suggested that my previous experience on Meteors and Canberras should equip me to take the sick pilot's place and fly the Javelin on

Below: A Hunter F.G.A.9 of No 20 Squadron with a white-painted nose cone operating out of RAF Tengah, the tropical climate having taken its toll on the rest of the paintwork. The aircraft has just landed—notice that the doors for the braking parachute are still open. The smudges around the Aden cannon ports are evidence of recent firing.

COURTESY JEREMY SAYE

Above: A No 20 Squadron Hunter T.7 attacks a simulated target in the Malayan jungle, February 1967. Notice the marker flare placed by a Forward Air Controller (FAC).

to Kai Tak. The navigator agreed to take the back seat and I could see no honourable way out. After a skeletal briefing, including, I recall, use of toe brakes for directional control on the ground which must have been new to me, I spent an hour with Pilots' Notes thinking, 'This can't be happening!' With the realisation that time was running out if we were to reach Hong Kong in daylight, wiser counsel came to my rescue and I think the sick pilot simply carried on at a lower altitude. The idea of attempting to land at Kai Tak, always tricky, on a first flight in daylight, let alone at night, still haunts me. But only now, as I relate this tale forty years later, does a thought occur to me: was I the victim of an outrageous spoof? Spoofing new arrivals at Tengah was a popular sport, and although I was considered immune from such tomfoolery when I arrived, was I, on this occasion, well and truly hooked, line and sinker?

With none of the overcrowding now experienced in Europe, the Tengah squadrons were able to plan training programmes virtually free from airspace restrictions and with a variety of readily accessible air-to-ground ranges, supplemented on occasions by splash targets towed by HM ships, available for regular practice in weapons delivery. Once a year, armament practice camps were held at Butterworth, near Penang, where, as a bonus, Australian Mirage

III squadrons were only too happy to engage in aerial combat. Elsewhere, air-to-ground ranges in Hong Kong provided continuity in weapons practice for those on detachment.

Air-to-air gunnery was rarely practised and, it is recalled, produced mixed results. It is now clear that, while the Hunter's four Aden cannon remained effective against ground targets, as an air-to-air weapon the gun was losing ground to the missile. However, high-level pilot interceptions and air combat featured regularly, to prepare pilots in the air defence rôle. It happened to be a time when the helicopter gunship was gaining prominence as a threat to ground forces, and No 20 Squadron, together with Army helicopters, took part in trials to develop helicopter-*versus*-fighter tactics. These led to the broad conclusion that by manœuvring towards a single fighter the helicopter would generally survive but that a pair of fighters working together could defeat it.

Simulated strike training ranged from the simple pair to four-ship formations with escort and 'bounce' aircraft sometimes in the form of Javelins. Such co-operation was easily set up at station level but occasionally Group exercises tasked composite operations when, for example, Hunters escorted Hunter/Canberra combined strike formations against targets defended by Javelin patrols. Airfields, communications centres, fuel storage depôts, ports and even small habitations (kampongs) were used as training targets, their distance from base determined according to whether the

ROGER AUSTIN, COURTESY JAK PUGH

COURTESY JEREMY SAYE

Above: The writer flying Mk 9 XG153—again a somewhat weather-beaten aircraft.

Left: A small number of No 20's Mk 9s were locally modified to mount an F.95 sideways-looking camera in the nose, providing a useful reconnaissance tool. This photograph was taken using such a camera.

Below left: A No 20 Squadron Hunter Mk 9 at low level along the Main Drag at Hong Kong. After No 28 Squadron, based in the colony, had its commission terminated in 1967, No 20's Hunters made frequent detachments there to conduct exercises and provide air defence.

Below right: RAF Kai Tak (Hong Kong), with a No 28 Squadron F.G.A.9 centre stage.

COURTESY JEREMY SAYE

route was flown at high or low level. Target recognition was facilitated using photographs taken by No 81 Squadron but, latterly, No 20 Squadron became self-sufficient when an ingenious local modification was introduced fitting an optical flat (window) in the side of the nose cone and mounting a port-facing F.95 camera in place of the nose radar and powered by the G.90 gun-camera supply. Only one or two aircraft were modified, but it added a useful fighter-reconnaissance capability and a capacity to expand the target library.

Devoid of man-made features, the jungle which covered much of Malaya away from coastlines and cultivated areas added to the uncertainty of pilot navigation, and topography assumed greater importance, particularly at low level. Another consideration connected with the jungle was that if a pilot had to eject, and if his parachute became entangled in the tree canopy, he would be left suspended high above the ground and unable to get down. Pilots therefore flew with a so-called 'treescape' buttoned to the flying suit consisting of a length of cord and a braking system to allow a controlled descent to safety. In the same connection, pilots were all given comprehensive training in jungle survival at the Jungle Warfare School.

The Squadron's standing operational task in rotation with the Javelins was to maintain air patrols in Borneo along the length of the Indonesian border. Detachments were based at Kuching in the west and Labuan in the north-east, from which patrols covered the centre and both ends of the 800-mile border. Starting at the coast west of Kuching, the border was ill-defined and wound its way through a ragged line of hills where ground forces were stationed in hill-top forts. After 400 miles it headed north-east over a desolate jungle-covered mountain range before turning east towards the coast with Sabah to the north.

At Kuching or Labuan pilots generally flew a combination of border patrols and simulated close air support sorties under the direction of forward air controllers (FACs) attached to the various Army formations stationed along the border. Pilots were provided with maps printed in black-and-white which we made more intelligible by colouring in the contours. Large expanses of the central region were unmapped and shown only by vague dotted contour lines. Venturing forth into the unknown for the first time and traversing a prehistoric landscape devoid of human habitation was a unique and truly memorable experience!

Torrential rain was a common feature of the weather in the tropics and could blot out the airfield for up to an hour, making landing hazardous if not impossible. Kuching's closest diversion airfield suitable for Hunters was the civil airport at Sibu, 170 miles to the east, requiring relatively large fuel reserves on recovery. However, storms were predictable and visible on radar so pilots could be warned of their approach, allowing a normal sortie length of about an hour and a half. Otherwise, flying was relatively unaffected by weather but on the one occasion when Hunters were scrambled from Tengah in response to a request from the Army for air support to flush out a group of insurgents who had crossed the border near Kuching, the planned dawn attack was defeated by low-lying mist and the Army succeeded where we failed!

Proving adaptable at each stage of its development, the Hunter had come a long way since the F. Mk 1 joined the Royal Air Force some ten years earlier. Its task in the Far East took it to new rôles in a fresh environment operating from diverse locations within a huge area and in vastly differing situations. Always a pilot's favourite, in the Far East the Hunter once more came up trumps, living up to its famed reputation and giving exemplary service.

SCORCHING THE SKY

Air Commodore Mac McEwen AFC

AEROBATICS have always been an essential part of a fighter pilot's training and were always a popular part of the curriculum for the Hunter. There were three basic types of aerobatics: the classical, smoothly executed manœuvres laid down in the flying manuals, all of which the Hunter could handle admirably and which had to be demonstrated to the Central Flying School examiners on their annual check of the Squadron; the aggressive, rather brutal manœuvres more suited to a lead-in to air combat training and dog fighting; and low-level display aerobatics. Each type had its own special techniques, and the Hunter was cleared for everything except spinning and flick rolls. The 'g' limits were +7 and –3.75, which gave plenty of scope. I loved dogfighting most of all, I suppose, but I had a penchant too for display flying, which I carried out for several years.

The supervision of pilots selected for solo display flying was rather casual in the early days of the Hunter, and you mostly just learned on the job. It was a beautiful aircraft to display, because it looked good, and it had enough power to be very impressive and yet not run away with the pilot. It also made a ferocious noise at full power.

A fighter display, to my mind, needed to show to the full the aircraft's acceleration, rate of roll and turning ability, and I always found that the way to get the crowd's attention was to frighten them right at the outset if you could manage it. The easy way to do this was to approach silently from behind at a fair speed, but with the throttle shut so they could not hear you coming. Then, a short distance from the crowd, the throttle had to be slammed up to full power. The engine would take a couple of seconds to wind up, by which time you would be right above the crowd and starting a high-'g' turn right in front of them and they would, you hoped, get the double shock of the Hunter seeming to have appeared from nowhere and then the deafening roar as the engine opened up.

I would then go into a tight loop parallel with the crowd along the runway line and plan to delay the pull-out—the recovery. In a low-level loop, there is always a moment coming down the back side, with the aircraft pointing vertically downwards, when it looks from the ground that the aircraft is not going to recover and will plunge straight into the airfield. It looks like that from the cockpit too sometimes, but the pilot has the advantage of having done it before many times, and he knows precisely for a given height and speed how much altitude he needs to recover to straight and level flight.

That vertical position was the moment, then, to delay the pull-out a little. It was similar to the old tricks an acrobat or high-wire artist in a circus would use, giving a bit of a wobble or two to make it appear that disaster was about to happen when, in fact, he was fully in control all the time. The hope was that the crowd would hold its collective breath for a moment, wondering if the aircraft was about to crash, and then sigh with relief as it pulled out safely after all and soared away into the next manœuvre. I found that this stunt worked as often as not, and it became a standard part of all my displays. I was surprised how many quite experienced pilots were taken in by it too.

Approaching from behind the crowd was barred in the end following the inquiry into the tragic death of John Derry at Farnborough in his D.H. 110, the forerunner of the Sea Vixen. His aircraft disintegrated at high speed and the engines ploughed into the crowd, killing 31 spectators and injuring many others. In the wake of that, it was decided that, henceforward, display aircraft were not to be allowed to point directly at the public. So I had to cut out the first bit of my display, approaching from behind, and rely on the scary loop instead to catch the crowd's attention.

In ways such as this, I modified my display sequence as the seasons went by until eventually I felt that I had a show that was just as effective as previous versions but a good deal safer. One of my earliest modifications was the direct result of a display I carried out before Air Commodore Sir Frank Whittle, the designer of the jet engine no less, who opened a big flying display at Exeter Airport on Saturday 28 June 1958. Flying Officer McEwen, in a Hunter, and described in the programme as 'one of

Right: *Sans pareil*: Hawker Hunters of 'The Black Arrows'—No 111 (F) Squadron—carve their distinctive signature in the sky.

78

COURTESY HOWARD N. TANNER Jr

COURTESY NIGEL WALPOLE

COURTESY HOWARD N. TANNER Jr

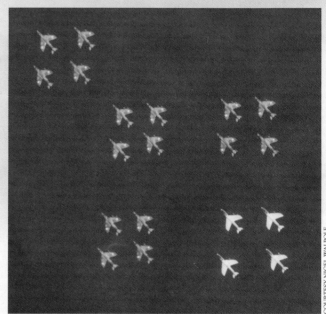

COURTESY NIGEL WALPOLE

COURTESY NIGEL WALPOLE

This page: An essential (and pre-requisite) discipline of aerobatics is the ability of pilots simply to hold formation, and this art is practised constantly by every squadron. A selection of examples of precision formation flying is seen here (clockwise from top left): No 257 Squadron's disbandment flypast at Wattisham in March 1957 (the author is up there somewhere!); No 8 Squadron's F.G.A.9s in Diamond Nine over HMS *Hermes*; a No 229 OCU Hunter flypast up from Chivenor; the Chivenor Wing airborne, with four Meteors in trail; and a flyover at Wattisham by Nos 257 and 263 Squadron Hunter F.2s. Opposite: Precision formation flying by thirteen Hunters of Nos 8 and 208 Squadrons, led by a T.7 trainer. A non-participant can be seen on the Khormaksar pan below, its cockpit shielded from the heat of the sun.

our most daring fighter pilots', was to finish up the show, following a very stylish performance by the No 56 Squadron formation aerobatic team, led by Squadron Leader R. J. S. Dickinson. In the circumstances, I felt beholden to put on as good a show as I could possibly manage.

One of the manoeuvres that I was particularly proud of at that time was an eight-point slow roll. It was quite difficult to execute, and it needed large control inputs, great bootfuls of rudder and a lot of negative 'g', but I felt that I had mastered it pretty well after a great deal of practice, and hoped that it would impress both the public and my fellow pilots. The display went as scheduled, and the only part that went wrong was the high-speed, low-level pass at the end, which was followed by a vertical climb, rolling first to the right and then to the left until the aircraft disappeared from sight into the bright blue

sky. This was always considered by solo aerobatic pilots to be the easy bit that anyone could do. Unfortunately, I cut the corner too much in the final turn and ended up with the speed not as high as I had intended, so I had to make it a really low pass down the runway, hoping that that would make it look faster than it was.

Afterwards, Sir Frank asked to see me, and I had hoped that he might comment on my eight-point roll. Instead, the great man shook my hand vigorously and said, 'Heavens! Whatever speed were you doing on that final run?' I was disappointed by this initially, since he seemed to have enjoyed most the only bit of the display that I hadn't done properly— the so-called easy bit! But then I reasoned that if someone as intelligent as Sir Frank Whittle couldn't tell what speed I was doing, then neither could anyone else, and I filed that away. In future, I would

COURTESY MARCUS WILD

just make sure that the final high-speed run was very low and not worry too much how fast it was; it would make life easier for me and tighten up the display somewhat—and no one would ever know the difference between 620 knots and 550 knots anyway. Later, I asked other pilots what they thought of my eight-point roll, and I got a fairly muted response. One said that he hadn't quite realised that that was what it was, and thought it was just a very, very slow roll. I decided there and then to drop the rather ponderous eight-pointer and substitute a four-point snap roll instead. It was much easier to do, and everybody told me that it was punchier and more in keeping with the rest of the display.

Above: In the first decades after World War II it was virtually *de rigueur* for squadrons to put together their own aerobatic display team, and No 43 (F) were quick off the mark with their new Hunter 1s. The team continued when the Squadron re-equipped with Mk 4s in the autumn of 1955, and the latter are seen here stepped down in tight *echelon*.

Below: *Echelon* is one of the less demanding formations to hold, principally because each pilot has, in essence, to fix his gaze in one direction only. It is nevertheless difficult to achieve perfection, and here No 208 Squadron's pilots are doing an excellent job in their Mk 6s in 1959.

It was the fashion then to include a slow-speed run past the crowd, followed by an opening of the throttle and then some dramatic manœuvre to demonstrate the aircraft's acceleration. In my routine, I would fly past just above the stall at about 200 feet with undercarriage and full flap down, and then raise them while putting on full power and holding the aircraft straight and level until I had enough speed (about 250–280 knots) to go into a slow loop.

Again, I found that it was impossible for people on the ground, even seasoned pilots, to estimate an aircraft's speed accurately; if I raised the flypast height to 500 feet, it was even more difficult. I changed my routine, therefore, so that I flew past at 500 feet with the undercarriage down, but with only two notches of flap and at 200 knots instead of 135 knots. I also gently fed in a little rudder to right and left, hoping that it would look as if the aircraft was wallowing as it usually did just before the stall. Then I would raise the undercarriage, leave the flap where it was and bang on full power. The acceleration was very rapid, and the trick was to make sure that the undercarriage limiting speed of 250 knots was not exceeded until the wheels had folded fully away. If it was exceeded, the undercarriage would probably stick halfway up and the display would be spoilt, even if the undercarriage was not damaged. Happily, that never happened to me. From the ground it appeared that one moment the aircraft was flying along with wheels down at the stall, and then a moment later it was pulling up into a loop from an impossibly slow speed. In fact, the speed was a healthy 280 knots as often as not, and although I sometimes ended up going over the top of the loop with no speed at all, the aircraft could cope with that and I never felt in any danger. Other pilots sometimes asked me what speed I started the loop at, but I always evaded the question.

Little by little I modified and tightened my routine, so that in the end it was much easier to do—and, I hoped, more impressive. People often suggested new manœuvres for it, but I never adopted any of the ideas. It was, after all, my neck that was at

COURTESY PHILIP JARRETT

stake and I wasn't about to incorporate anything not entirely safe. I remember flying in a two-seater one day with a good friend, Flying Officer Bob Manning, and he wanted to show me a manœuvre that he thought I might to try. We were at 10,000 feet and he pulled the Hunter vertical and throttled right back so that the speed fell quickly off the airspeed indicator altogether and we hung there in an eerie silence. He then pushed the control column fully forward and the aircraft slowly rotated about its axis and ended up, still with no speed, pointing steeply

downwards. I was too busy looking at the nose position to notice the height we achieved at the apex of the manœuvre, but it took an eternity before the speed registered again on the ASI and we could start pulling out of the dive in a desperate attempt to recover before we hit the start height—which we didn't, ending up 2,000 feet lower than we had started! I thanked him for the demonstration but said that, while I didn't mind being vertical with no speed at 10,000 feet plus, I wouldn't feel comfortable doing the same thing at low level with solid East

Opposite, top: Four Hunter Mk 6s of No 92 Squadron *en echelon*.
Below: From early 1961 No 92 Squadron formed the official RAF Aerobatic team, 'The Blue Diamonds'. Their displays were usually initiated by a mass take-off, as here, the Mk 6s led by two T.7 trainers.

Above: The 'Blue Diamonds' in action. The aircraft were finished in royal blue with white wing tips and fuselage stripes, with the Squadron's emblem of cobra and maple leaves flanked by the traditional red and yellow chequer-board on the nose.

Anglian terra firma so close below, and the subject never cropped up again.

As with any mode of flying, one never ceased to learn about low-level aerobatics. On one occasion I carried out a display at Biggin Hill before a huge crowd and was due to take off, do my bit, and then depart back to my home base. Unfortunately, although the Met forecast had been quite rosy, a lot of dark and lowish-looking cloud began to appear as the start time approached, and I was first on the programme. It seemed pretty obvious that I would have to do a flat, rolling display beneath the cloud, cutting out the looping parts, but I needed to know more about the extent of the cloud before I could decide on the finishing manœuvre. A transport aircraft landed as I taxied out, so I asked him what the cloud was. He said the base was 1,500 feet out of the rain showers, and the tops 4,000 feet.

I decided, therefore, that at the end I would do a vertical departure, and hope to get in one vertical roll before I disappeared in cloud. All went well and I came round the final turn in a torrential rainstorm but with a fair turn of speed, shot across the airfield, and wrenched the aircraft vertical. From the ground, it appeared quite spectacular apparently, because the

Hunter became a ball of condensation while turning through the rain shower, with only the fin and the wing-tips protruding from it, and they were trailing persistent vortices. The cloud base was higher at the far end of the airfield, and I started rolling just as I entered cloud at 2,000 feet. I checked the control column forward, centralised the ailerons and waited for the cloud tops to appear at 4,000 feet and for the aircraft to burst out into the bright sunlight.

But 4,000 feet came and went and I was still in cloud. The climb indicator showed full up-deflection and the altimeter was winding up furiously past 8,000 feet in no time. All the other flight instruments had toppled, however, and were spinning uselessly. I had no idea what attitude I was in, but at least I was climbing fast. 12,000 feet came and went

Below: No 43 Squadron groundcrew engaged in fitting pyrotechnic flares to a Hunter Mk 4 in preparation for an aerobatic display at Fiumicino, Italy. These gave an orange trail but, as one of No 43's pilots admits, a somewhat insipid one.
Right: A couple of years later the trail was much more effective and longer lasting, the smoke now being generated by burning derv located in a tank strapped to the top of the Aden gun pack and pumped by a booster pump from a Meteor to an outlet just above the tail pipe. The system was pioneered by 'The Black Arrows' and the spectacular results are evident in this photograph of 'The Blue Diamonds' searing through the sky during one of their displays.

COURTESY MARCUS WILD

and I started to become disorientated and a little worried. The speed was falling fast through 300 knots, when Air Traffic came on the radio and asked if I had finished. I was inclined to say that I might be reappearing on the end of a parachute in a minute if things did not improve, but I said nothing, held the controls central, and waited.

Air Traffic kept on calling, and the aircraft reached 18,000 feet, with the speed below 200 knots. I was just beginning to push the control column forward in the hope that I might recover some semblance of control, when I fell out of the side of the huge cumulonimbus cloud I had just been in for what had seemed like an eternity. The nose was very high, but I was in the clear now and called Air Traffic—in what I hoped was a calm voice—and told them that I was clearing their airspace.

I could see that the general cloud-tops were 4,000 feet as the transport pilot had told me, but he hadn't mentioned that Biggin Hill was underneath a thunderstorm cloud, a cumulonimbus that reached to 30,000 feet. That explained the dark cloud down at ground level and the torrential rain that I had flown through at the end of my display. I learnt about flying from that and never again did I perform solo aeros without first establishing properly what the cloud base and tops were. Back to the old format, it seems: 'Don't assume—check.'

Finally, I learnt about more things than just flying matters during my period as a display pilot. I was on No 56 Squadron at Nicosia, Cyprus, in October 1959 and had to do a display before the Israeli Air Force Chief of Staff, who was on a formal visit. He was a fighter pilot, no more than 35 years old, and looked very young compared to the RAF hierarchy we were used to. I determined, therefore, to let him see what we RAF chaps were made of.

In the event, I got rather carried away and foolishly threw most of the rules by which I was bound out of the window, ignoring all the height limits. At the southern end of the main Nicosia runway was a deep dip in the ground, and only a few days before, one of our pilots, Flying Officer Max Walters, had landed normally, thinking he had a 15-knot headwind, but the wind had turned through 180 degrees while he was on the final approach—a not unusual occurrence

Left: 'The Black Arrows' in action. The 'Treble-One' team, in its Hunter 6s, set new standards in aerobatic performance that even today, fifty years on, the world's air forces strive to emulate. The most famous achievement of the team was that in which twenty-two aircraft were simultaneously looped—a record for the greatest number of aircraft to carry out this particular manœuvre and one that has never been broken. Its Leader, Squadron Leader (as he then was) Roger Topp, writes about the event on pages 98–101.

in the hot Mediterranean climate. No one had told Max this, and, as the runway was longer than the 2,000-yard strips we usually operated from, at the end of the landing he opened his hood and started doing his after-landing checks, unaware that the 15-knot tailwind was sending him rapidly to the end of the runway. He realised it too late and rolled off the end of the runway and down the steep slope into the dip, in which there was a barbed wire fence. The barbed wire rode up the Hunter's windscreen and, as the cockpit was still fully open, cut into Max's face, scratching him rather badly, and came to rest at the top of the ejection seat. Here, the barbed wire contacted the sear which operated the ejector seat top handle, and half pulled it out of its housing. Had it pulled it fully out, Max would have been ejected, probably with fatal consequences.

I knew about this big dip from this incident, and in my final turn dived into it so that momentarily I disappeared from the view of the VIP party watching from the control tower. I then reappeared and headed straight for the VIPs I could see leaning on the railing outside Local Control. I think it was the fastest and lowest I had ever been, and I passed over their heads and zoomed upwards, rolling until I was out of sight.

When I taxied in, the Squadron Commander met me at the aircraft and it was clear that he was, to put it mildly, extremely unhappy. He tore me off a strip in front of the rather surprised groundcrew and said that I was grounded until further notice, would never fly with No 56 Squadron again and was to await further penalties once it was known how the Nicosia Station Commander felt about my disgraceful behaviour.

I was crestfallen. I knew that I had been very foolish. However, the Israeli CAS came round to the crewroom later and demanded to see the aerobatic pilot. He slapped me on the back and congratulated me enthusiastically, and the Station Commander, too, was full of praise and congratulated the Squadron Commander also on a job well done. I was somewhat nonplussed and not sure where I stood, until the Squadron Commander called me in later and said that it seemed that my display had been well received after all, and so I was clear to carry on flying, but that I was to abide by the rules in future.

What I learnt about life in the RAF from this incident, therefore, was not about flying at all, but human nature. Luckily, I had learnt the lesson for myself that day, and I would never carry out a sortie like that again!

Last Words *Air Vice-Marshal Peter Latham* CB AFC

On Treble-One Squadron, whenever operational training, our primary task, allowed, we carried out full aerobatic rehearsals over the airfield using the Air Traffic Control Tower as the focus. Each rehearsal was filmed with a cine gun-sight camera, adapted for hand-held use. The film was seen in negative during the post flight debriefing, which also included frank comments from Flight Lieutenant Colin Hardy, the adjutant and show commentator, who watched every rehearsal. One manœuvre mid-show consisted of a nine-ship loop towards the spectators at 45 degrees to the crowd line. It finished with a steep, near vertical, low turn to starboard in front of the crowd at a hundred feet or less, giving a good plan view to the spectators before straightening on a heading 45 degrees away from the crowd and pulling up into a second change formation loop.

In the debriefing Colin Hardy remarked on Flight Lieutenant Clayton-Jones having 'a bit of a folly' during this manœuvre. A 'folly' described a momentary loss of steady formation-keeping, with a few rapid adjustments to regain proper positioning. Clayton-Jones was an outstanding member of the Squadron, a fine aerobatic pilot, a great chap for a party and possessed of a remarkable ability to remain silent in almost any circumstances. It was for this reason that he was always known as 'Clam'. I could not see any of the team members while leading but I remembered this moment because there was some indecipherable R/T natter at that time. The only R/T we used during a show was an instruction to the team, a safety acknowledgement or, *in extremis*, a call that required an answer.

'Clam' flew on the extreme right of the formation and so would have been the chap closest to the ground during this manœuvre and would, of necessity, been concentrating his gaze upwards on my wingman and not able to see his proximity to the ground—perhaps a couple of wing spans away. 'Was that you?' I asked him. 'Yes,' he replied. 'Well, what were you on about?' I asked. 'Nothing,' he said. 'I just wanted to die talking.'

Three Hundred Yards of Cornfield *Squadron Leader Brian Weeden*

This, my second tour on the Hunter 6, was interrupted by three months on the Day Fighter Combat School course at West Raynham and then being posted to the Hunter OCU at Chivenor as its first Fighter Combat Leader. I arrived in June 1958 and left in February 1959; however, I flew with the Squadron from June to October. My new Boss at Stradishall was Squadron Leader Les de Garis. It was a busy four months and seemed to be full of displays of one sort or another. The Squadron's rôle was the same as that of No 65 Squadron, my previous posting—that is, day fighter air defence.

At long last I got some concentrated 30mm Aden firing on the range at Leuchars, but soon after that we were into the 'silly season'. On 26 July 1958 I was leading a box of four Hunters behind three boxes of Javelins and ahead of two other Hunter boxes, all in close formation—six boxes in line astern. After several practices and some pretty rough flying from the Javelins in front of us, the formation flew low over the Empire Games Stadium at Maindy in Cardiff as the Games were to be opened by HRH The Duke of Edinburgh. It was an occasion for cockpit laughter I won't forget. We orbited to the north of Cardiff until we got our 'two minutes' call and, as planned, ran in for the low-level flypast. At 30 seconds to go—and committed to this timing—we were asked to delay for 30 seconds as things were running a bit late! Even 'The Red Arrows' would have blown them a raspberry at this stage, but our leader was politeness itself as he explained that this was impossible. Did the Duke get rapidly hustled onto the daïs? I somehow doubt it!

Soon afterwards I was chosen to be one of the flight leaders for the great Hunter/Javelin squadrons flypast at the SBAC Show at Farnborough. There were several leaders'

practices, including very memorable one on 25 Aug 1958 when thunderstorms were starting to form. By the time we returned (to Duxford) a very heavy storm was leaving the airfield, having put the runway awash, and we were all very short of fuel, with little more than enough for one circuit. I was third to land and put my Hunter down as slowly and smoothly as I dared. With full brake applied, there was virtually no deceleration and 2,000 yards later my aircraft flashed passed the two ahead of me (which had burst tyres) and went off the far end. After about 300 yards of cornfield I came to a halt and leaped out. Despite my protestations and the runway controller's opinion that I landed when only just over the runway threshold and slower than any other aircraft, I was found to blame for landing too fast or not braking hard enough. As my Station Commander said when he interviewed a very disgruntled me, 'It must have been your fault. Chalk it up to experience.' A year later I was re-interviewed by my Station Commander and exonerated. The RAF had discovered 'aquaplaning' on high-pressure tyres and the (boiling) bubbles on my tyres clearly indicated that they were at a virtual standstill when the aircraft was doing 100mph (and yet they didn't burst, despite their 180psi pressure). The moral, my friends joked, was to stop being a smoothie!

Farnborough finished on 7 September and the Boss told me I was to be the station's Hunter aerobatics pilot. This sounded fun but the next show, at Honington, was only a fortnight away and I hadn't done a low-level air display since the Hicks Aerobatic Trophy at Cranwell (in a Balliol and 'not below 1,500 feet'). I had four practices and then did the Show. There are three strong memories. I was sitting in my Hunter waiting to take off (so that I could give my final practice to get Les de Garis's and the Station

Commander's okay) and watched the final practice of the Javelin display crew—and they spun in at low level and were both killed. 1 was cleared for take-off and flew through the smoke from the blaze below. My final practice wasn't as low as the earlier ones had been!

In fact, I had had a great idea: as well the loops, rolls, Derry turns, slow-speed pass, etc., I thought of arriving for the first pass inverted and fast. I had never seen anyone else do this. I tried it out at about 5,000 feet and 450 knots and worked out what the initial elevator trim setting should be and then dropped down to 3,000 feet and 500 knots, and then 550 knots—with an increasing lack of enthusiasm for the idea. As I decreased height still further, I became increasingly disillusioned with my great idea and persuaded myself that I hadn't been given sufficient time to prepare (otherwise known as 'I chickened out'). I've often wondered whether any other Hunter pilot had a go at this. On Battle of Britain Day I did the usual manœuvres and finished my final fast run with an 'upward Charlie' through the only big cumulus in East Anglia—with not much speed left as I came out of the top. I have heard of display pilots running out of speed and dropping back through the murk; I'm glad it didn't happen to me!

A few days later I was off to the Fighter Combat Leader's Course at West Raynham (and then on to the OCU staff at Chivenor) with no thought of ever returning to Stradishall, but No 2 Squadron of the OCU always became No 145 Squadron in war (and on annual exercises) and once more

I found myself back at Stradishall. On 12 July 1961, during a lull in the 'war', two of our QFIs, flying a twin-seat Hunter T.7, got caught out in a nasty rainstorm, ran short of fuel and were about to bail out when they spotted a disused wartime airfield—and grabbed it just in time. Martin Chandler, then Boss, sent me over to the airfield (Witchford, just south-west of Ely) to assess the situation and fly it back if possible. When I got there (and the two QFIs went home), I was met by OC Flying Waterbeach who kindly drove me around the airfield to let me choose the best runway for the attempt. The place was shoulder-high in weeds, the tarmac was starting to break up and the entire airfield looked like a builders' yard—and the best take-off run I could get was estimated as about 1,000 yards. Meanwhile, the groundcrew checked the aircraft, changed the wheels and put in sufficient fuel to get me home. Waterbeach's runway sweeper was pressed into service (as were the groundcrew) to get rid of as much debris was we could, and when I decided that we'd done the best possible job I climbed in, started up, wound up to full power and rolled through the undergrowth.

I was airborne with about 100–200 yards to spare and was quite startled when I saw the number of people and vehicles who had come to watch the 'show'. It seemed like Battle of Britain Day! I flew back to Stradishall with the undercarriage kept down and landed uneventfully; a tyre burst was on the cards, but it was only back in dispersal that both tyres went flat! Tough aircraft, the Hunter!

Above: The problems associated with landing a Hunter on a rain-soaked runway were very significant and could lead, as here, to aquaplaning.
Right: A Hunter F. Mk 4 of No 229 OCU, in the 'shadow' markings of No 145 Squadron, 1960.

Zero Airspeed Flight _Commander Simon Askins FIMechE_

While I never flew this magnificent aircraft operationally, it was an integral part of my flying career in the Royal Navy as it was the aircraft on which I did my 'swept wing conversion' flying in 1960 and thereafter used for continuation flying and instrument flying. Then, when at RNAS Brawdy as the resident Maintenance Test Pilot, I regularly flew the squadron aircraft on air tests and for annual test flights. Thus I flew some fifty different airframes of both the Mk 11 and the T. Mk 8 types.

As part of the aerodynamics instruction on swept-wing aircraft it was firmly emphasised that a major hazard for such aircraft was getting too slow, as, instead of resulting in a nose-down stall, it would instead 'pitch up' as the wing tips stalled and the centre of lift moved forward and further reduce the airspeed. Therefore, stalls—and, more importantly, spins—were a big 'no-no'. The Hunter had a reputation for developing an inverted spin and being difficult to recover from any spin; our aircraft actually had a white datum spot painted on the instrument panel to show 'stick central' as being the first part of the recovery from any spin.

Likewise, under the paragraphs on 'Spinning' in the Pilot's Notes, it did actually state that '. . . an inverted spin may result from a poorly executed stall turn manœuvre . . .' With this in mind, when conducting air tests which required a check of low-speed handling to ensure that there was no wing drop at the pre-stall buffet, I naturally approached the check with due caution, although I had found that although the Notes said that this should occur at about 130 knots, I had found that 110 knots was quite possible and controllable.

Then, on one occasion when flying with a QFI, he agreed that 110 knots was a controllable speed, and asked if I had ever seen zero airspeed. This interested me, as I had never tried getting to zero. He demonstrated it by going into a vertical climb, taking off the power, then applying full aileron. The airspeed did indeed fall to zero—but, due to secondary effects of aileron drag, the aircraft would perform a very convincing stall turn.

Thereafter, I naturally added this manœuvre to my repertoire in order to offer some variation to normal aerobatics. I did try the same routine in other swept-wing aircraft—but not all were as docile as the Hunter!

Left: A two-seat Hunter T.7 in the early 'silver' scheme with yellow training bands, similar to that in which Brian Weeden made his hair-raising take-off from Witchford, described on pages 90–91.
Right: A Fleet Air Arm Hunter G.A. Mk 11 powers upwards in a vertical climb.

COURTESY TONY BUTTLER

Beating the Bang *Air Commodore Ken Goodwin* CBE AFC

My aeros career started from EFTS (Elementary Flying Training School), where air sickness prompted a cure, which included aeros on every solo sortie! I joined No 92 Squadron (Meteor Mk 4s) in late 1949, and my Boss noticed all the aeros activity and nominated me Squadron Aeros Rep—me, with all of 100 hours on jets! My CO, the late Squadron Leader Ray Harries DSO DFC (better known as 'The Spitfire Napoleon'), suggested a routine which included a half roll on take-off, retracting the undercarriage while still inverted and thence a push into a bunt up to around 2,000 feet with no airspeed remaining before 'pulling through'. On the way down I picked out my crash site on the banks of the River Ouse and felt surprisingly calm until I had bottomed out below said river bank, out of sight of my disappointed spectators, who were expecting a 'mushroom'. There followed the onset of quite violent physical shakes, which meant abandoning the rest of the practice! I asked my Boss what height he had achieved on the bunt, to which he replied that he had never actually done it!

I continued flying Meteors and Vampires until I was posted to No 118 Squadron at Jever and brand new Hunters, where, once again, Wing Commander 'Hammer' West nominated me as Station Aeros Rep, and after a demo competition for the AOC I was appointed individual solo pilot for the 2nd Tactical Air Force—with no minimum height limit! For the next two years I flew in a multitude of shows, ranging from Helsinki in the north to Avignon in the south.

One of my early shows was an impromptu affair at the USAFE base at Étain-Rouvres during a three-day NATO detachment of six No 118 Squadron aircraft. The refuelling nozzles would not fit our Hunters! The Boss, Norman Buddin, suggested that I do something for the Americans— with only 1,600 pounds of fuel (enough for eight minutes' aeros). During take-off the aircraft did not feel right and, in a roll off the top, having pulled up over the last few feet of

the 10,000-foot runway, the Hunter reached the proverbial 'nothing on the clock' and seemed motionless. Perhaps we had stayed up to late the night before? Things improved with the nose down and acceleration began to feel normal. However, without ram air the performance deteriorated to the point where the entire demo was having to be conducted at a funereal pace—something that impressed the onlookers hugely and won me a return visit for the US Armed Forces Day! The engine problem had been the failure of the swirl vanes, and to cure this a new ram jack had to be fitted.

It was at another Armed Forces Day two years later that I had a 'nasty'. The weather was atrocious and nothing much was happening. However, when the cloud base lifted to 500 feet I volunteered to do a 'flat show' in the absence of anything else. Soon after take-off, and during an inverted run, the engine ran down. I pulled up into cloud and foolishly asked the tower for a reciprocal dead-stick on 24, all the while pressing the relight button. Oh joy—Mr Rolls-Royce proceeded to wind up again! I was quite certain that the negative 'g' bag had punctured, so I was able to give a bit more of a display—only right side up!

I tagged along as the Number Five or Six to the No 93 Squadron aerobatic team at quite a few shows. When weather permitted, I would often break off from formation and climb to 40,000 feet. As the formation carried out its bomb-burst I would put the nose down, aim at the show line and slip through Mach 1. Holding a very high rate of descent, it was possible to 'beat the bang', causing the uninitiated to think that the Hunter was supersonic in straight and level flight. This manœuvre came close to disaster at the opening of Amsterdam International, where

Below: Mk 4 XE665—the 'Boss''s aircraft on No 118 Squadron; notice the Squadron Leader's pennant beneath the cockpit. This Hunter was later transformed into an 'Admiral's Barge' (see page 184).
Right: Aeros with No 93 Squadron—and the writer, flying the sole Hunter from No 118, WT760, in the Number Five position.

COURTESY PHILIP JARRETT

Main image: Excellent *echelon* formation by the four Hunter Mk 4s of No 93
Squadron's aerobatic team.
Opposite, bottom: The writer taxies out for his solo display in WW660, a
Hunter Mk 4, at an air show in 1956. The No 118 Squadron markings—
stylised waves—recall the unit's considerable success in attacking enemy
shipping during World War II.

perfect weather heralded a sonic boom—which, fortunately,
hit the target. Had the Air Attaché been alerted to the
boom bit he would not have sanctioned it with hundreds of
acres of greenhouses surrounding the airport: to have
missed the target would have been somewhat expensive. It
was lucky for both of us that I didn't!

I went to Helsinki with the team as part of a British sales
drive which included many pretty lady ambassadors. The
weather forecast was terrible for flying but excellent for
entertaining young ladies. Imagine our dismay the next
morning to discover blue everywhere and no rain either!
The show was going fine until a junior team member lost
touch after the bomb burst (though was eventually rounded
up) and yours truly exited his lovely Hunter only to be
collared by the local Chief of Police ready to arrest me for
sonic-booming the place without permission!

As one continued to move from show to show one
tended to run into old friends. On one occasion I promised
the leader of the F-86 'Skyblazers' a go in the Hunter in
exchange for a ride in the Sabre. The American got his part
of the bargain although, being unused to our braking
system, he left my tyres in a bit of a mess. Moreover,
although I had flown F-86s before, I never got my half of

the deal. The French came to my rescue and let me loose
with a Mystère 2.

With my return to England in 1958 there were still
demos to be flown. I think that the Battle of Britain show
at Biggin Hill must have been my swansong with the
Hunter, but, fortunately for me, I was posted to the Air
Fighting Development Squadron at the Central Fighter
Establishment (where, incidentally, I started another love
affair, this time with the Lightning via OCU, Lightning
Conversion Squadron, No 74 Squadron and RAF
Wattisham, all as CO). At AFDS I joined in the conduct of
further trials with the Hunter. The most important of these
took place in Aden, in the quest for the most suitable
aircraft to replace the Venom in that theatre (the other
trials aircraft being the Jet Provost and the single-seat Gnat).
At that time we did not have 230-gallon tanks for our
Hunters and so the deployment was more than interesting!
It included finding Wadi Halfa, a desert oasis, with almost
non-existent D/F. This was on the leg from El Adem,
around the outskirts of Egypt and over the Sahara, beyond
radar coverage. It was amazing how many hitherto
unencountered rumbles emanated from the back end of the
aircraft! We were equipped for desert survival, but as the

desert rescue team were limited to a 150-mile radius of operations, my Boss, Colin Coulthard, handed me a .38 revolver for possible use in the event of an emergency bale-out. It should be said that the aircraft were interim Mk 9s, with drag 'chutes, improved air conditioning and 'sawtooth' leading edges to the wings.

And so to Khartoum and Aden, for three months of flying, principally to determine the effects of severe temperatures on both aircraft and pilot. Diplomatic problems dictated a return home via Salah, Masirah, Sharjah, Teheran, Cyprus, El Adem and Orange to West Raynham. The planned stop in Turkey did not materialise owing to a lack of comms and bad weather and so, as can be imagined, both our Hunters landed at Nicosia with tanks about empty. Of the three trials aircraft, the Hunter came out a winner, and the occasional presence of Company Chief Test Pilots providing rather nice hospitality in no way influenced the outcome of the trial.

I feel that I have explored the performance envelope of the Hunter more or less to its limits. To have taken off in the box of a vic of five is an experience never to be forgotten—and how forgiving the aircraft to a pilot more prepared to undertake such a manœuvre in hurricane-force winds at furnace-like temperatures!

Going for a Loop *Air Commodore Roger Topp* AFC**

A few minutes ago we took off from Odiham in Hampshire, formed our glossy black Hunter fighters into a tight arrowhead formation and headed for Farnborough.

Weeks of relative obscurity in the Suffolk skies have prepared us for this occasion. Today is the start of the Farnborough Air Display, a world class air show and a big event. Our formation is big too, for we are about to demonstrate something audaciously new in the realm of fighter aerobatics—a loop by a formation of no fewer than twenty-two aircraft. Rapidly we approach Farnborough, which lies dead ahead at four miles. The airfield stands out clearly and we can see the many brightly polished parked aircraft, the blue and white striped awnings of the numerous marquees and the dark mass of the crowd.

Three miles to go. We enter a shallow dive, aiming to bring us about one hundred feet above the ground at the airfield boundary. Alter course slightly to adjust for wind and maintain our correct approach path. Gently does it—small movements of the lead aircraft require much greater movements by the aircraft at the extremities of this large formation.

Press the radio button and call our man in the control tower, the squadron adjutant; soon now he will take over Oliver Stewart's task as commentator, a concession not easily extracted from this doyen of Farnborough. Our man tells us that John Cunningham, flying the Comet, is completing his display and we shall be clear to commence on time—and we *are* on time, to the second!

Down below, the compelling voice of the commentator keeps the attention of the spectators riveted on the Comet on its final approach; they have not spotted us yet, skimming low over the heather of Laffans Plain, even though we are less than a mile away. Gracefully, John Cunningham eases his magnificent aircraft on to the runway, Oliver Stewart reluctantly relinquishes his microphone to our man, who invites everyone to look now to their left, where they will see . . . !

This is it then. We are on stage. For the next few minutes the skies over Farnborough are ours; we must make good use of them.

We have about a hundred yards to go. We are low. The rearmost aircraft, flying beneath the slipstream of those in front is the lowest, some fifty feet above the ground. But the pilot ignores the ground: he, like all the others, fixes his eyes on the aircraft on which he is formating, concentrating to the exclusion of all else on maintaining his correct position. In every cockpit there is an atmosphere of tense but professional anticipation.

Main image: 'Tremblers' abreast: five Hunter Mk 6s of 'The Black Arrows' in immaculate formation—XF416 (nearest), XG189, XG194, XE653 and XG170. As, latterly, on at least some of the Squadron's F.4s, a small Union Flag was carried on the starboard fuselage forward; the port side carried a miniature of the Squadron crest.

Opposite top: On the way down: five 'Black Arrows' Hunters caught during another impressive loop.

COURTESY PHILIP JARRETT

In the lead aircraft I make quick final checks: fuel—enough to complete the display and return to base; airspeed about 420 knots—good; engine power 7,200rpm—enough to give eighty-five per cent power. Don't touch the throttle again now: the others will have enough to do without chasing my throttle movements. Down below, the airfield boundary flashes by. Now is the time! Radio a soft warning of intent to the formating pilots and ease firmly, steadily, back on the control column. As one, twenty-two Hunters rise from the background of the heather-clad dunes and point skyward.

As we zoom upwards the airspeed falls. Resist the temptation to apply more throttle: we have sufficient speed and inertia to fly over the top of this loop provided

COURTESY REG WYNESS

we keep the radius correct. Do this by maintaining the right back pressure on the control column. Too much or too little and we shall stall. I dismiss from my mind any disturbing thoughts of what could result from twenty-two aircraft stalling in close formation.

A glance in my mirror confirms that all aircraft are still in perfect formation. So far, so good. All the Hunters are now standing vertically on their tails. For better or for worse, we are now virtually committed to completing this loop in some fashion or other. From this altitude there is little one can safely do with so many aircraft other than loop them—it is the point of no return!

Looking forward along the nose of my aircraft, all that can be seen is the clear blue of a cloudless sky; the earth's horizon has disappeared. It is difficult now to keep the path of the loop absolutely perpendicular to the ground, for the limitless sky provides nothing by which direction can be gauged. If the loop is not maintained in the vertical plane, then the formation will turn and those aircraft on the inside of the turn must, to stay in position, fly more slowly than those on the outside—perhaps too slowly for comfort. Furthermore, if the loop turns, then its position relative to the ground moves laterally, and although started in line with the runway will finish well displaced to one side, perhaps over the crowd—a position not renowned for its popularity with the show organisers, let alone the spectators. But surely by now we must be nearing the summit. I throw my head well back and look for the horizon. Ah yes! There it is, and level too—we have kept our flight path vertical and all is well.

As we come to the top of the loop, the half-way point, we encounter a further difficulty. An aircraft flying line astern of another must keep below the jet efflux and slipstream of the one ahead. Consequently, the flight-path arcs for the aircraft at the rear of the formation are much greater than for those at the front, and to maintain their station those at the rear require much more engine power. Unfortunately, at the top of the loop airspeed is low, which results in poor thrust response to throttle movements.

To keep in formation is difficult; to regain position once it is lost is impossible. But this is not all. As we reach the summit the aircraft in front begin to descend, the speed ceases to fall and under gravity we are about to accelerate quite rapidly. This is only true, however, for the leading aircraft because those behind have yet to reach the top and so are still decelerating. The result is a tendency for the spacing between aircraft to increase and the shape of the formation to be spoiled. We must prevent this happening.

In effect, those of us in front must wait for those following to reach the top of the 'hill'; but if we in front reduce engine power we do not achieve the desired result because the effects of gravity on our acceleration would more than compensate for the reduction in thrust. Moreover, the use of air brakes would cause too much air turbulence for precision flying. Fortunately there is another method. We in front delay our downward plunge by holding our aircraft, inverted and virtually level with the horizon by relaxing the back pressure on the control column until the positive 'g' is only just sufficient to prevent us ceasing to 'sit' and hanging in our shoulder straps instead.

Below: 'The Black Arrows' at Odiham prior to the Farnborough display, the pilots in 'twenty-two' formation with CO Squadron Leader (as he then was) Roger Topp at the head. The Hunter in the centre background is one of the 'borrowed' aircraft, retaining its standard day camouflage scheme.

Above: Going for a loop: twenty-two Hunters on the upward leg of their heart-stopping feat.

Glance again in the mirror. It reveals an impressive sight. As each aircraft in turn tops the 'hill', the sky appears to fill with Hunters each poised, floating, inverted, on the horizon. There is a capriciousness in their attitude, as though they themselves anticipate the exhilarating dive to come as much as the pilots. Very well then. Here we go. Ease back again on the control column and we swoop rapidly downwards, diving for the runway beneath. The speed builds up, giving a renewed crispness to the feel of the controls. If anything, the formation packs closer together than before. Mere feet separate wing tip from wing tip. The airfield grows rapidly larger as we hurtle downwards, and as the runway becomes near life-size our impressive formation ceases its downward plunge and sweeps above the airfield no more than a few feet above the ground.

One can sense the lightness of spirit and the pride in every cockpit. We cannot judge whether the loop was immaculate, but we know that it was pretty good. One day perhaps, somewhere in the world, another squadron might perform a loop with twenty-two fighter aircraft in tight formation and close to the ground, and in public at an international air show but . . . well, we were the first! We swing swiftly through to the completion of our demonstration, including a barrel roll with a diamond of sixteen

black Hunters, and then, in a matter of moments, we are clear of Farnborough and streaking for Odiham.

We land and quickly debrief. We are nonchalant. Everything went as planned and practised, so what is there to talk about? Come on. Pile into our cars and hare over to Farnborough. Rumour has it that there is, somewhere among those marquees with the blue and white striped awnings, some free beer.

Twenty-two to one we shall find it!

Right: A 'Treble-One' pilot in his 'office', fully connected and ready to fly. The aircraft's serial number is stencilled on the headrest of the ejection seat.

WEAPONS AND TACTICS

Air Commodore Mac McEwen AFC

THE rôle of the Hunter was primarily that of a high-level air-defence fighter and secondarily as an air-to-ground attack aircraft. It was well equipped to carry out both tasks. The basic armament was four 30mm Aden cannon, with a total load of 600 rounds and a rate of fire of 1,200 rounds per minute. In one second, therefore, it could pump eighty high-explosive (HE) 30mm rounds into a target and the destructive power of that was formidable indeed. It had about 7½ seconds' total firing time and needed only short bursts to be fully effective, so the basic weapons fit was flexible, too, and could handle a variety of tasks.

In the air defence rôle, the weapons system consisted of the guns, a standard Mk 5 gyro gun sight and a radar-ranging facility mounted in the nose cone. None of these was particularly sophisticated or complicated, and all proved to be robust and reliable once the engineers had overcome the serious initial problem of the engine stopping when the guns were fired. This was done simply by modifying the fuel systems.

The Swedish Air Force saw fit to add Sidewinder missiles to their Hunters, which would have given our aircraft an enhanced capability in the air defence rôle as well, but the Air Ministry never agreed to that, probably because they had an eye on the Hunter replacement, the Lightning, which already had an impressive all-weather missile capability, as did the Javelin, which carried four infra-red Firestreaks. A missile retrofit for the Hunter was therefore deemed to be too expensive.

The main problem with the gun-only fit was that the 30mm round was not effective beyond about 600 yards. Against other fighters in combat, that was fine, because the weapons were harmonised for just over 200 yards anyway, and no one would want to fire outside 600 yards. The intention was mostly to get in as close as possible before opening fire. Against a bomber target, however, with radar-laid, small-calibre tail guns that could fire back and be lethal out to 1,000 yards and more, it was a different problem. We would practice endlessly carrying out quarter attacks and were very proficient with these at low and medium altitudes, up to about 30,000 feet. For a quarter attack we would fly parallel with the target and, when abreast, turn towards it, reversing the turn when the target reached the dead-ahead position and then following a curve of pursuit which terminated in a position line astern. Pilots could fire

Below: The Hunter as originally issued to the squadrons—four 30mm Aden cannon and a camera gun in the nose, and nothing else. The first 'excrescences' resulted from the trouble encountered with spent cartridge links, which, when ejected, bounced along unpredictably in the airflow. Faired collectors—the famed 'Sabrinas'—were the answer.

BAE SYSTEMS

at high angles-off in this way—and without coming into the arc of fire of the tail guns. Above 30,000 feet, though, the air was much thinner and the radii of turn increased significantly, so that it was very difficult to end up line-astern of the target at close range. That meant that a bomber could fire at the fighter for several hundred yards before the fighter could get in range for the kill.

With no prospect of a missile fit forthcoming, high-level targets had to be coped with by carrying out what became known as the 'slide technique' attack. This involved slipping across the target horizontally at very close range and blasting away from one wing tip to the other. It was difficult to get the initial positioning right for this, and it was something of a miracle that no mid-air collisions occurred during training, but there was little alternative.

The tactic most used against the principal threat during the Cold War was known as the Lane Technique Procedure. The Soviet threat was so overwhelming that it was expected that in the worst case the Ground Controlled Interception (GCI) radars would be largely destroyed quite early on, and all that might be left would be a general-purpose broadcast control that would go out on all frequencies and give a rough idea where enemy targets might be. It was based more on intelligence information than live radar plots. The lanes would radiate out from the British Isles at ten-degree intervals over the expected approach direction, and aircraft would be scrambled to 'gates' at the beginning of each lane. When a pilot heard that the mass raid was, say, 170 miles offshore, he would start his stopwatch and fly out along the lane at Mach 0.9. Assuming the target was cruising at Mach 0.8, there would be a closing speed of seventeen miles a minute, and so after ten minutes the Hunter pilot would know that he was close to the target area and would go into a search pattern. With no height information to go on, and possible weather complications, and the Hunter navigation relying on out-of-date Distance Measuring Equipment (DME) beacons in the days before TACAN was introduced, it was an optimistic tactic to say the least, and could even be thought to have been born of desperation. That, however, applied to a lot of things that happened during the years of the Cold War, and there was really no alternative. The remarkable thing is that the tactic was tried on several large annual exercises and shown to be very effective.

Below: As the design was developed, so did the Hunter's rôle, and taking on the task of ground attack meant the external carriage of weapons and stores. This F.6 has 100-gallon drop tanks and twenty-four unguided rocket projectiles—a typical load for the mark. The link collectors for the cannon are also prominent in this head-on view.

Air-to-air firing was practised against flag targets. The latter were about twenty feet long and six feet deep and were towed by a Meteor on a long, nylon rope. It was a purely academic exercise, but to score well the pilot needed to be able to track the target smoothly, and it was a good test of ability. The tips of the shells were dipped in brightly coloured paint, which left a mark round the hole in the flag if it hit. Each aircraft was given 100 rounds to fire, and the pilot's score was calculated simply by counting the number of holes with his colour. A score of 25 per cent was considered good, and 50 per cent or more would be exceptional.

Cine film of the gun-sight picture was taken on all attacks, and these images were analysed in great detail. The minimum angle-off limit was fifteen degrees, for to fire at less than that put the towing aircraft and its pilot at risk. As it was, the tug pilot could often hear the cannon shells humming past his cockpit even at bigger angles-off. We had a squadron pilot once who registered twelve zero scores in a row and was told that unless he scored on his next flag sortie he was to be sacked. He attacked the flag

with great gusto, but, alas, no more skill than he had shown previously; he managed to get one shell in the flag—but two in the starboard engine of the Meteor tug several hundred yards away. The tug pilot was not best pleased, and the pilot left for pastures new the next day, despite complaining that it was unfair since he had broken his duck at last!

Opposite, top: Four Hunter Mk 2s of No 257 Squadron in loose *echelon* formation over East Anglia.
Below: A Hunter F.5 in the markings of No 41 Squadron.
Above: An F.G.A.9 with modifications to its gun troughs—baffles to direct the blast downwards in an attempt to cure the tendency of the Hunter to dip its nose when the Adens were fired.

COURTESY PHILIP JARRETT

Apart from the tendency to attack from near line-astern positions, a tendency to fire from below the flag was also actively discouraged. This was because, if the turn was too tight, the deflection at the firing point would be too high and the shells would go in front of the target. Sometimes the nylon tow rope would be cut and the flag would fall off. If the pilot was attacking from above, that was not a problem, but if he was coming up from slightly low, the flag could hit him, and it had a solid metal spreader bar at the front weighing several pounds. Flying Officer Ted Newton (No 257 Squadron) suffered this on a low-level flag sortie one day, and striking the spreader bar at 400 knots or so caused his tailplane and rudder to come off. He ejected hurriedly, and severely damaged his back doing so. He had to spend most of the following year in hospital and, when he did eventually return to the Squadron and bravely resume his flying career, he surprised us all by

marrying his nurse. He is still married to her to this day, so it turned out happily in the end, but his story is always quoted as a cautionary tale of why one should not attack the flag from beneath.

To improve air-to-air gunnery scores, squadrons had to attend an Armament Practice Camp (APC) at RAF Acklington, where we did nothing but air firing for two weeks. Scores did pick up to start with, but Acklington then became renowned more as a Mecca for social activity than a place for weapons experts. Legendary tales were told of how young pilots had to toil with the physical demands of firing sorties the day after nights of wild passion at the Red Row Village dance hall. The scores dropped off for a while, but recovered again eventually. In later years, when Mrs Elizabeth Dacre presented the Dacre Trophy, to be awarded annually in memory of her son Kenneth, who was killed in the war, to the best RAF fighter squadron, APCs (and MPCs, or Missile

COURTESY PHILIP JARRETT

Top: Almost a full underwing load for a No 20 Squadron Hunter F.G.A.9, with practice bomb racks nestling between the rows of rocket projectiles. The stiffening struts necessary when full 230-gallon underwing tanks were carried are clearly in evidence.
Left: The Hunter trainers were equipped with a single Aden only, mounted in a fairing on the starboard side, chiefly in the interests of saving weight and space. Some later Naval trainers were unarmed.
Opposite: A pair of ground-attack F.G.A.9s, again from No 20 Squadron. This unit's rôle in the Far East is recalled on pages 74–77 and 126–129.

Practice Camps, as they came to be known) assumed great importance once again and became a vital part of the training year.

The gyro gun sight was a well-proven piece of equipment. The pilot had to set the wing span of the target on the front of the sight, which would display an aiming point, or 'pipper', surrounded by graticules which formed a circle. The circle could be increased or decreased by a twist grip on the throttle, and this in turn altered the power fed to the ranging coils. To get the range right, the pilot had to adjust the size of the circle so that it matched the wing tips of the target, and then all he had to do was move the pipper on to the rear of the cockpit, keep it there until he felt he was close enough, and then squeeze the trigger. It sounds easy, but it wasn't—especially if

the target was evading furiously, trying to get away. If the radar ranging was working well, however, it certainly made life much easier.

We once had the opportunity of conducting mock attacks on a giant US Air Force Convair B-36 Peacemaker that was making one of its rare visits to Britain. This aircraft first flew in 1946 and was the biggest combat aircraft ever. It had a wing span of 230 feet, could carry ten times as many bombs as the original Flying Fortress, the B-17, and had a range of well over 6,000 miles. It had six 'pusher' piston engines and four jet engines hung under its wings, and the pilot endeared himself to us by announcing that he had 'six turning and four burning'. Two hundred and thirty feet was well beyond the limit of our wingspan setting scale, so we set 85 feet and

encircled the two inner engines instead. The fighters looked like Lilliputians diving in on this Leviathan of the skies, and in the crew room afterwards there were excited stories of how everyone had only just missed crashing into the target because of its size. In fact, when we analysed the film, hardly anyone had got in range and, had it been for real, most of our cannon shells would have fallen well short.

The Hunter could also carry 24 three-inch rockets, and the combination of rockets and cannon was used to achieve spectacularly successful results during operations in the Radfan area of Aden in the 1960s. Finally, the Hunter could carry bombs on hard points under the wings, and accuracy in both low-level attacks and from steep angles was good.

The Hunter had no rôle as a night fighter, but pilots had to be kept current in night flying in order

Above left: Four three-inch R/Ps fitted beneath a Hunter's starboard wing. These projectiles were always carried on the outboard stations.
Above right: A full battery of twelve R/Ps. The addition of underwing pylon mountings required the relocation of the wing-tip whip aerial from the under to the upper surfaces.

to be able to redeploy to other bases at night, and to cater for the occasional late returns from sorties that ended up in the dark—and, sometimes, the pre-dawn take-offs that were called for; moreover, a certain amount of night-time formation flying had to be practised. The aircraft was such an easy instrument flying platform, and the cockpit lighting was so good, that it was simple to fly at night, but the actual touch-down was a bit hit-and-miss. There was no landing light, and at the round-out point you disappeared into a black hole, which was disconcerting at first. I always found that an extra five knots on the final approach speed was useful, because it enabled

one to feel for the ground a moment longer. A taxying or landing light would have been useful, too. I diverted to RAF Bentwaters just after it had got dark on one occasion, and while taxying in I had a near-miss or two with private cars zooming round the taxiway on their way home. I told the Local Controller, who asked, 'Why don't you put your taxi light on then so they can see you?' When I told him I didn't have a taxi light he was speechless. He didn't say so, but I could tell that he was thinking what a crazy lot we British were.

In general, however, night flying did not present a satisfying challenge as it did later with aircraft such as the Lightning, which did most of its business in the dark, and it was not all that popular. We used to plan to do a set number of sorties on night-flying nights, and didn't pack up until we had done so. If all went well, we could close the airfield and all be

back in the bar well before last orders, but often the flying would drag on and we would be waiting for the groundcrew to produce a final aircraft.

On one such night I was programmed to be second from last off and Flying Officer Eddie Mussett last off, but the aircraft were delayed interminably with minor servicing problems. We were in the crew room looking at our watches and drumming our fingers, when Eddie suggested that to pass the time we should toss a coin to see who would take the next aircraft to be serviceable. We did so, and he won, so I slipped to the end of the queue. The aircraft were ready to fly soon afterwards, and he took my aircraft and I took his, roaring away into a very dark night fifteen minutes after him. We were

Below: Hunter G.A.11 XE689 of 764 Naval Air Squadron releases a three-inch rocket from its port underwing rack during a training sortie. These projectiles had 20-pound warheads.

COURTESY TONY BUTTLER

Combined Elements Colonel Howard N. Tanner Jr USAF

When I arrived at RAF Wattisham to take command of No 257 Squadron I learned that the RAF made night deployments by single aircraft only because no night formations were being flown. I felt that, if the Squadron were ordered to be deployed during darkness, it would be a long drawn-out process, and so I requested, and received, permission to train the Squadron in night formation flying. In the early practices the Squadron took off to form a long, in-trail formation so as to give the pilots an idea how the aircraft appeared at night and to make them aware of other aircraft in their vicinity. The in-trail formation was flown with smooth maneuvers, in order gradually to acquaint the pilots with the type of flying that would be carried out; these sequences also provided those on the ground with some spectacular sights! After the pilots became comfortable

with the basic introductions to night flying the training changed to a two aircraft flight ('element'), and as we became more and more proficient, the elements were combined to form flights of four aircraft. I imagine that the palms of the pilots' hands became sweaty on occasion, but they all performed in an outstanding manner and I was extremely pleased and proud of them.

Our training paid off during a London Defense Exercise which saw two flights of the Squadron on alert. The pairs were 'scrambled' at sundown, but, shortly after the Hunters took off, the fog rolled in and Wattisham was closed—as indeed were all RAF stations in the vicinity except Duxford. Fortunately the flights were able to get to RAF Duxford before it closed and to receive landing instructions, although the Tower Controller was somewhat nonplussed to see eight aircraft on the runway instead of only two!

Left: A four-ship of Hunter Mk 2s of No 257 Squadron.

Left: The World-War II-era rocket projectiles were phased out during the 1960s, to be replaced by podded rockets, as seen here on a Hunter test aircraft. By the time these packs entered widespread service, however, the RAF's Hunter fleet was being run down in favour of more modern aircraft.

AD HOC COLLECTION

Left: The 1950s was the age of the jet fighter and also marked the coming of the air-launched missile. The Fairey Fireflash beam-riding missile was tested on a Hunter but the programme did not proceed to production status, losing out to the Firestreak in acceptance trials. It required radar guidance from the aircraft.

Below: A manufacturer's present-ation of the complete panoply of ordnance and stores available to the Hunter F.G.A.9 customer. Fire-streaks and Fireflashes are included in the suite.

COURTESY PHILIP JARRETT

BAE SYSTEMS

Right: The De Havilland Firestreak infra-red homing missile was tested underneath the wings of a Hunter, but RAF Hunter squadrons never took it into service. It did, however, equip Javelin all-weather fighters and, later, Lightning interceptors. The Firestreaks carried here are mock-ups.

Below: Probably the last of a long line of 'excrescences' added to the RAF's Hunters as the years went by were the prominent fairings on the upper surfaces of the wings, housing jettison 'guns' for the outboard pylons. One can be seen here on the port wing of a No 1 TWU Hunter T.7.

both doing a rather dull high-level night cross-country exercise, and mine went normally. When I landed, however, I was upset to learn that Eddie's aircraft had crashed soon after take-off and that they were still looking for him.

It transpired that his engine must have had a catastrophic failure in the climb and the Inquiry team concluded that he probably had fire indications and a seized engine and must have ejected at a speed in excess of 450 knots. The jolt on hitting the airflow caused his parachute release box

to operate, and when the seat operated automatically and released him from the seat he was released from the parachute too and fell 10,000 feet or more to his death.

No one will ever know the full circumstances, but I have felt guilty about this ever since, because I think that I would instinctively have delayed the ejection until I had reduced the speed, and I might have survived. In any event, I will not make the same mistake again and have never tossed a coin for anything ever since.

SOPs, Bingos and Jokers *Squadron Leader Brian Weeden*

NO 257 Squadron's Hunter 2s were troublesome in service and so the Squadron was disbanded before my first tour had been completed (at that time tour lengths were expected to be 2–2½ years).

Duxford is a famous RAF airfield with old-style hangars— which have just enough height to allow a Hunter 6 tail through their wooden doors. Initially, the Boss was Squadron Leader Jack Ives and he was replaced in September by Squadron Leader Geoff Hermitage. I was treated as one of the more senior pilots and, on most sorties, briefed and led.

At that time (1957–58), No 65 Squadron had a day fighter rôle much the same as No 257's. The Hunter 6 still lacked a working radar-ranging facility but it had more fuel than the Mk 2, was equipped with the more powerful (and much more reliable) Avon 200 series engine, had new 'sawtooth' leading edge wings (resulting in a tremendous improvement in 'dog-fighting' capability) and could fire its four powerful Aden cannon with devastating effect. There was no doubt that the Hunter was turning into a useful fighter aircraft but it was, of course, still very much a day fighter. No 64 Squadron's Javelins 'down the road' had a night/all-weather capability, and although we could run rings around them and kept ourselves in night flying practice, the Hunter didn't have the kit to intercept night or dirty-weather intruders.

A typical 'winter' training sortie for a pair of Hunters might have been a close formation take-off and climb on a given vector through cloud to, say, 30,000 feet, opening out into battle formation when above cloud. On the climb, contact would be made with GCI fighter control and the pair took turns in being the attacker and the target. Sometimes the fighter controller might be under training and these attacks (and any response) might be rather sedate, but, with experienced controllers, it could much more testing— and much more fun. This was particularly so when the new 44-channel VHF radio sets were fitted and (fighter/target) controllers were able to use separate frequencies.

When experienced pilots were doing the attacking and defending, the target aircraft were permitted to evade robustly once they had spotted the attacker, but with attacking JPs (junior pilots) still learning their trade, the evasion might be limited to sedate turns or weaving. The 'robust stuff' would be introduced as their experience and capabilities progressed. A 'Bingo' fuel call was usually an indication that RTB (return to base) time had arrived. The ensuing descent and high speed made a tail chase excellent training value, its robustness dependent upon the experience of the

JPs (who had to take acceptable cine film proof of their prowess —without supplying this proof at the post-flight debrief a miss would be scored). A 'Joker' call would bring the fun to an end and signified that 'going home' minimums had been reached. The sortie lengths were typically 40 to 50 minutes.

If the weather was fine (perhaps a cloud base of 1,000– 1,500 feet and three miles' visibility), the returning pair would fly below cloud with the Number Two staying almost abreast in battle formation 500 to 1,500 yards away. Assuming a left-hand pattern at the airfield, the Number Two would be flying on the right-hand side of the formation and both aircraft would break left simultaneously when over the airfield, followed by stream-landing (with, say 1,000-yard spacing between aircraft on touch-down). If the weather was foul, ground radar might talk the pair down to landing, either as a pair or suitably spaced for a stream landing. Debriefing the sortie might normally take only a few minutes, but it could sometimes be lengthy, the length largely depending on the complexity of the sortie and how well it had been flown.

As the JP became more experienced, the briefing for a sortie like this would become littered with the term 'SOP' (short for Standard Operating Procedure). These procedures were routines to be learned and always to be followed unless briefed differently, for example if radio silence was in force, 'Ready to Start Up' was a thumbs-up signal to the ground

crew who passed it on to the formation leader, and his signal to start up would be to rotate his hand/finger above his helmet (and for the ground crew to repeat this to the formation members). Variations on types of start-ups might be a clearance call from Air Traffic Control or a tele-scramble call from our controlling GCI station, miles away. Perhaps the most obvious hand signal given by the ground crew was a sawing signal to the throat—'Cut engine(s) immediately!'

Other SOPs might cover the action to take if, whilst flying in close formation in cloud, you lost contact with your leader, or your leader's aircraft developed a serious problem, or your radio failed, or your undercarriage failed fully to lock down; the list is long

but not endless. However, they all needed to be learned whilst on the ground—a large library doesn't fit too well in a single-seat fighter aircraft cockpit, and if you are scrambled to intercept a potentially hostile aircraft you need to be certain what your options are before you get there!

Generally speaking, the briefings got shorter the more experienced the pilots became and they then concentrated on things that changed from one sortie to the next, for example the weather forecast and general conditions, radio contact frequencies, weaponry fit and special tactics.

Main image: A four-ship of Hunter Mk 6s from No 65 Squadron, up from RAF Duxford, led by a well-weathered 'Oscar'. The new aerials associated with the upgraded communications fit described by the writer can be seen under the aircraft's bellies.
Below: A close view of No 65 Squadron's emblem—the fifteen swords of which recall a memorable dogfight during the closing weeks of World War I when the Squadron disposed of that number of enemy aircraft.

BOTH PHOTOGRAPHS: COURTESY PHILIP JARRETT

113

A Heady Mixture *Air Commodore Peter Johnson* OBE

I arrived at RAF Khormaksar in Aden at the tender age of 20 on 6 May 1965 with 307 flying hours total—163 on Jet Provosts, 73 on Meteors and 70 on Hunter F.6s and T.7s, having left RAF Chivenor a week or two earlier. My first flight with No 8 Squadron was in a Hunter T.7 with the Squadron QFI, Ian Porteous. My first F.G.A.9 flight was on 11 May.

What were my first impressions? Well, it was unbearably hot. May is just into the monsoon season and temperatures were well over 35°C with ninety per cent humidity—quite a contrast from North Devon! The talk was of 'acclimatis-ation', which seemingly needed to be done as soon as poss-ible. Then there was the unfamiliar flying kit—very thin green Australian flying suits, 'noddy' boots and two internal g-suits. In my innocence I thought two suits to be rather generous until it was explained that because of the inner rubber bladders they could not be washed; nor could they be exchanged for new. This meant that one suit was worn until it reeked so badly of sweat that you were forced to change to the other, wearing that while the first one dried out, in the process forming a delicate layer of salt residue. Then you swapped them again. Those two suits lasted me for twenty months, by which time they were indescribable!

What else? Well the maps of Aden were not quite like those back home. They were nicknamed 'chocolates' because ninety per cent of the terrain was coloured brown with the legend 'Reliability poor' written all over it. So navigation, using dead reckoning in the days before inertial and GPS systems, was an art not a science. For some unaccountable reason we were issued with a holster but no gun; perhaps The Powers That Be thought that we would shoot ourselves or each other rather than the bad guys. But we were given a 'goolie chit' to keep us safe. This little card supposedly relayed, in Arabic, the information that if the holder of the chit was unharmed by whoever captured him after baling out of his jet, the capturer would be hand-

somely rewarded by the British Government. Frankly, I didn't have much faith in it, but, being young and in-destructible, dwelt little on the consequences of chit failure, which, as the nickname implied, was reputed to be term-inally harmful to one's prospects of fatherhood.

And so to the Hunter. I'd flown some fifty hours or so in the F.6 already at Chivenor on the OCU course and the F.G.A.9 was little different apart from the drag 'chute and the ability to carry 230-gallon drop tanks on the inner wing pylons. These latter were used for what were termed Extended Long Range (ELR) sorties, the first of which I flew on 13 May 1965. It lasted 1 hour 30 minutes—the longest I'd been airborne in a fast jet. I remember one or two such ELR trips to the Wadi Hadramaut, a spectacular rift valley some 300 or so miles north-east of Aden, with the legendary white-walled towns of Shibam and Saywun rising dramatically out of the sides of the mountains. The last sortie I had to the Hadramaut was in a Hunter F.R.10 on loan from No 1417 (Recce) Flight, also based at Khormaksar and part of Strike Wing which rather incongruously included Mk 3 Shackletons equipped with 20mm cannon and 25-pound practice bombs.

The real differences came in operating the aircraft. There were two Hunter F.G.A.9 squadrons in Aden at that time, No 43 (F), the 'Fighting Cocks', and No 8, which had been in Aden since 1945 and equipped with Hunters since 1960. The two squadrons shared aircraft and each jet wore both squadron markings. The idea was to get maximum utilisation from the aircraft without overstressing pilots in the heat of Aden. So, typically, we would start flying from early in the morning and get in two (or, exceptionally, three) sorties before midday, when the jets would be turned over to No 43 Squadron to fly all afternoon. They would

Below: XF429, a Hunter F.R.10 of No 8 Squadron on low-level patrol off the Arabian coast near Aden. Markings enthusiasts will notice, apart from the Squadron colours carried high on the rear fuselage, the white tips to the wings and to the inboard 230-gallon external tanks.

COURTESY NIGEL WALPOLE

COURTESY NIGEL WALPOLE

Above: A No 8 Squadron F.R.10 photographed by another F.R.10. Notice that the air brake beneath the rear fuselage has been deployed.

then fly them the following morning and hand them back to us at midday—and so on. That meant a whole afternoon on the beach every other day and a whole morning to recover from a hangover, also every other day. And it was a matter of pride for each of the squadron's groundcrew to hand over a set of fully serviceable aircraft each lunchtime. The system worked well, and perhaps the idea was replicated elsewhere in the RAF although I never saw it again.

The other operating differences came about because of sand corrosion. Our rôle was mostly low level, and front windscreens became sand-blasted, needing to be replaced regularly. In the heat haze of a summer afternoon, with cockpit temperatures at low level off the clock and in visibility of only a mile or less, a sand-blasted front windscreen presented a very formidable problem. Sand also affected equipment. Radar ranging, which I had used at Chivenor for air-to-air cine and gunnery, did not work in any of the squadron aircraft, it having been deemed too difficult to maintain in the dusty conditions. So we had to learn the art of estimating the range of other aircraft by eye during air-to-air combat and cine exercises—often with remarkably good results.

Our task was a heady mixture of air defence and ground attack. We had an air-to-air rôle using the four 30mm Aden cannon, but because there was no banner-towing capability in Aden all the air-to-air practice gunnery work was against other Hunters using cine film instead of bullets. This we practised assiduously down to fairly low levels, becoming expert at ranging visually using the gyro gun sight 'diamonds' controlled from the throttle twist grip. Starting with 1v1 combat we worked up to 4v2, mostly using conventional 'stick and search' tactics in pairs in tightly echeloned fighting wing formation.

Although Aden had a rudimentary ground-to-air radar system available to assist with air defence missions, the Hunter's operational rôle was day only. However, we did do some night flying—which I found terrifying. At night the random lights in the desert from Bedouin camp fires looked exactly the same as the stars above, hence disorientation was a real threat. New pilots had the worst job of trying to formate, either in close *echelon* or in fighting wing, on the experienced leader, whose Hunter was singularly ill-equipped with lights. You just had get through this and become a pairs leader yourself to then earn the easy bit!

For the air-to-ground rôle we were equipped only with the 30mm Aden cannon and 3-inch 'drains', unguided and fearsomely unreliable rockets launched from the outer underwing pylons. For practice we threw ourselves most days at the gunnery and bombing range near the beach just off the end of the Khormaksar runway. We usually fired the guns in pairs but on one occasion I did inadvertently fire all four. The aircraft nearly stopped dead with the recoil, circuit breakers popped and the cockpit filled with the heady smell of cordite. I didn't do it again!

Three-inch rockets came as practice or live. Practice rockets had concrete heads whilst the live ones had 60-pound HE heads. They were aimed using the 'bottom diamond' in the gyro gun sight and accuracy was given to few; most of we junior pilots were ecstatic if we got anywhere near the target, or even the ground! Simulated attack profiles (SAPs) were flown mostly as four-ships with two pairs in fighting wing formation about a mile line abreast—tactics left over from World War II days. Typically we would combine rôles by flying a four-ship low level out to a couple of simulated targets in the desert or in the numerous wadis, usually isolated buildings or small desert airstrips, and then climb up for a bout of 2v2 combat before returning to Khormaksar. Low level was notionally 250 feet, but since nobody ever complained about noise we often flew much lower. Seeing sand rising from where a jet pipe had come very close to the ground was not uncommon!

The main problem with air-to-ground was the Guns/RP switch in the cockpit. This had to be selected to the appropriate setting for gunnery or rocketing, which sounds simple but which was made really confusing because the switch could be found in the cockpit of various aircraft in no fewer than twelve different positions, including upside down! I guess this was because all the F.G.A.9s were modifications of earlier marks, not 'designer' built as Mk 9s. So many were the occasions when a rocket came embarrassingly off the rails rather than shells from the Aden cannon, and *vice versa*.

Operationally, we represented the last gasp of British colonial rule through air control. Emerging victorious but exhausted from World War I, Britain had had to deal with restive populations and disorders of all sorts in its Empire. Uprisings against British rule, tribal warfare and border problems seemed endemic in the Middle East, in Africa, and along India's North-West Frontier. The expense of large ground-force expeditions to maintain order in the Empire was becoming increasingly burdensome and the doctrine of air control was developed in the 1920s as a cheaper way of pacifying unruly populaces.

It began in the 1920s in mandated Iraq, where the RAF bombed Kurds and Arabs when they rebelled against Britain's attempts to control them. As the RAF became more experienced in using aircraft to maintain order in places such as Iran, Somaliland, Aden, the Sudan, the North-West Frontier, Palestine and Transjordan, air control

became more sophisticated, principally using the concept of 'minimal violence'. This usually involved dropping leaflets on truculent villages warning the occupants to behave or else face the threat of bombing. That concept of air control ended essentially with the British withdrawal from Aden following an insurgency against British rule known as the Aden Emergency. The Emergency began with a grenade attack by the communists' National Liberation Front (NLF) against the British High Commissioner on 10 December 1963, killing one person and injuring fifty, and ended on 30 November 1967 when the British finally pulled out.

Nearly four years earlier Hunters had been in the thick of operations in support of ground forces during the Radfan Campaign. In February 1964 our troops came under heavy attack in the Jebel Radfan area, some ninety miles north of Khormaksar. A makeshift brigade-size force including Royal Marines, Paras and 'A' Squadron SAS, led by Major (later General Sir Peter) de la Billière, was assembled and pressed into action, supported by Hunter ground-attack missions using guns and rockets. The campaign

Below: Some tidy flying by Nos 8 and 43 Squadrons as they formate in 'Diamond Nine' over the desert. Navigation in this theatre could be a challenge—the Hunter pilots' area of operations comprised literally hundreds of square miles looking exactly like this.

lasted until 27 June 1964 and Nos 8 and 43 Squadrons between them flew over 600 sorties, delivering 2,500 rockets and expending nearly 200,000 cannon shells.

Although the Radfan Campaign was successful in temporarily halting rebel insurgency, it was not long before armed struggle against the British resurfaced, predominantly now targeted against civilians and military personnel in the Aden township itself. At the same time there was growing concern about support to the NLF (and other anti-British factions) from what was then known as the Yemen Arab Republic, to the north of the Aden Protectorate. The threat came from a poorly equipped but determined Yemeni Air Force flying MiG-15s and -17s. Thus the operational task became one of sporadic support to ground forces facing insurgency incidents up country, mainly to the north of Aden, coupled with armed 'flag waves' along the border with the Yemen designed to deter incursions into South Arabian airspace by Yemeni fighters.

The latter campaign was successful. Legend has it that a few MiGs were sighted but in my time none actually penetrated our airspace so our Hunters must have frightened them off! I flew 35 operational sorties during my twenty months in theatre, most of which were 'flag waves'. A few were in support of our troops on the ground, but one particular mission sticks in my mind. On 13 September 1966 I was scrambled along with a more experienced pilot to attack targets in Wadi Bana, not far from the Radfan area, in support of troops who were coming under heavy fire. Under control from a helicopter-based Forward Air Controller, we had identified our targets and my leader was about to tip into the dive for a rocket attack, with me following, when over the radio we received an order from the authorities in Aden to cease fire.

At the time I could not understand why we had been stopped in our tracks, probably leaving our troops on the ground to their fate, but later events, and my dawning realisation of the political situation, went some way towards explaining this awful incident. Briefly, in February of that year the British Government had told pro-British Federal Government leaders that South Arabia would be granted full independence and all British Forces withdrawn by no later than 1968. This announcement was designed to bring the opposing parties together around the conference table. In fact, the cause of the Federal Government became

Below: Four Hunter F.G.A.9s in 'Box Four'. As in the photograph opposite, the aircraft carry composite fuselage flashes consisting of black and white chequers (No 43 Squadron) and sand (upper), blue and red bars (No 8).

COURTESY PETER JOHNSON

Left: A settlement in the Wadi Yahar, used as a base by rebel tribesmen, following a rocket attack by Khormaksar-based RAF Hunters.
Below: Standing out starkly against the pale desert background, a Hunter F.R.10 plies its trade over southern Arabia. The markings borne on the nose are those of No 1417 Flight, which comprised the RAF Khormaksar station emblem (a dhow against a large sun) set within an arrowhead device in black, blue, yellow and green.
Right: Hunters of the Aden Strike Wing offer a demonstration of their firepower.
Opposite, bottom: One of No 8 Squadron's Hunters flying over Little Aden.

COURTESY NIGEL WALPOLE

hopelessly lost. It had never enjoyed widespread support, but once it was clear that it would receive no further military aid or continue to enjoy economic support derived from the British base, it was helpless before an organised and committed terrorist campaign. Strident external forces, from the Yemen and from Egypt in particular, fuelled this opposition, and the collapse of the Federation swiftly became a *fait accompli*. To my mind, those troops on the ground were victims of a disingenuous attempt on the part of politicians to appear supportive of our campaign against the insurgents whilst at the same time washing their hands of an increasingly nasty mess. Later events surrounding the mutiny in June 1967 by members of the South Arabian Police Force in Crater, the Arab town in Aden, where support to our troops under lethal attack was denied by the authorities, bore further witness to this duplicitous policy.

Notwithstanding this inglorious chapter at the tail end of British colonial history, life was a ball for a young Hunter

COURTESY NIGEL WALPOLE

pilot with few thoughts other than to enjoy flying. One day towards the end of my time in Aden my Flight Commander said to me, 'Peter, you don't realise how good this tour is!' And he was right—I didn't realise it until much later. The flying was fantastic, water-skiing from the sandy beaches was great, my sun tan was permanent and the booze was cheap. I flew over 400 hours during my time on No 8 Squadron, over 350 of which were in F.G.A.9s, and I left in a VC-10 on 8 February 1967 to become a QFI, ending up as an instructor on Gnats at RAF Valley in Anglesey before moving on to Phantoms and, later, Jaguars.

I flew Hunters again briefly later in my RAF career, but that experience on the aircraft during my first operational tour left an indelible mark and fond memories that I continue to cherish. The Hunter was, and still is, a classic aircraft which, despite its peccadilloes, was a delight to fly and, thankfully, forgiving of even the most ham-fisted of irresponsible young pilots. I am privileged to have flown it.

The Perfect Vehicle *Group Captain Nigel Walpole*

In the Cold War, high-level strategic photographic recon- naissance (PR) was all about cameras, but photography was only one component of fighter (armed) recce (FR), a potentially invaluable asset to first- and second-echelon troops involved in a fast-moving battle, and to the inter- diction and counter-air campaigns. For this purpose the Hunter F.R.10 was ideal, a worthy successor to the Swift F.R.5, which had set the pattern for armed recce in the Cold War. I had cut my teeth on FR at RAF Gütersloh, on No 79 (F) Squadron, in the second half of the 1950s, flying the Swift F.R.5—a much maligned fighter but a superb aircraft at low level—before progressing to the F.R.10 six years later, again at Gütersloh and in the same rôle, on No II (AC) Squadron.

After a very satisfactory evaluation of the embryo F.R.10, the RAF ordered 33 of these aircraft, converted from Hunter F.6s. The result was an aircraft very similar to the F.G.A.9 but incorporating port, starboard and nose-facing Vinten F.95 oblique cameras; the gunpack was retained with its four 30mm Aden cannon but the radar ranging was discarded to make room for the cameras, and there was no provision for bombs or rockets. Armour plating gave some protection to the pilot and increased the weight in the nose to keep the centre of gravity within bounds; the Mk 9's brake parachute was included, and a gearing system was introduced to dampen aileron sensitivity at high indicated airspeed when flying at low level. The external tank capacities mirrored those of the F.G.A.9, but fuel in the 230-gallon tanks on the inboard pylons was gauged. Distance Measuring Equipment (DME) gave way to a miniature radio compass, as did the very high frequency (VHF) radio to ultra high frequency (UHF) equipment. The rôle equipment included a voice recorder.

The cockpit layout of the F.R.10 differed markedly from that of the F.G.A.9, its ergonomics being optimised for low-level FR operations. The upper port centre panel of the F.G.A.9, which contained the weapons and stores jettison switches, was moved to the port wall, where it remained easily accessible, while a fixed gun sight was offset to star- board, both modifications greatly improving forward vision. The radio controls were also moved from the port shelf into the space vacated by the panel and gun sight, enabling the pilot to change frequencies without the distraction of look- ing down into the cockpit. An independent stopwatch holder, fuel warning 'bingo' lights and F.95 camera oper- ating and footage indicators were also positioned to be seen at a glance, again minimising the need to bury the head in the cockpit. The all-important G4F compass was moved up and to the left from behind the control column, for quicker reference (also helping instrument flying). All this made low flying easier and safer, allowing the pilot to concentrate on his look-out, map-reading and visual observations. The cockpit layout of all the RAF F.R.10s was the same, a boon to flight safety while lessening the risk of selecting the wrong switch ('switchery pigs')—an all too common problem in other marks of the aircraft. Combining all these attrib- utes with high performance made the F.R10 a perfect vehicle for armed recce.

The F.R.10 was powered by an Avon Mk 203 or 207 axial-flow gas turbine engine, developing 10,000 pounds or

10,150 pounds static thrust, respectively, at sea level, as a result of which the aircraft could easily achieve its maximum permitted speed of 620 knots. The special gearing, provided in anticipation that powered aileron control would be undesirably light for the rôle, was rarely used, the pilots soon getting used to the aileron sensitivity. The 'follow-up' tailplane, most relevant to manœuvring in the upper airspace, was retained but not used in high-speed, low-level FR operations. The Swift gave a steadier ride at very low level, with the pilot able to fly almost 'hands off' at speeds up to 600 knots in an aircraft which could generally sustain greater damage from bird strikes and other incidental problems inherent in operational low flying. The Swift could also out-accelerate the F.R.10, but only by using its very thirsty reheat, and could decelerate faster with its air-brake-cum-flap, but the Hunter F.R.10 could go further, had better manœuvrability and employed a brake parachute to shorten landing runs; moreover, the Hunter had double the firepower and a greater combat potential at all levels. All things considered, the F.R.10 was the better aircraft of the two for the job.

The only obvious visible differences between the F.R.10 and the F.G.A.9 were the three camera ports and, perhaps, the external tank fit. The F.R.10 invariably carried 230-gallon drop tanks inboard and 100-gallon tanks outboard, whereas the Mk 9s were normally fitted with four tanks for ferry flights only and were seen more usually without the outboard 100-gallon tanks, enabling them to carry rockets or bombs and permitting better manœuvrability.

Having competed in international competition against the F.R.10's contemporaries—the RF-84F (which equipped the majority of NATO air forces in Europe at the time), its replacement the RF-104 Starfighter and the USAF's RF-101

Voodoo (I also flew both Starfighter and Voodoo, the latter on an exchange posting)—I found that the F.R.10 had the edge over them all in the short-range, daylight, armed recce role. The RF-84 may have had longer legs, but it was less manœuvrable and was ineffective (with its two 20mm cannon) in combat against the latest front-line fighters, while neither the RF-104 nor the RF-101 carried weapons and they too were less manœuvrable; they relied heavily on their higher top speeds to escape from hostile aircraft. The Hunter's F.95 camera fit was far superior in terms of continuous photographic cover and definition, in the very-high-speed, ultra-low-level regime, than those of any of its contemporaries.

In the mid-1960s, when I joined No II (AC) Squadron, we expected a war in NATO's Central Region to take us in our F.R.10s into the former East Germany, out as far as the border with Poland. The planned war tasks consisted largely of route searches for enemy activity moving west to support their troops in contact, and airfields considered of immediate importance to the opening stages of the conflict. Thereafter, the targets would have included pre- and post-strike recce of bridges, missile sites, airfields, troop concentrations, storage dumps and the like, all of which were grist to the mill for our Hunters and the experienced

Below: Hunter F.R.10 'Sierra' was the personal mount of Squadron Leader David Thornton when he was OC No II (AC) Squadron from 1962 to 1964. His rank pennant is displayed alongside the camera window.

pilots we had on our squadron. While our F.95 photographs could provide more detail, there was always a chance of camera failure, operator error (rare!) or failure to get back to a home base (or to a base with film-processing facilities), and there would always be a time delay before the customer received useful information from our film. Even if all went well, and our skilled photographic interpreters (PIs) were able to glean the necessary information from negatives displayed on light tables perhaps one hour after the aircraft had overflown the target and get this in a 'Hot Report' to the front line without any delay, the information might not have arrived in time to influence the battle. While serving with 16 Parachute Brigade, I do not recall the prints requested becoming available in time for them to be of use in the conduct of an exercise battle, although they could help to plan the next moves and were wonderful for VIP displays. On one exercise, purely to impress the Army, we arranged for a Hunter F.R.10 pilot to photograph our partly camouflaged location and return to Gütersloh with all speed for an operational turn-round and return to our site to drop a package of prints to us from his aircraft's airbrake. True to form, the Hunter was back overhead an hour and a half later, supposedly with the package, but by then the Brigade HQ, fearing imminent attack, had 'crashed out', leaving me to collect the cherished prints. Sadly, there were to be no prints, our conscientious pilot having checked his airbrake operation when taxiing out, releasing the package on to the taxiway—for no lesser person than the Station Commander to find!— and putting an end to this innovative but officially unauthorised practice in Germany. Fortunately, the pilot had passed impressively accurate visual observations directly to me, on a planned UHF frequency, in an In Flight Report (IFREP). IFREPs could be invaluable additions or indispensable alternatives to photographs, but their efficacy depended on an efficient and well-rehearsed network of ground and airborne communications, and in this we had less confidence. Such

Above: Shipping reconnaissance was part of the Hunter F.R.10's rôle—but this particular 'find' was unusual.
Right, upper: Line astern in a Norwegian Fjord, Dave Bagshaw catches 'Puddy' Cat on his forward-facing F.95.
Right, lower: Keith Holland of No IV (AC) Squadron had a multiple brake failure at RAF Gütersloh, but his F.R.10 would fly again.

reports might not be sufficiently detailed to satisfy the peacetime perfectionist but, as I found out while serving with the Brigade, they could render all we wanted to know in a fast-moving battle—'tanks lying in wait over the hill', 'bridge ahead down' and so on. Brevity in an IFREP was essential to avoid jamming, and encoding in many cases was unnecessary.

Although we could not carry bombs or rockets on the F.R.10, it had been proved that the four Aden cannon could have a devastating effect against many lucrative targets, enabling us to join the battle at the front—preferably under the direction of Forward Air Controllers (FACs)—or to be re-tasked in the air by various means. We might also be authorised to use our discretion when sighting high-value, fleeting targets (a nuclear missile convoy, for example) and use our guns against them. With map-reading our forte, and ultra-low-level the *modus operandi* for all our tactical aircraft in the Central Region, we could also call up and lead a strike force to a target and mark it with our guns. There were likely to have been many occasions in a European war in which such immediate action could have been crucial and would have been justified, any delays, such as waiting for photo confirmation, almost certainly rendering subsequent follow-up action superfluous. My friends in the Voodoo force proved the point many times during the 1960s conflict in South-East Asia. Nevertheless, the cardinal principle was that an FR mission should only be diverted to another purpose when the need was significantly greater—in order that so valuable an asset should not be put to any unnecessary risk. It followed that, although the F.R.10 pilot had the capability to engage in

combat with most hostile fighters at that time, in visual flight conditions at low level, he would have done so only *in extremis*: his primary task was to return with the information he had been tasked to gather.

Operational training for the Hunter F.R.10 pilots on No II (AC) Squadron at Gütersloh was geared to all these rôles. Above all, their objective was to reach and acquire the targets, note their details visually while operating their F.95 cameras to best effect, and get home safely with the required information, taking only those offensive or defensive measures deemed necessary.

In war, if only for economy of effort, single-aircraft missions would surely have been the norm, but this would also allow an F.R.10 pilot to manœuvre his aircraft to its limits in terrain such as the Sauerland, Harz or Teutoburgerwald, in marginal weather, down 'in the weeds' and

at very high speeds, without concern for a wingman. He would not, however, have the benefit of defensive cross-cover or redundancy of a wingman. That said, it was not unusual for No II (AC) Squadron to fly pairs of F.R.10s on operational training sorties, on a competitive basis in a standard 'trip of the day', *inter alia* removing any temptation to relax into more comfortable peacetime ways—such as flying at slightly less than operational speeds, a little higher than would be prudent in war or taking a quick second peek at the target. The wingman did not get off lightly; while the onus was on the leader, both pilots would be required to complete their route planning, covering up to three targets, in a total of thirty minutes, and to carry out full target recces. Moreover, a wingman might be given covert orders to re-task his leader in the air, perhaps to another target or an immediate diversion to another

airfield. Most sorties required IFREPs to be passed, to dedicated army cells if they were in the field or back to the Squadron via an ARC-54 UHF radio secreted below its operations desk. In addition, both flyers might get a surprise reminder of the need for constant vigilance, when a third aircraft was authorised to 'bounce' them in a safe area, committing them to evasive combat. Regular use of the Aden cannon in self-defence and offensive action was also on the agenda. Although the F.R.10 lacked radar ranging, its pilots became very proficient in air-to-air gunnery, training at ranges off the Frisian Islands on detachment to Leeuwarden, and in Britain using the Chivenor ranges. Moreover, when the weather precluded low flying, the Squadron's pilots would climb into air combat training areas to hone their skills at all forms of combat. In principle, the Squadron also devoted one week a month to air-

to-ground gunnery, usually combining it with a recce sortie covering two or three targets, terminating at any range available and concentrating on first run attacks (FRAs).

By all these means, the fighter-reconnaissance pilots continued to develop all their fast-jet skills and exploit the versatility of their Hunters to the full. In every type of NATO or national competition ('Royal Flush', 'Big Click' and 'Sassoon') or evaluation (Taceval), the pilots and aircraft of the two F.R.10 squadrons in Germany excelled, but this was in a wholly training environment. It was left to the F.R.10s in Aden to prove themselves in battle—and this they did.

Below: A brand new Hunter F.R. Mk 10 on a pre-delivery flight prior to joining No II (AC) Squadron in Germany in 1961. It is painted in the standard day fighter scheme of Dark Sea Grey with disruptive Dark Green camouflage, with High Speed Silver undersurfaces, all in glossy finish.

Blessed Indeed *Group Captain Jeremy Saye FIMgt*

The Hunter squadrons in the Far East in the 1960s (Nos 20 and 28 Squadrons) were equipped with the latest DF/GA (Day Fighter Ground Attack) Mark 9 variant. I was posted to No 20 Squadron at RAF Tengah in Singapore in mid-1966 as a third-tourist, initially as the Squadron PAI (Pilot Attack Instructor) responsible for all weapons training and delivery and later 'promoted'—in hierarchy, not rank!—to command 'A' Flight in early 1968. At this distance in time, some forty years after I left the Squadron, one's recollections become clouded with nostalgia, and probably also a number of inaccuracies, for which, dear reader, I can only apologise: the advancing years play tricks on one's addled brain-cells! However, I am not addled about the Hunter's rôle as part of Tengah's Strike Wing during the latter days of the Confrontation with Indonesia.

Our rôle on No 20 Squadron was, principally, to deter, and by default to attack, any intruders by air, sea or land against Malaysia or Singapore. To this end, we trained in practice interceptions (PIs) at high and low level, close air support (CAS) in support of ground forces, and strike (though not as in NATO's nuclear 'strike') missions against ground targets anywhere in Malaysia. These would, had actual hostilities developed, have typically included convoys, troop concentrations, lines of communication, command and control centres, supply depôts etc. In the more benign environment that prevailed in the late 1960s, such targets had, of course, to be simulated, suitable ones being few and far between in the sparsely populated areas of mainly jungle over which we operated. Over time we built up quite a library of strike targets—bridges, kampongs, small clearings used as football pitches (!), isolated buildings etc. Many of

Below: A pair of No 20 Squadron's F.G.A.9s pass Castle Peak in the New Territories, February 1968.
Right: An R/P-armed Hunter Mk 9 in No 20 Squadron markings. The Squadron served in the Far East from 1961 until 1970, thereafter re-equipping in RAF Germany with Harriers.

these we established using our own F.95-equipped Hunters (see above, pages 74–77), but we were grateful for the support of the PR Canberras of No 81 Squadron, co-located with us at Tengah. A typical training strike sortie, involving a four-ship armed with simulated 3-inch rockets and four 30mm Aden cannon, against a target up-country would, because of the distance involved, require a hi-lo-hi profile. The profile would include a climb-out and transit at high level for about 30 minutes, a let-down for a 20-minute, low-level approach and attack, and a 30-minute return at high level. Sounds simple enough, and not materially different in concept from standard hi-lo-hi profiles practised in other theatres. Except . . . except that navigation in FEAF was something of an occult art! First, the Hunter had no sophisticated navigation aids that make life so easy for today's generation of fighter/attack pilots. Satnav had yet to be invented, as had any sort of inertial navigation equipment or moving-map display, as later seen in the Jaguars and Harriers that superseded the Hunter. We had to rely on the time-honoured principle of heading/speed/distance to give time en route, hoping that the forecast wind was accurate. Add to this, of course, a map, the details on which were hazy at best ('areas uncharted'), and jungle beneath one that, to the untutored eye, seemed completely featureless. Many experienced Hunter pilots, new in theatre, were humbled to become 'temporarily uncertain of their position' (and I certainly counted myself amongst their number), whereas a first-tourist with a year or so in theatre was able to find the target. One quickly got to learn that skill and experience were no substitute for local knowledge.

We devoted at least 25 per cent of our training time to weapons delivery, and this was always a highlight of the programme. In addition to using local ranges at Ulu Tiram, Asahan and China Rock, once a year the Squadron moved up to the RAAF Base at Butterworth in the north-west corner of Malaysia, opposite Penang, for its Armament Practice Camp (APC), using primarily the coastal range at Song-Song, about which more in a moment. One of the more contentious weapons that we trained to deliver in theatre (though not up at Butterworth) was napalm, a fire bomb that, as a result of some unfortunate footage from Vietnam, media 'hype' described as the 'indiscriminate burning of women and children'. Consequently, our training was never described as 'napalm delivery' (although we had stocks of 100-gallon tanks of the stuff), but it would be right to place napalm in context, as it was hardly a new weapon. Napalm was, in essence, a fire-bomb/fuel gel mixture, designed to stick to, and burn, its target rather than to spread widely. It was composed of polystyrene plus benzene to solidify the gasoline, and was, despite fears to the contrary, remarkably stable, requiring an igniter to set it off. Napalm had been used since World War II, most notably in reducing much of Dresden to ashes in early 1945, and it has been widely used, although not much reported, in every war since. Had we been called upon to use it, it would have been controversially effective in clearing jungle hide-outs etc., whilst demoralising the enemy. The preferred method of delivery was a level drop from 50 feet and 420 knots as the target disappeared under the nose—hence our training in this method of delivery with 25-pound practice bombs, the aerodynamics of which were designed to be similar to those of the napalm tank. However, sometimes things do not go as planned and a 'switchery pigs' ensued. The practice bombs were crutched in pairs into an open bomb carrier, usually mounted on the Hunter's inboard pylons, if the range was close enough not to need the external fuel tanks. The Hunter's armament circuits were pretty basic: if the pilot selected the appropriate pylon, armed that circuit and pickled the release button, the store on that pylon would release. Easy! Except that, if the practice carrier were on that pylon, it would be necessary to check that an additional switch within the pylon was set to ensure that the release pulse went to the bombs and not to the carrier. Obvious, really—and certainly this requirement was repeatedly reinforced to all armourers and pilots. Does anyone see Murphy's Law coming into play here? Sure enough, both armourer and pilot screwed up one day, with the result that, when the pilot pickled, the carrier released with both bombs still aboard, and plummeted to earth well short of the target—'unscoreable at six'. Despite protestations from the pilot about an 'inadvertent release' (and thus not recordable), I insisted that the scores for both bombs stand, and that both armourer and pilot retrieve the carrier from the range. They did so with considerable loss of dignity!

Song-Song was an unpretentious over-water range, a short flight to the south-west of Butterworth, but with limited facilities. It did have, however, some excellent, clearly defined, fifteen-foot-square hessian targets that were ideal for air-to-ground gunnery, and for which we carried sixty rounds of 30mm ball ammunition, using one of the selectable four Adens. Each pair of aircraft normally had a fifteen-minute range slot, which allowed for one practice ('dry') run plus up to five live ('hot') runs to fire off the rounds. The Range Safety Officer (RSO), Whose Word Was Law, strictly controlled time on target, and he, rightly, never allowed any of us to extend the range slot to accommodate anyone who had been unable to 'bring their guns to bear' in the allotted time. One of the features at Song-Song was the crosswind, which was usually benign at dawn but increased steadily throughout the day. Every pilot, naturally, wanted the first slot of the day, and, as the PAI in charge, I was responsible for ensuring that each had his fair share, me included. To add spice to the event, the APC featured an inter-Flight competition, with the groundcrew running a

'book' on the outcome, plus a sweepstake on each individual pilot. I was sufficiently young, arrogant and confident to fancy my chances as an individual winner, and thus lead the Flight to victory—pride before a fall, indeed! On the morning to which this story relates, I led our pair to the range for the first slot at 0900 hours. The weather was perfect with not a breath of wind. I had selected a well-harmonised aircraft, firing an inner gun, and was fully expecting to 'fill my boots'. However, we arrived to find the range closed: a Malay fishing boat was illegally casting its nets just within the Danger Area, and the RSO would allow no firing until it had cleared off. Steam rising from every orifice, I cajoled and pleaded, even abusing such authority as I had as the Squadron PAI—which cut no ice at all—to shift the whole morning's programme by thirty minutes. I then lost control, and threatened to fire a warning shot across the boat's bow to encourage him to move on, whereupon I was told to 'Leave the range immediately'. Oh what shame and humiliation! Later, I grovelled an apology to the RSO and to my Boss, and was lucky that this potential international incident did not turn out to be entirely career-limiting!

Following the withdrawal of No 28 Squadron's Hunters from RAF Kai Tak, Hong Kong, in 1967, No 20 Squadron was authorised to detach a Flight up there twice a year to 'maintain an RAF presence'. On each detachment, because there wasn't much else to do in such a restricted area, we used Port Shelter Range, a flat, rocky promontory on the

COURTESY TONY BUTTLER

Above: A No 20 Squadron Hunter Mk 9, in a photograph probably taken immediately after an engine change. The nose cone, tail cone and Aden cannon equipment are absent, as is the fin panelling covering access to the rudder control linkage. The drooped air brake is probably a result of slightly leaky non-return valve in the hydraulic circuit.
Opposite page: Spot the Hunter! A Mk 9, wheels down, on the approach to Runway 13 over Wan Chai Harbour, Hong Kong, in late 1968.

eastern side of the New Territories coastline. The range included a 'dive circle' shaped like a dart board, in the centre of which was a prominent Bull's Eye, the striking of which was awarded a DH (Direct Hit) together with much kudos. This was an ideal target on which to practise our 25-degree rocketry. That day, when I was assessing the morning's results, I noticed that the scores were all over the place, few pilots apparently having been able to fire even remotely accurately. The cine film from the cameras recording the image through the gun sights displayed a lack of concentration, leading to sloppy tracking and poor accuracy. And then the story emerged. Apparently, on the night before, a posse of pilots had made a foray into downtown Kowloon to sample the delights therein. After probably more libations than was wise, they had been lured into the back streets to see a 'movie' (colour not specified). The star of this movie was a young lady of ample charms and dubious virtue, who was performing 'an unnatural act' right there on top of the Port Shelter Bull's Eye. The following morning on the range, the young pilots, when turning in to attack, were diverted from their purpose of tracking the target by haunting images of this young lady performing on the Bull's Eye. Clearly, this was a novel diversionary tactic that offered great potential for an enemy to develop. The mind boggles.

And finally, although nothing to do with weaponry (but everything to do with flying in Hong Kong), we turn to night flying—a nemesis for most day-fighter boys. For reasons that escaped me at the time (and even now leave me bemused), we were tasked to go night flying whilst based at

RAF Kai Tak, where, let it be remembered, we shared the only runway with all Hong Kong's civil airline traffic, the latter invariably expecting priority for landing. The night in question was overcast with light rain, and with a strongish wind from the south, making for a tricky approach and landing on the duty Runway 13. The approach on the base leg to this runway, heading north-east, was over the middle of Kowloon—a mass of flashing and disorientating neon lights. One headed for what was known locally as the Checker Board, fortunately illuminated and easy enough to see, but itself mounted on a hillside immediately to the front, and directly in the windscreen. When you picked up the runway lights to your right, you turned on to finals, passed the high-rise buildings on your wing tip, and man-œuvred to make a successful landing. On a clear day, it certainly concentrated the mind, but on a dark and rainy night with a crosswind, it was sufficient to make one contemplate a change of underwear. I have been lucky enough to have survived many dicey landings before and since, but none was scarier than that first night landing on Kai Tak's Runway 13.

How should one sum up flying Hunters in the Far East in the 1960s, as opposed to flying them in any other theatre? Flying a Hunter anywhere was always a joy, because it was truly a gentleman's aircraft, but it was especially a joy in the Far East because of the frisson of the rôle within the large Strike Wing that included four other squadrons at Tengah. In those days one could fly almost anywhere, and at any height (within reason), as very little of the airspace was controlled and most of the terrain was uninhabited. There was always a sense of purpose, with a grumbling Indonesia to the south and a full-blown war to the north in Vietnam. Add in a colonial lifestyle in the splendid Officers' Mess, together with the many social and sporting delights in Singapore itself, and those of us privileged and lucky enough to have been a part of them were blessed indeed. Those were the Golden Years!

129

THE GROUNDCREW

Air Commodore 'Mac' McEwen AFC

WHEN I had been on my first Hunter squadron for about a year, a publicity team from the Air Ministry came down and said that they wanted to interview all the pilots in order to get ideas on how to advertise the Royal Air Force and attract the right sort of people. When my time came, an earnest publicity journalist, who, clearly, had already decided what form the advertising should take, tried to put words in my mouth by saying, 'If you were asked what is the best thing about your job as a fighter pilot, you would say it was the feeling of exploring the frontiers of science with the challenges of supersonic flight, wouldn't you?' I said that that bit was great, but what really attracted me was the *esprit de corps*, the camaraderie, that was the very essence of a fighter squadron. The spirit was hard to put into words, but it was like being in a large family where everyone was friends, and flying was more like a sport than a job. We were in the bar every night celebrating something or other, so it was like being at a permanent party, and I loved it all. The interviewer looked down his nose at this and disagreed with me, and when the new series of advertisements came out much later, there was no mention of *esprit de corps*. I thought this was wrong, and found

throughout my career that spirit was always the most important issue. I still do think that.

It was not just a matter of comradeship among the pilots that was important, however; it applied equally well to the Squadron groundcrew as well. They were a wonderful group of men, highly professional, but full of good humour and always totally flexible. I have always found that one can tell a good fighter squadron from a bad one straight away by looking at the relationship between the pilots and the groundcrew. The RAF has always advertised itself as a great example of teamwork, and so it is, but in any organisation there are always tensions of some sort between people in branches performing different functions, simply because they are all humans and all have loyalties of their own persuasion and to their own kind. Hunter squadrons, however, were comparatively small units, and in my experience nearly always had good morale, although there were, to be sure, exceptions.

Below: A groundcrewman checks the cockpit of a No 34 Squadron Hunter Mk 5 at RAF Nicosia during the Suez Crisis of October–November 1956. No 34 participated in hostilities along with the Mk 5s of No 1 (F) Squadron, but operations were hampered by the aircraft's limited range. The distinctive (and unofficial) 'invasion stripes', in yellow and black, were characteristic of many of the British and French aircraft employed during the operation.

BAE SYSTEMS

Above: The first Hunter prototype, WB188, is refuelled from a bowser in preparation for a test flight. The vital rôle of the groundcrew is often overlooked—without their industry, no aircraft can fly.

A warning sign was when not everyone knew everyone else's name. This is much less evident in the Royal Navy, where everyone is, literally, in the same boat, and if they sink they all go down together, nor in the Army, where units are totally dependent on one another for their very survival. In the Royal Air Force, however, the NCOs and airmen do their job of preparing and looking after the machines, and the officers (with the sole exception of the engineering officer) do a completely different job in flying them. There is always the potential for a gulf between aircrew and groundcrew, therefore, and it can only be bridged by a common respect and understanding. Much of this can be achieved by common courtesies, of course, such as referring to groundcrew by their names and showing interest in what they have to do, rather than treating them as just another piece of equipment. But the real secret for success is to convince them that they have your complete confidence in them, and to let them know that you are all on the same side. There is no substitute for mutual trust.

This is sometimes more difficult than it may seem, because pilots and groundcrew have such a different outlook on flying. When you hear a pilot say, for example, 'The weather was so bad, I didn't know I was down until I heard the groundcrew clapping', everyone knows instantly that this is a huge joke, because the groundcrew would never in a million years applaud a landing in bad conditions. That is the rôle they expect the pilot to be able to carry out properly as a matter of course, in the same way that the pilot expects the groundcrew to be able to change his engine correctly. It's just a fact of life.

One day an edict came down From Above indicating that the groundcrew were not being told enough of what the pilots did in the air. Henceforth, pilots

131

were to tell their starter crews in detail what it was they were going off to do and, after they had landed, tell them how it had gone. This was one of those edicts based on a total misunderstanding of how fighter operations worked—and something of a misunderstanding of human nature itself. Time was always of the essence, and there just wasn't the time to brief the groundcrew in this way, especially if at the time your head was full of facts and figures you needed to recall about the imminent sortie. Furthermore, after you had landed, the groundcrew didn't want to hear all about it; they simply wanted you out of the cockpit and out of the way as soon as possible so that they could get on with refuelling and re-arming. The clock was always ticking on a fighter flight line. After a very short time the edict was withdrawn and we went happily about our normal ways. The fact was that, by and large, the groundcrew did not want to know what we were up to in the air; they just wanted to know if the aircraft was fully serviceable and, if not, whether it was a snag that could be left until the end of the day.

When relationships did get strained, the pilots were often the cause, because they did something that caused the groundcrew to doubt that they knew what they were talking about. This often manifested itself in the way defects were reported in the Form 700, the serviceability log. A defect had to be reported clearly and accurately, so that the engineers could know where to start looking for the cause. Thus if a pilot wrote a vague comment such as 'Something loose down the back end', the engineers would feel quite entitled to write in the log's rectification action column, where they had to demonstrate how a fault had been corrected, 'Something loose down the back end tightened up.'

Many a hornets' nest of recrimination started over something as unimportant as that. There was a case where a pilot made such a nuisance of himself by continually snagging aircraft for minor defects that could never be traced and wasted everybody's time that the Warrant Officer in charge of the line wrote in exasperation in the rectification column. 'Pilot changed and aircraft found satisfactory.' There was another famous occasion when a pilot started his take-off and noticed that the airspeed needle was winding backwards and that the altimeter was unwinding. He abandoned the take off and switched off in dispersal, announcing that the pitot static lines behind the instrument panel must have been

Opposite: Groundcrew of No 56 Squadron feverishly at work, attending to the Aden gun pack of one of their Hunter F.5s; notice the special winch designed to aid the pack's removal. Removing the pack changed the aircraft's centre of gravity—hence the tail prop to keep the Hunter stable.
Right: A closer view of the Hunter's Aden gun pack and the latter's winch and cradle. A well-practised crew could remove a spent pack and install a new, fully loaded one in about a minute. The quartet of 30mm cannon could fire at a rate of 1,200 rounds a minute and the pack's capacity was 600 rounds—formidable destructive power indeed.

COURTESY PHILIP JARRETT

connected the wrong way round, because that was the only way this inverted operation of the instruments could be explained. The instrument tradesman involved was called, and he was adamant that he had connected the lines properly and tested them, so the pilot must be mistaken. The 'Chiefy' (Chief Technician) running the line that day said that, to save time, they would prove it one way or another: he would blow down the pitot head himself. The pilot and the instrument mechanic would watch from the cockpit, and then they would see who was right.

The 'Chiefy', who was a gnarled old expert of many years standing, positioned himself at the pitot head and the pilot and instrument mechanic at the cockpit waved to indicate that they were ready for the test to begin. All this would have been a good idea, but unfortunately, when he taxied back in, the pilot had left the pitot head heater, which stopped the head from freezing at altitude, in the 'on' position and had also left the battery switch on. While the discussion about the instruments had raged, therefore, the head was getting hotter and hotter, and when the 'Chiefy' pursed his lips and applied them to the end of the tube to blow, it must have been close to red hot. The result was that, instead of the instruments moving, an anguished howl came from the pitot head area and the 'Chiefy' recoiled

clutching his mouth and saying words that are best left unrepeated. It was later shown that the pilot was right and the instrument mechanic wrong, but, because the after-shutdown checks were not done properly, the pilot did not come out of the incident well.

I climbed into a Hunter once and went through the normal left-to-right cockpit checks, which, quite early on, involved pressing the relight button on the HP cock to check that it was working. You could tell that it was working because the ignitors could be clearly heard, crackling merrily away in the engine. The groundcrew would also listen at the engine intake to confirm that all was well. At this stage, the LP cock would be on but the HP cock closed. On this occasion, however, when I pressed the relight button the starter cartridge fired with its usual deafening bang, making the groundcrew jump out of their skins. Since my hand was already on the HP fuel cock, I pushed it open and snapped on the booster pumps, and the engine started normally. I did the rest of the checks and taxied out, and I must say I wondered a bit about the electrics on this particular aircraft: when I closed the hood electrically, for example, would the undercarriage select 'up'? But all was normal.

The aircraft behaved perfectly throughout the sortie, but I recorded it as unserviceable in the log because of the relight button problem. I went back to the pilots' crew room and was having a quiet coffee when a sergeant electrician from the Station Electrical Section, whom I had never met before, appeared with a large electrical chart under his arm and told me in no uncertain terms that my experience with the relight button could not possibly have occurred. He opened the chart in front of everybody and showed that, for good safety reasons, the relight circuits and the engine ignition circuit were completely separated. This seemed irrefutable evidence, and I was quite taken aback. He said that I must have had a mental aberration, and that, instead of pressing the relight button on the left-hand side of the cockpit, I must have operated the harness go-forward lever and leant forward to press the engine starter button on the opposite side of the cockpit. We went out to the aircraft and checked the relight switch again, but he was right—the main cartridge didn't fire when it was pressed. He then said to me rather condescendingly, 'You've perhaps been flying a bit too often lately, eh, sir? Perhaps you'd better take a spot of leave.'

I felt baffled and rather humiliated and went out to the line to put the aircraft fully serviceable. I watched the next pilot start, and the aircraft behaved normally—and, in fact, it continued to do so for the next three months. Then the fault reappeared. Investigation showed that, although the two electrical circuits were designed to be quite separate, physically the wires crossed one another in the fuselage, and with all the vibration that always came with the Sapphire engine the insulation must have worn away so that bare wire touched bare wire and the circuits were joined. During the sortie I flew after my incident, further vibration must have caused the wires to separate again, and they did not join up once more until three months later. I went triumphantly off to the Station Electrical Section to beard the sergeant I had met in his den and to let him know that I was not such a ninny after all, only to find that he had been posted and left the service. So I was denied the infinitely satisfying experience of telling him, 'I told you so!' I had learnt a good lesson, however: if you witness something and know it happened, never let anyone persuade you that you did not. I have stuck to that ever since, and it has often stood me in good stead.

In my early days flying the Hunter, we had a corporal on No 257 Squadron, an expert who used

to do the work of ten men. One lunchtime one of our aircraft took off and the undercarriage failed to retract properly. It appeared that the sequence valves had malfunctioned, because the doors closed before the undercarriage legs had been raised and the whole lot jammed in the half-closed position. We had never had this emergency before, but I was the duty pilot at the time, and after we had arranged a flypast over the tower so that we could examine the under-carriage position through binoculars, and had got another aircraft to have a close look at him, I told the pilot to orbit overhead while I consulted with the Squadron duty engineer—who happened to be the corporal in question. We discussed it, and he agreed that if the pilot overrode the normal system by selecting the emergency 'down' lever, the 1,800psi in the emergency system air bottle should blow the undercarriage back to the 'down and locked' pos-ition without any problem. This duly happened, and I told the pilot to switch off at the end of the runway to be towed back, in case there was a further hydraulic problem. I then went out to meet him, collecting the corporal on the way. Because this was a curious incident, Wing Commander Flying and Wing Commander Engineering went out to meet the aircraft in another Land Rover, following on a

few hundred yards behind. As we neared the parked Hunter, the corporal said to me, 'I know what's happened. I had to do some undercarriage retraction checks on that aircraft, but I had to do it on my own because everyone had gone to lunch. So I had to wire the sequence valves off with piano wire. When I took the jacks away afterwards, I forgot to take the piano wire off and we'll find them still there in the undercarriage bay. That's why the sequencing didn't work. It'll only take me a second to whip out the piano wire, though, and nobody will ever know.'

I was in a quandary. It was typical of that corporal that he should have pressed on with the retraction checks on his own over lunchtime and made no fuss about it, and he was such a staunch and loyal member of the Squadron that I didn't want to see him fall foul of his Engineering Wing Commander, who was right behind us, but if I let him remove the evidence the aircraft would be subjected to endless futile checks—none of which would reveal anything—and be out of commission for a long time. It would, moreover, be dishonest.

We got out of the Land Rover, and, sure enough, there was the tell-tale piano wire sticking out of the sequence valves. A quick snip and it would disappear for ever, and nobody would ever know why that emergency had occurred. Wing Commander Flying's Land Rover was still 100 yards away, and so I had about thirty seconds to decide. I had always been brought up to believe (and I still do) that honesty is the best policy, however, and so I said, 'Sorry, ——, we'll have to leave the wire in,' and went out to meet

Below: The pilots of No 257 Squadron start the Sapphires of their Hunter Mk 2s, line groundcrew in attendance as always, to ensure that all is well. The Squadron chinthe emblem is now prominently displayed on each aircraft—compare these markings with those illustrated on pages 6–7.

the two wing commanders. The corporal was recognised as an excellent engineer and he was given only a token rebuke over this incident in the light of the wonderful work he did for the Squadron, and it didn't affect his career afterwards. I never discussed it with him subsequently, but I have no doubts that I did the right thing, and I hope he forgave me.

Finally, in this little discussion about aircrew/groundcrew relations, I found that if the groundcrew ever offered advice— which was rare—it was worth listening to. During 1960 Wattisham had to be closed for three months for runway resurfacing, and its squadrons moved to Stradishall, also in Suffolk, the personnel commuting from their homes each day so as to minimise the upheaval. Aircraft in very deep servicing were left behind at Wattisham, but there was one Hunter which did not quite fit that category. It had been something of a rogue aircraft and had not been fit to fly for a long time, and the engineers wanted to get it across to Stradishall so that they could sort the problems out. Eventually, after a maximum effort by the groundcrew, who worked all night, it became serviceable on the last day that the Wattisham runway was to remain open. I was deputed to collect it and to deliver it to Stradishall, thirty miles away.

I read up on the long history of faults on this aircraft and noted the many attempts that had been made to rectify it. The Warrant Officer, who had been left behind specifically to get this aircraft serviceable, fell into step beside me as I walked out to the flight line, remarking, 'I'd appreciate it as a special favour to me, sir, if you handled things gently in this one and didn't do one of your hairy take-offs.' At that time I was the Station's low-level display aerobatic pilot, and I was working on what I hoped would be a spectacular take-off routine once I had practised it enough. I would hold the Hunter down on the deck after raising the undercarriage, and then go straight into either a low-speed roll off the top (but using twenty degrees of flap) or a 180-degree climbing roll, depending upon the venue and the crowd position. I had never been given a word of warning like this before, however, and, coming as it did from a worthy such as the Warrant Officer himself, I was suspicious right away and demanded to know what it was that was really wrong with the aircraft. The Warrant Officer swore that it was fully serviceable but added that I should take it easy because he had 'a feeling in his water'.

I was a bit spooked by all this and double-checked everything as I taxied out, but it all seemed perfectly normal, so I called for take-off clearance. The nosewheel came off the ground normally, and the aircraft felt fine on lift-off, but some instinct

Below: Shorn of its wings and tailfin, a Hunter F.R.10 of No IV (AC) Squadron is loaded on to a 'Queen Mary' for dispatch either to a maintenance unit or to the manufacturers for attention.

COURTESY NIGEL WALPOLE

COURTESY NIGEL WALPOLE

Above: A No IV (AC) Squadron Hunter F.R.10 undergoing maintenance, with its nose cone removed to reveal the mountings for the F.95 cameras. The canopy has been removed to permit full access to the rear of the cockpit and ejection seat systems and parked on a special cradle across the fuselage spine.
Below: Flying completed, the Hunters are left to the maintenance boys to lavish their attention on their precious charges. No 257 Squadron once more.

told me not to raise the undercarriage too quickly—which was just as well because, as I reached out for the undercarriage button, there was a loud *clunk*, the power controls went into manual and the emergency warning panel lit up with a total hydraulic and electrical warning indication.

I cruised quietly over to Stradishall, lowered full flap on the emergency system, and landed without incident, but I was grateful for that timely word of advice I had been given. The next time I went across to the Sergeants' Mess (an officer could only go there if specially invited) I had a heart-to-heart with that Warrant Officer, but he was still insistent that the emergency was a coincidence, so I never did get to the bottom of the mystery. Come to think of it, I never got to fly that particular aircraft again, and that really *was* a coincidence. Some people might call it fate.

COURTESY HOWARD N. TANNER Jr

Fun, False Locks, and Frame 32 *David Applegate*

The Hawker Hunter was a beautiful machine, and it introduced a new standard of visual attractiveness for a warplane: we had admired the beauty of the Mosquito and the Spitfire, but these were now old-timers. It was time for the 'moderns'. And what 'moderns' they were—Comet, Swift, Canberra and, the darling of them all, the Hunter, which set all our hearts racing! Clean of line, superbly graceful in the air, symbolic of the fresh and exciting 1950s, we loved its aura of complete efficiency. Even when they added the 'Sabrina' panels and the air brake, it won all round. What glamour! And it was British—and what pride it generated!

There were some early maintenance problems—hydraulic pipes, especially those serving the air brake, which fatigued merrily, producing difficult control and braking problems for the pilots; the aileron hydroboosters, which could give a 'false lock', possibly leading to restricted aileron control; the way rain hammered and tore off the rubberised coatings on the nose and fin radomes; the tyres, with lives of nearly ten (!) landings—until they introduced inner tube base supports, when rubber consumption dropped by two-thirds! The Mk 6, with these problems beaten, began to arrive at North Weald for No 111 Squadron in 1956, and as Squadron Engineer Officer I considered it a real privilege to work on the aircraft, to become intimate with them, and to treat them as somewhat wayward friends. They sometimes did as we asked, although some new features did their best to drive a wedge between us.

The engine starter accelerated the Avon 203 to 'self-sustaining speed' in ten seconds, powered by isopropyl nitrate; its own turbine ran quickly up to 44,000rpm. There has never been a hiss like that starter; indeed, I still hear it in my tinnitus. Strange things happened. For example, the exhaust pipe, being almost flush with the bottom of the

fuselage, pushed some of the very hot gases into the adjacent servicing bay, with fiery results, and it was decided from On High that the door to this bay should be kept open during the start cycle, but hooked up with wire. This wire went the way of all loose articles, and, fearing FOD, the door was just left to hang. But this door had the starter control box mounted on it, and collected quite a lot of heat from the gas, such that it dried up a bit and caused the start to recycle before it had finished, so that the hiss turned into the sound of the *Sir Nigel Gresley* leaving King's Cross with the night mail! So we had to find those pesky bits of wire, and use them!

One interesting day during a start, part of the top of the spine of, I think, XF446 blew off, looking for all the world as though the drogue gun had fired. But no—we found that, due to a misalignment between engine and starter which could occur as the engine was trundled home after a change, the still-explosive exhaust swept up into the spine and exploded as the jet pipe warmed up. Such fun!

The aircraft suffered structural cracking at Frame 32, just aft of the wing roots. This was the result—in my opinion—of the design of the power train from the engine offtake to the hydraulic pump and the generators, situated on the front face of a 'turret gearbox' at the base of Frame 32. The power train consisted of a straight driveshaft from the engine, with a quick-release coupling, to the 'turret box', through two right angles and lengthy shafts and casings. This seemingly flimsy arrangement vibrated and resonated enough to cause the frame to crack, which could not be tolerated because it might break up and lead to complete hydraulic and electrical failure, or worse. It was a threatening occurrence, and caused much hangar work, with many tails off, engines out, repairs, refit engines and tails—all very time consuming.

Below: Four of 'Treble-One''s Hunter F.4s. The aircraft nearest the camera, WT739, was that in which CO Squadron Leader Roger Topp set the Edinburgh-London speed record on 8 August 1956, completing the distance from Turnhouse to Northolt in 27 minutes 52.8 seconds—flying the 331.6 miles at an average speed of 717.5mph. Red wing tips identified aircraft of 'A' Flight of the Squadron; white tips identified those of 'B' Flight.

Right: No 111's Mk 4s were supplanted by Mk 6s in 1957–58 and it was not long before the aircraft appeared in their trademark all-black finish—at first, without white surrounds to the roundels and fin flashes. The expertly executed displays of this world famous aerobatic team demanded incredibly hard work and dedication by the 'boys in the background'—the groundcrews.

COURTESY REG WYNESS

The microswitches in the noseleg door often went u/s, causing unscheduled steep climbs after take-off, and there was the endemic problem of air in the hydraulics; some aircraft were sick with air much of the time. So many bleed screws, so much unwelcome effort! It was all because of the high hydraulic oil interchange between jacks and too small a hydraulic reservoir.

Later experience showed me how very important component interchangeability is, and how much design and inspection effort must be put in by manufacturers to achieve what Henry Ford managed before World War I—to get all the parts to go together. The Ministry mantra of fit, form and function may sound good, but when you could not even fit a new wing tip because there were no attachment holes the principle seemed to have been forgotten. Once, in very hot weather at Cameri, in Italy, a leaking elevator hydrobooster necessitated a change, and so we asked base to send one out. This they did, but it would not fit—it

COURTESY PHILIP JARRETT

was a different mod state. Another had to be flown from North Weald (by our intrepid US exchange officer in a Meteor 7), and that did fit. But why was so little thought apparently given to the severe effects on operations that poor interchangeability might have? The end is rich, too: at base, they could find no fault with the original; I thought, 'So much for product environmental testing!' And people wondered why there were so many maintenance hours per flying hour!

We all learned a lot. The pilots did, too: apart from their professional flying, they saw that in order to have clean aeroplanes a lot of elbow grease had to be applied. We did manage to keep our aircraft clean-ish, and I'm sure that their being black helped! At Le Bourget in 1957 we had the pleasure of hearing our Station Commander refer to the US Thunderbird Aeros team as having 'dirty aircraft'! The French major domo of the flight line there could not understand why we needed trolley 'accs' (les batterie-accumulateurs) for our 'self contained' starter systems, and much difficulty was experienced trying to explain that the internal batteries could only provide one start attempt and that in order to avoid flat batteries and embarrassing changes in a foreign field we needed trolley accs.

The Hunter looked superb, and I loved it. The need to get five, or seven, or nine aircraft on the line all the time concentrated the mind, and was a real change from the old Meteor days. I did wonder sometimes just how much care and professionalism had been put into ensuring that the Defence of the Realm was properly furnished with first class equipment, considering the snags we met. However, the achievement of ensuring that enough serviceable aircraft were on the line for aeros practice, or a show, was challenging and satisfying. I would not have missed it for worlds!

I have always regretted not collaring a pitot head for a standard lamp: goodness knows, enough of them had to be changed because of in-flight touches. And although we had a Meteor 7 on the Squadron which the Boss used (with me in the back) to pave the way for shows in France, Norway, Italy and all points east, I never got a ride in a Mk 7 or 8 Hunter. If anyone has one, and would like to offer me a trip, do call!

Maltese Air Cover *Senior Aircraftman David Sell*

I was a National Serviceman between February 1955 and February 1957 and served my two years in the Royal Air Force. In September 1955, after completing basic training and trade training at RAF Hednesford and RAF Yatesbury, respectively, I had the good fortune to be posted to RAF North Weald. On arrival I was sent to work in the Central Signals Section, but after three weeks I was told that there was a vacancy for an air radar mechanic on No 111 Squadron. 'Treble-One' was the only regular squadron at North Weald at the time, the other two units being were Royal Auxiliary Air Force squadrons, which flew Gloster Meteor Mk 8s.

I duly reported for duty to Treble-One and for the first time saw the magnificent Hawker Hunters close up. These gleaming aircraft took my breath away—the elegant, streamlined shape, the sheer raw power of the Rolls-Royce engine on take-off—and to this day I still recall vividly the first time I saw a pair of 'Treble-One' Hunters taking off from the far end of the long runway, roaring up towards the station buildings with ever increasing speed and, two-thirds along the runway, lifting up clear and folding their wheels into the their wings in one movement. That ear-pounding, gut-wrenching roar as the pair soared clear of the hangars before going into a steep climb! Over the following months that awesome display of power as the Avon engines hurled the Hunters into the sky was a spectacle that never ceased to thrill.

The 'Boss' on 'Treble-One' at that time was the legendary Squadron Leader Roger Topp, and it was through his drive and vision that the Squadron developed from being the nominated Royal Air Force display squadron to becoming 'The Black Arrows' of world renown. While I was on the Squadron he increased the number of Hunters in the display from five to nine. Each time he wanted to add another Hunter to the display formation a delegation from Air Ministry would come from London to North Weald to watch the demonstration flight: there was sufficient 'scrambled egg' around for all us groundcrew to enjoy a cooked breakfast! The hangar would be suitably 'bulled' and all the aircraft polished. However, few complained, because it was an exciting time to be on No 111, seeing history being made before our eyes as the displays became ever more complex and daring. I still remember the first time I saw the 'bomb burst'—a heart stopping moment for us all as the individual Hunters broke, diving to different points of the compass.

One Friday afternoon in September 1956 the Squadron was informed by Air Ministry that a detachment from 'Treble-One' was required to transfer to Malta with six aircraft and back-up groundcrew and spares. This deployment was to be made apparently at the behest of the Maltese government, who had insisted upon the provision of air cover for the island: Colonel Nasser had blocked the Suez Canal and declared it nationalised for Egypt, and there was to be a build-up of British forces on Malta prior to an invasion of Egypt to reclaim the Canal Zone. Thus six Hunters were prepared for the long flight and the selected groundcrew—two from each trade group, a fitter and a

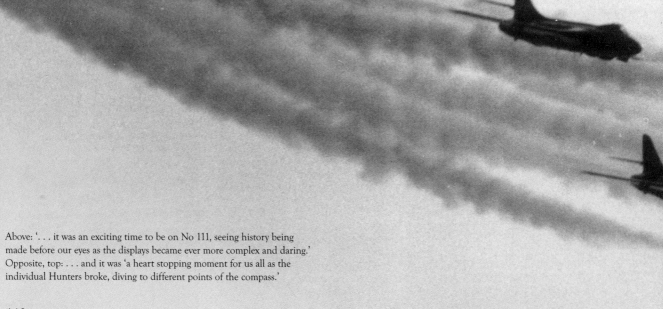

Above: '. . . it was an exciting time to be on No 111, seeing history being made before our eyes as the displays became ever more complex and daring.' Opposite, top: . . . and it was 'a heart stopping moment for us all as the individual Hunters broke, diving to different points of the compass.'

mechanic—were sent to the Station Medical Quarters for the appropriate injections! I was fortunate enough to be selected to go as air radar mechanic, with Corporal Tony Brown going as fitter.

That weekend was frantic, each trade group assembling its kit and spares, as the groundcrew and their equipment were due to fly out at 0600 hours on the Monday morning. Three large aircraft from Transport Command flew in to North Weald to be adapted and loaded. The groundcrew flew off in a Hastings which had had the seats removed down one side to accommodate a spare Avon engine. This was fastened with chains to secure it, and I well remember, later on the Monday morning after we had taken off on time (and dressed in 'best blue' as there was insufficient time for us to be issued with khaki drill uniforms), listening to the creaking of the chains securing the spare engine as

we flew over the snow-covered Alps thinking, 'Blimey! What a place to crash if that engine comes loose!'

We arrived safely in the late summer afternoon sun at RAF Luqa in Malta and I was delegated to disembark from the Hastings carrying the groundcrew cricket bat! I descended the steep steps from the aircraft into the very warm Mediterranean sun with kitbag in one hand and cricket bat in the other and wearing my thick No 1 Dress Uniform complete with 'Postman Pat' cap. It must have been a bizarre sight. We were placed in temporary accommodation in Nissen huts that got very hot during the day as the sun beat down. That first night witnessed a heavy rainstorm and no one slept as the water thundered down on the tin sheeting: it was like trying to sleep inside a kettledrum!

Being a small detachment, we found that the trade groups blended to a certain extent. Radar 'bods' helped the wireless chaps with some jobs, and vice-versa. Moreover, as the Hunters flew armed with live ammunition, we helped

Above: RAF Luqa in the mid-1960s, with seven Vulcan bombers on the 'pan' at left. The airfield was one of a number on the island that were vital to British power projection from the earliest days; Malta was also, of course, a major base for the Mediterranean Fleet. The facility is now Malta International Airport, the British presence having been terminated in 1979.

the armourers by filling the belts which went into the gun packs with cannon shells and winching the packs up into the aircraft's bellies. We all took turns in escorting the pilots to their aircraft and fastening each of them into their Martin-Baker ejection seats (and making sure that the safety pin was removed).

The Hunters on detachment had their Avons started by cartridges, and after take-off the groundcrew would gather up the empty cases, which were then used to capture the small lizards that roamed around in the sandy, rocky soil at the edge of the airfield. While the aircraft were airborne 'race meetings' took place, with bets being made on the speedy lizards as they scurried away after being released from their temporary 'stables'. This was an alternative pursuit to a game of 'one wicket cricket' using, of course, the Squadron bat!

In the afternoons and evenings we would go in to Valletta using either the local buses (an exciting experience in itself) or the taxis which used to wait at the main gate of the Luqa camp. We had been warned to negotiate the price for the taxi ride before we got in: we were told that the local drivers inflated the charges for innocent young 'erks.' We quickly learned the art of 'haggling'. Three of us would negotiate the price and then, once agreement had been reached, the driver would start off before suddenly realising that he had five passengers in his taxi! When he protested, our argument was that, as it was downhill to Valletta, he could take his foot off the accelerator and clutch and freewheel—the extra weight of two airmen would make the car go faster as it built up momentum without using petrol!

The only other incident I can recall from that time was when the instrument fitter, a junior technician on the

detachment (who shall be nameless), was apprehended by the Maltese police. Apparently, after spending the evening in Valletta he found that he needed to relieve himself but was unable to find a public lavatory. In view of the urgency of the situation he found a quiet little alleyway to perform his natural function, but unbeknownst to him two Maltese children saw him and informed the local constabulary. As a result, our colleague was arrested and set to appear before the Valletta magistrates. There was great hilarity prior to his appearance in court as we had all been issued with the minimum of odds and ends of khaki drill on arriving at Luqa and thus had to sort out our kit to make him present- able for the occasion. He was found guilty and fined a nom- inal sum; the charge sheet, which had the offence described in Maltese on one side and English on the other and claimed that the defendant 'was observed urinating in a place not appropriate for that purpose', became a piece of 'Treble-One' folklore and was pinned up on the notice board in the temporary small building we had as a Squad- ron HQ.

The Hawker Hunters performed impeccably on the detachment, and I feel proud to have made a small contrib- ution to the effort. As history shows, the whole Suez action ended in ignominy for the British Government and marked the end of an era. For myself, I returned to North Weald and carried on doing my job on the Squadron until I was demobbed in February 1957.

A Cunning Plan *Squadron Leader Roger Hymans*

In January 1958 I joined No 111 Squadron, who were at the time the Royal Air Force aerobatic team. With our black Hunter 6s we visited many different places in Europe, and on one occasion we were scheduled to go to Oslo. My great chum Richard Clayton-Jones—known as 'CJ', or 'Clam'—decided from looking at the map that there was quite a lot of sea between us and Norway, and he came up, long before Baldrick, with a rather cunning plan. 'CJ' was one of the world's great characters. A very talented pilot, he had a marvellous sense of balance and could put several bar stools one upon the other before climbing to the ceiling and signing his name with a lit candle. He seemed to have no sense of self preservation. I was tasked with trying to restrict his more extreme activities, and so, as Officer i/c Clayton-Jones (a sort of secondary duty), I was rather careful when a new idea was formulated.

He had decided that the sea in springtime could be chilly, so what if one of us had an engine failure on the way to the land of the Trolls? His plan was to put the nose of his aircraft in the exhaust of the afflicted Hunter and push him home. Yes, I said, quietly sipping my pint, but would it work? What about slipstream etc? Okay, he said, what we will do is go up to about 30,000 feet, you flame out your engine, and I will see how close I can get. My immediate reply was fairly but firmly negative, but after a few more beers I was persuaded to give it a go. However, there was no way I would flame out the engine: I would merely throttle back.

The next day we each boarded our Hunters for some 'general handling' and climbed to 30,000 feet. I then brought my engine back to idle and gently started to glide down. I could feel some slight yawing and pitching as 'CJ' moved in behind me. I then noticed that the jet pipe temperature was gently rising as his nose restricted the exhaust. After a while he moved out to my left and said that he did not think that it was such a good idea after all. As I looked across at his aircraft I realised that his nose was missing much of its black paint! I advised him to taxy behind the hangar after landing.

We had a word with our superb ground crew. The old 'Chiefy' shook his head in disbelief but got the problem fixed before the Boss found out. Apparently the canopy was a bit distorted by the heat, and this was more difficult to solve. Nothing more was said, however. We were so lucky to have such people take care of our much abused aircraft!

Below: The nose of a 'Black Arrow' —without the modifications brought about by the 'cunning plan'!

THE NAVAL BARGAIN

Commander David Hobbs MBE

THE Royal Navy operated two versions of the Hawker Hunter in significant numbers from 1958 to 1995, both in their designed rôles and in others that were not even considered when the Admiralty first identified the requirement for a swept-wing conversion training aircraft. Virtually every Fleet Air Arm fixed-wing pilot flew the type during that period, some of them completing several tours as instructors and amassing thousands of flying hours.

The Admiralty took note of the RAF's decision to procure a high-performance swept-wing conversion trainer and monitored the development of the Hunter T.7—which was based on the F.4 airframe and was powered by the 'small-bore' Avon 100-series engine—because the Ministry of Supply expected a number of F.4s with low airframe hours to become available for conversion. This proved to be the case, but 55 new-build T.7s were ordered in 1955. The Navy elected to procure its own version of the Hunter trainer in the mid-1950s because it had transonic performance and involved no very great development cost, and because the side-by-side seating arrangement was ideal for applied flying training since both pilots would have an excellent view ahead through their gun sights. While the RAF would have preferred a trainer based on the Hunter F.6 with its 'larger-bore', 200-series Avon, the Navy was quite content to keep costs down by relying on rebuilt F.4s.

Basic and Part One of the advanced flying training syllabus for all naval pilots was carried out within the RAF's flying training organisation using straight-wing aircraft such as the Vampire T.11. However, with the imminent arrival of the transonic Scimitar and Sea Vixen in service, neither of which was to have a training version, the need for a conversion trainer of adequate performance to cover Part Two of the advanced syllabus and weapons training was urgent. Since all training, standardisation and instrument rating checks were carried out ashore, there was no requirement for training aircraft to embark in carriers, and Hunter trainers were an effective way of providing an aircraft capable of converting new pilots from straight to swept-wing

techniques and teaching them to use aircraft as a weapons system. The naval version of the Hunter trainer was designated T.8 and differed from the T.7 in having naval radios and an arrester hook stressed to take cables on an airfield runway (but definitely not on a carrier).

The prototype T.8, WW664, was a converted Hunter F.4 and the ten new-build aircraft that followed it were taken from the RAF production batch and modified on the line. Two of these equipped 764 Squadron at RNAS Lossiemouth in July 1958 after brief service trials. The first, XL581, was lost accidentally within a month but the second, XL580, continued in service with the Royal Navy in a variety of rôles until 1995 and survives today in the

Below: The Royal Navy operated both single-seat and two-seat Hunters, and this is a brand new Hunter G.A.11, freshly converted for the Fleet Air Arm.

Fleet Air Arm Museum at RNAS Yeovilton. The type had a very high utilisation rate, and despite the loss of four of their number in accidents, the first eleven Hunter T.8s flew 22,500 hours in their first six years of service. Further batches of T.8s were acquired from 1963 onwards; the later aircraft were all converted from F 4s. The ten new-production aircraft were built, like the T.7, with a single 30mm Aden cannon but this was subsequently removed; none of the conversions was so armed. T.8s equipped 759 Naval Air Squadron (NAS), the Advanced Flying Training School, first at RNAS Lossiemouth and then at Brawdy.

In addition to the conversion trainer, the Navy wanted a robust swept-wing aircraft that could be used for the tactical and weapons training of new pilots, a rôle that would now be referred to as 'lead-in' training, bridging the gap between basic flying training and the front line. Again, the Hunter F.4 was an attractive prospect, with large numbers of surplus airframes available. Many had been purchased with US 'Offshore Procurement' funds, and the Admiralty had to buy the aircraft from the US Government as well as fund the conversion; they were still, nevertheless, a bargain, and many gave the Navy thirty years of service. Conversion involved stripping out all four Aden cannon and the gun packs and installing the TACAN navigation system, naval radios and an airfield arrester hook. The new aircraft was designated G.A.11, and it could carry a variety of air-to-surface weapons and drop tanks on four wing pylons (the lack of air-to-air weapons led to the absence of an 'F' in the designation). Some G.A.11s were further modified to accept an F.95 camera in the nose and designated P.R.11 for use in teaching reconnaissance techniques. Although the G.A.11 retained the 'small-bore', 100-series Avon of the original F.4, it was lighter and had a performance approaching that of the F.6, which had the larger 200-series engine. A total of forty G.A.11s were converted for the Navy; ten more were cancelled, most of these being bought back by Hawker and sold to the Swiss Air Force.

Hunter G.A.11s equipped 738 NAS first at RNAS Lossiemouth then at RNAS Brawdy, where they were used to train pilots destined for the Scimitar, Sea Vixen, Buccaneer and Phantom. The type was also used by the Air Warfare Instructors' School, 764 NAS at Lossiemouth, which operated a mix of T.8s and G.A.11s. Following the ill-advised political decision to run down the Royal Navy's

carrier force in the late 1960s, the Royal Navy's three Hunter squadrons were disbanded between 1969 and 1972.

The aircraft's usefulness was far from over, however, and they were used to replace Sea Hawks of the Fleet Requirements Unit at Hurn and the Sea Venoms of the Air Direction Training Unit at RNAS Yeovilton. The two organisations were combined in 1972 to form the Fleet Requirements and Aircraft Direction Unit, based at Yeovilton. FRADU Hunters were used by the Royal Navy's Fixed-Wing Naval Flying Standards Flight, also based at Yeovilton, for a variety of tasks, including standards checks for front-line pilots, instrument checks and the provision of dissimilar targets for disembarked fighter squadron training. FRADU continued to use Hunters until they were replaced by Hawks in 1995, thirty-seven years after the type first entered naval service.

Over the years colour schemes changed. G.A.11s were originally finished with Extra Dark Sea Grey upper surfaces and white underneath. From 1983 they were sprayed grey overall with low-visibility markings. T.8 s were originally silver with yellow bands, then Light Aircraft Grey with 'dayglo' red panels and finally, after 1983, overall grey like the single-seaters. Three T.8s XE665, XL580 and XL584, were finished as 'Admiral's Barges' with high-gloss, dark blue upper surfaces and white undersides. A Rear-Admiral's flag was painted on the nose and they were used individually by Rear-Admiral Percy Gick when he was Flag Officer Flying Training at RNAS Yeovilton as transport between his inspections at the then many naval air stations in the country. Naval Hunters carried a variety of weapons under their wings ranging from live and practice bombs, 2-inch and 3-inch rockets, and rocket pods

and flares. Some were experimentally wired for Sidewinder and Bullpup missiles. A number of T.8s were refitted with cockpit instrumentation similar to that fitted in the Buccaneer and used for Buccaneer pilot conversion. Later three were modified to accept Blue Fox radars and Sea Harrier instrumentation, and these were designated T.8M. They were used initially for trials and later by 899 Squadron at RNAS Yeovilton to train pilots as there were no radar-equipped two-seat Sea Harriers.

Royal Navy squadrons formed several temporary aerobatic display teams during the Hunter's service life, among them the 'Rough Diamonds' of 738 NAS at RNAS Brawdy in the 1960s and the 'Blue Herons'

Below: Three Hunter G.A.11s of 738 Naval Air Squadron, based at RNAS Lossiemouth, where they were employed to train pilots destined for front-line fast jets in navigation and weapons-release skills. The Squadron later moved to RNAS Brawdy.

COURTESY DAVID HOBBS

of FRADU at RNAS Yeovilton. The latter was unusual in that it was one of only a few display teams made up of civilian pilots, albeit under contract to the Royal Navy.

I missed out on flying the Hunter in the advanced flying training school at RNAS Brawdy because I was one of four RN pilots who were exchanged to fly the Gnat T.2 at RAF Valley in an experiment looking at future changes in the military flying training system. I subsequently flew both the T.8 and G.A.11 while serving in the Naval Fixed-Wing Flying Standards Flight at RNAS Yeovilton and considered both, but especially the G.A.11, a joy to fly. Like many pilots before me, I found the Hunter to be light, responsive and very much a pilot's aircraft. The cockpit could be described as an ergonomic 'slum', but the same could be said of many of its British contemporaries and one rapidly got used to it and learned to find switches instinctively. The aircraft was easy to fly on

Below: The cockpit of a Royal Navy Hunter T.8, showing the student's controls and instruments The notices affixed beneath the coaming to the left are checklists for communications frequencies. The TACAN control unit at the top of the right-hand vertical white line surrounding the blind flying panel is set on Channel 47, the Yeovilton beacon. The gun sight has been removed and replaced by an IFF control unit.

COURTESY DAVID HOBBS

Above: XL580, one of the three Hunter T.8s known unofficially as 'Admiral's Barges' and employed as FOFT's personal transport at RNAS Yeovilton. The luxurious appearance was confined to the exterior paintwork! This particular Hunter was later converted to T.8M standards and fitted with Blue Fox radar to assist the training of Sea Harrier pilots. It is now part of the Fleet Air Arm Museum's collection.

Below: Two Hunters were modified to become T.8Ms and this is the other aircraft, XL603, seen here sporting 230-gallon underwing tanks with high-visibility markings.

instruments in 'actual' conditions or at night, and aerobatics in a clear sky were great fun. In simulated 'engine-off' recoveries with the throttle closed, after the inevitable 'practice pan' call, the aircraft covered a mile for every 1,000 feet of height lost, and the ensuing 'one-in-one' glide, having checked the TACAN read-out for range and bearing to see if one could get back on to the runway at Yeovilton during a 'trapper's sortie', was always a fascinating challenge. Advancing the throttle 'to check that the engine was okay' could sometimes stretch the glide when necessary.

In another incarnation I flew Hunter F.G.A.9s on an exchange appointment with an RAF squadron at RAF Chivenor. Rather grandly titled the Senior

COURTESY PHILIP JARRETT

Naval Officer Chivenor, I was in fact the only naval officer there at the time. By comparison with the G.A.11, the F.G.A.9 was much heavier, and the 230-gallon drop tanks on the inboard pylons seemed huge by comparison with the smaller 100-gallon variety on the G.A.11. The cockpit had more in it, too, and seemed to be more cramped, but it is difficult to remember what the precise differences were. The runway at Chivenor was much shorter than the main east/west runway at Yeovilton, and stopping could be exciting, especially when there was little wind and the runway was wet.

The Hunter T.8 had the luxury of a tail parachute. We tended not to use it often; I think that the reason for its inclusion was to teach pilots moving on to aircraft like the Phantom the technique. It was considered polite at Yeovilton to tell the tower, as part of the 'downwind call', that its use was intended so that a sailor could be dispatched in a Land Rover

to pick up the parachute once the aircraft had turned off the runway. A little bit more power than usual had to be selected while taxying, in order to keep the 'chute deployed.

During my flying career I flew an unusual variety of aircraft, ranging from the Gannet in A.E.W.3 and C.O.D.4 versions, five marks of Hunter, Canberras and Wessex helicopters. If I had to choose one to fly in again it would be the Hunter G.A.11 every time—although I have fond memories of the Gannet and 849 Squadron!

Above: The prototype Royal Navy T.8 two-seat trainer; it wears the original trainer finish of High-Speed Silver, with yellow bands. The position of the single Aden cannon can clearly be seen. This particular aircraft had previously seen service (as a Mk 4) with No 26 Squadron.
Below: Another 738 NAS Hunter G.A.11, with white trim applied to its standard RN paint finish and the Squadron's pegasus emblem on the nose. This aircraft was one of the four 'Rough Diamonds' Hunter aerobatic team that performed between 1965 and 1969.
Right: 'The Blue Herons'—another well-known Royal Navy Hunter aerobatic team—execute a formation loop.

COURTESY TONY BUTTLER

HUNTER SQUADRONS

SOME thirty Royal Air Force front-line squadrons were at one time or another equipped with the Hawker Hunter, and several others operated the aircraft in an auxiliary rôle; in addition, a number of RAF and Fleet Air Arm second-line units flew the type, principally on training and allied duties. Several squadrons, for example Nos 43 (F) and 54 (F), enjoyed a long association with the aircraft, progressively re-equipping with more advanced marks as new variants were developed; others flew Hunters only very briefly, No 245 Squadron, for example, taking them on establishment for mere months.

The aircraft was introduced into service in 1954 to great acclaim and general approval (albeit qualified by those who had identified the shortcomings of the early versions), but three years later its seemingly unstoppable success was severely jolted by the British Government's now notorious 1957 Defence White Paper: seduced by the apparent efficacy and invulnerability of unmanned missiles, the politicians of the day decided that the manned combat aircraft had little if any future. The paper caused uproar at the time—and, half a century on, it can be seen even more clearly how ludicrous a proposition this was—and, although its proposals were not executed in their entirety, its effects were far-reaching, one being the immediate disbandment of many Hunter units.

There is not the space in this book to offer a detailed examination of the squadrons with which the Hunter was equipped, and the scope of the volume does not permit consideration of the many overseas air arms that flew the aircraft: what follows, therefore, is a brief summary of the RAF, FAA and Government-run establishments that were at one time associated with the Hunter, together with a selection of representative images.

Left, upper: A Hunter F.G.A.9 of No 1 (F) Squadron. It was common practice from the early 1960s onwards for Hunters to display their fuselage serial numbers in white rather than black. Notice the white wing tips, and the partially open air brake.

Below: A No II (AC) Squadron Hunter F.R.10 being flown by our contributor Squadron Leader (as he then was) Nigel Walpole, the Squadron OC 1964–1967, whose name appears on the nose of the aircraft, above the unit crest.

ROYAL AIR FORCE SQUADRONS AND OTHER UNITS FLYING HUNTERS AS PRIMARY EQUIPMENT

Unit	Principal location(s)	Equipment	Remarks
![] No 1 (F) Squadron	Tangmere, Nicosia, Stradishall, Waterbeach, West Raynham	F.5s (00/09/55–00/06/58), F.6s (00/07/58–00/03/60), F.G.A.9s (00/01/60–00/07/69)	Disbanded 30/06/60 but re-formed next day out of No 263 Sqn. Took part in Suez operations 1956.
![] No II (AC) Squadron	Jever, Gütersloh, Brüggen	F.6s (01/01/61–21/03/61), F.R.10s (00/03/61–00/03/71)	Fighter-reconnaissance rôle. Mk 6s used briefly for type conversion.
![] No 3 Squadron	Geilenkirchen	F.4s (00/05/56–00/06/57)	2TAF RAFG.
![] No IV (AC) Squadron	Jever, Gütersloh,	F.4s (00/00/56–00/00/57), F.6s (00/00/57–30/12/60), F.R.10s (01/01/61–00/05/70), F.G.A.9s (01/09/69–00/05/70)	2TAF RAFG. Disbanded 30/12/60; re-formed next day from No 79 Sqn. Mk 9s as West Raynham *echelon* only.

continued p. 154

COURTESY TONY BUTTLER

Above: A pair of No 3 (F) Squadron Hunter Mk 4s shortly after delivery to RAF Geilenkirchen, the unit markings—yellow-outlined green rectangles—and call-signs having yet to be applied.

Right: No doubting the tenancy of this Hunter. As can be seen from this photograph, RAF combat aircraft based in Germany at this time (1960s) carried their major warning notices, though not the smaller airframe stencilling, in German. The triangular 'blade' atop the nose is a TACAN aerial.

COURTESY PHILIP JARRETT

153

Above: A Hunter F.G.A.9 in the marking of No 8 Squadron, with a full complement of drop tanks. The Squadron was unusual in carrying the unit flashes either side of the fuselage roundel in swallowtail form during part of its commission.

Bottom: XJ646, a Hunter F.6, was for a period allocated to No 14 Squadron, whose blue diamonds (on a white field) are carried on the after fuselage in typical form—though here, as was often the case in Hunter units, raised from the roundel's centreline. Notice the three diamonds on the nosewheel door.

Unit	Principal location(s)	Equipment	Remarks
No 8 Squadron	Khormaksar, Muharraq	F.G.A.9s (00/01/60–00/00/71) F.R.10s (00/04/61–00/00/71)	Part of Aden Strike Wing 1961–1967. See also No 1417 Flt (below).
No 14 Squadron	Oldenburg, Ahlhorn, Gütersloh, Jever	F.4s (00/06/55–00/04/57), F.6s 00/04/57–17/12/62)	2TAF RAFG.
No 19 (F) Squadron	Leconfield	F.6s (00/10/56–00/02/63)	
No 20 Squadron	Oldenburg, Ahlhorn, Gütersloh, Tengah	F.4s (00/11/55–00/07/57), F.6s (00/05/57–30/12/60), F.G.A.9s (03/07/61–13/02/70)	2TAF RAFG until 30/12/60; thereafter part of FEAF.
No 26 Squadron	Oldenburg, Ahlhorn, Gütersloh	F.4s (00/06/55–10/09/57), F.6s 00/06/58–30/12/60)	2TAF RAFG.
No 28 Squadron	Kai Tak	F.G.A.9s (00/06/62–00/01/67)	FEAF (sole Hong Kong-based fighter unit).

continued p. 157

COURTESY PHILIP JARRETT

Above: One of No 19 Squadron's Hunter F.6s, its blue and white chequerboard markings aligned centrally with the fuselage roundel; the Squadron crest, flanked by miniature chequerboards, appears on the forward fuselage, and a blue lightning flash adorns the white-painted wing tip.
Below: The personnel of No 20 Squadron pose in informal style with Mk 9

XG153 'Lima' to mark 3,000 hours of flying. The name presented above the squadron emblem reads 'Flt. Lt. O. J. Page'.
Bottom: A formal portrait of No 26 Squadron personnel at Ahlhorn in 1958, with one of the unit's Hunter F.6s in the background. The springbok emblem recalls the Squadron's original composition of South African pilots.

COURTESY JEREMY SAYE

MICHAEL HALL, COURTESY ROGER LINDSAY

Above: A brand new No 43 (F) Squadron F.1 illustrating the early practice—soon abandoned—in some units of applying individual call-signs to the flanks of the tailpipe.

Below: XE706 was a Hunter Mk 4, with which the Squadron re-equipped in 1956, by which time the decision had been taken to reposition the call-signs and raise the black-and-white chequerboard markings. The Squadron's famous emblem—the 'Fighting Cock'—was still carried on the port side of the forward fuselage.

Below: Like No 43, No 54 Squadron enjoyed a long association with the Hunter and, successively, flew all the Avon-engined marks. This is a Hunter F.G.A.9, identifiable by the housing for its braking parachute and the fact that it is carrying both 230-gallon and 100-gallon external fuel tanks.

Opposite: No 56 was one of the few squadrons to operate Sapphire-engined Hunters, with which it was hastily re-equipped following the decision to withdraw its Supermarine Swifts from front-line service. A Sapphire-powered Mk 5 is depicted in the upper photograph and an Avon-engined Mk 6, with typical 'encumbrances', in the lower. Chequered wing tips, in the Squadron colours of red and white, were a feature of both marks taken into service.

Unit	Principal location(s)	Equipment	Remarks
No 34 Squadron	Tangmere, Nicosia	F.5s (00/02/56–10/01/58)	Participant in Suez operations, 1956.
No 41 (F) Squadron	Biggin Hill	F.5s (00/08/55–16/01/58)	Last RAF fighter squadron to be based at Biggin Hill.
No 43 (F) Squadron	Leuchars, Nicosia, Khormaksar	F.1s (00/07/54–00/08/56), F.4s 00/03/56–00//02/57). F.6s 00/12/56–00/00/60), F.G.A.9s 00/00/60–14/10/67)	First squadron to receive Hunters. Part of Aden Strike Wing 1963–1967. See also No 1417 Flt.
No 45 Squadron	West Raynham, Wittering	F.G.A.9s (01/08/72–00/06/76)	Served principally as operational training facility for crews converting to SEPECAT Jaguar.
No 54 (F) Squadron	Odiham, Stradishall, Waterbeach, West Raynham	F.1s (00/02/55–00/09/55), F.4s 00/09/55–00/01/57), F.6s (00/01/57–00/03/60), F.G.A.9s 00/00/61–00/09/69)	
No 56 (F) Squadron	Waterbeach, Wattisham	F.5s (00/05/55–00/11/58), F.6s 00/11/58–00/01/61)	Previously sole front-line Supermarine Swift F. Mk 1 unit.

continued p. 162

COURTESY PHILIP JARRETT

COURTESY ROGER LINDSAY

157

The Privilege *Air Chief Marshal Sir David-Harcourt-Smith* GBE KCB DFC

The Hunter has been described as the most graceful jet aircraft to enter service in the Royal Air Force; to me it was the Queen of the Skies. It had the looks, and it was a joy to fly. This is hardly surprising as it came out of the same stable as the Hurricane, under the design leadership of Sir Sydney Camm.

I first came face to face with the aircraft in July 1956 at the Central Fighter Establishment at RAF West Raynham. I was at that time a Flight Commander on No 8 Squadron at RAF Khormaksar in Aden and had been selected to attend No 35 Day Fighter Leaders' School. I had never flown a Hunter—No 8 Squadron was equipped with the Venom F.B.4—and therefore arrived at West Raynham a week ahead of the other members of the course who had flown the aircraft in various squadrons in Fighter Command. I remember quite vividly meeting one of the DFLS staff members in the Officers' Mess bar one Sunday evening, having Pilots' Notes thrust into my hands and told that the first conversion sortie would be early the following

morning. As these were early days in the distinguished career of the various marks of Hunter that were to see service over the coming years, it was a Mk 1 into which I climbed on the Monday morning. It was truly a short-range fighter, with remarkably little fuel and probably the best power-to-weight ratio of any marks of the aircraft. My first take-off was exciting, and it must have been about 3,000 feet before I had managed to select the undercarriage up! Most of the sorties on the course over the next six weeks were of little more than 30 or 35 minutes' duration, and I note from my log book that by the end of the eight conversion sorties I was doing cine attacks at 45,000 feet as the main emphasis on the course was Air Defence/Fighter, with Battle Formation, Simulated Air Combat and Fighter Sweeps the order of the day. All this was a far cry from flying the Venom in Aden, where most of the sorties were around an hour and a half in duration, were nearly always flown at low level and frequently involved firing live ordnance. The course was thoroughly enjoyable, demanding and professional, but with a touch of the 'Battle of Britain spirit' both in the flying and in the bar afterwards. I hope I learned something about leadership in the air during my 44 sorties and 26.45 hours on the Hunter Mk l. On completion of the course I returned to join No 8 Squadron, not in Aden but at RAF Akrotiri in Cyprus,

Left: No 54 (F) Squadron had a long association with the Hunter, starting with the Mk 1, four of which are seen here during practice formation aerobatics. One aircraft has a yellow lightning flash on the tailfin and another a blue flash, and all four appear to have blue wing tips.
Below: The Squadron in a formal portrait taken during the period when the writer was Officer Commanding, 1963–1965. The aircraft are now F.G.A.9s

where the Squadron had been deployed for the ill-fated Suez Campaign that took place in the November.

At the end of my tour in Aden in September 1957 I returned to England (with a new bride), and after a spell of leave was posted to No 54 (F) Squadron based at RAF Odiham in Hampshire—civilisation at last, after more than two years in the heat and dust of the Arabian peninsula. Little did I realise that on arrival at Odiham I would discover that the Squadron were on a lengthy detachment at RAF Nicosia in Cyprus! At the end of November I flew out to join the Squadron, over half way back to Aden, and spend yet another Christmas away from home. No 54 were by this time equipped with the Hunter Mk 6. The aircraft had an uprated Avon engine, giving greater thrust, had a slightly increased internal fuel capacity and was equipped with hardpoints under the wings. The aircraft now had a reasonable ferry range, although it was still not possible to fly direct to Malta for deployment to Cyprus: a refuelling stop in the South of France, sometimes with an overnight stay, was necessary. Although this was a pleasant way to deploy, it was not acceptable operationally as it made transit times longer and often resulted in technical snags arising during the turn-round. The rôle of the Squadron was also confusing. The Hunter was not well equipped for air defence, having only four 30mm cannon and a gun sight with radar ranging. At the same time the defence requirement was turning increasingly towards

support of the Army, and here the limited weapons capability was a problem.

How lucky I was to return to No 54 Squadron four years later, this time as CO. The Squadron was now at West Raynham—where this story started. The importance of Army support had been recognised, and No 38 Group was formed to provide this service. The Hunter had been modified with strengthened wings, permitting a greater external fuel load and, more importantly, an increased weapons capability. I was back in the 'mud moving' business that I had enjoyed in Aden. It was now possible to deploy to the Eastern Med with only the one stop in Malta. We made regular detachments to El Adem for rocket firing (still with the 'Three-Inch Drain Pipe') and air-to-ground gunnery, as well as low-level skip bombing. Perhaps the most unusual aspect of the tour was the decision by No 38 Group to authorise ultra low flying—down to fifty feet in certain parts of the low-flying system in England, Scotland and Wales. Before Squadron pilots were cleared to fly down to this height, however, they had to do a check in the T.7 with either one of the Flight Commanders or myself. It is fun flying oneself at very low level, but sitting in the right hand seat of a dual aircraft while somebody else does the work is something different!

Main image: Close up to No 54 Squadron's Hunter F.G.A.9 'Tango', displaying the Squadron colours—blue and yellow—on the nose and also above the call-sign on the nosewheel door.

Above: The officers of No 54 Squadron prepare for the AOC's inspection, early 1960s. Er, sorry— wrong photograph.

The people on any squadron are very important and I was very lucky to have a good bunch. I like to think that we were efficient in doing our job and that we enjoyed a good spirit both on and off duty. I was particularly lucky to have two exchange officers, Farooq Khan from the Pakistan Air Force (who subsequently became CAS of the PAF) and Captain Jake Sletten from the Royal Norwegian Air Force. In addition, the Squadron had it own Ground Liaison Officer (GLO), the splendid Major Price.

Command of a Squadron should be a great privilege, a challenge and great fun. As far as I am concerned it most certainly was all three.

Unit	Principal location(s)	Equipment	Remarks
No 58 Squadron	Wittering	F.G.A.9s (01/08/73–04/06/76)	As No 45 Sqn.
No 63 Squadron	Waterbeach	F.6s (00/11/56–24/10/58)	
No 65 (F) Squadron	Duxford	F.6s (00/03/57–31/03/61)	
No 66 (F) Squadron	Linton-on-Ouse, Acklington	F.4s (00/03/56–00/01/57), F.6s (00/01/57–00/09/60)	
No 67 Squadron	Brüggen	F.4s (00/04/56–06/04/57)	2TAF RAFG.
No 71 (Eagle) Squadron	Brüggen	F.4s (00/05/56–30/04/57)	2TAF RAFG.
No 74 (F) Squadron	Horsham St Faith, Coltishall	F.4s (00/03/57–00/11/60), F.6s (00/11/57–00/11/60)	
No 92 (East India) Squadron	Linton-on-Ouse, Middleton St George, Thornaby, Leconfield	F.4s (00/04/56–00/03/57), F.6s 00/02/57–00/04/63)	'The Blue Diamonds' aerobatic team, 1961–1963.
No 93 Squadron	Jever	F.4s (00/01/56–00/03/57), F.6s (00/03/57–00/12/60)	2TAF RAFG.
No 98 Squadron	Jever	F.4s (00/04/55–00/07/57)	2TAF RAFG.

continued p. 164

Left: RAF Horsham St Faith, late 1957, and a pair of shiny, recently delivered Hunter F. Mk 6s. The artwork on the No 74 (F) Squadron hangar is impressive too.

Top: A quartet of No 92 Squadron's F.6s up from Middleton St George and in their original (standard disruptive camouflage) colour scheme, their maple-leaf-and-cobra emblems flanked by red and yellow chequers.

Above: With the nomination of the Squadron as the RAF's Aerobatic Team in 1961, No 92's Hunters were repainted royal blue overall though retained

the unit emblem on the nose. The wing tips and fuselage 'zip' were white. As the successors to 'The Black Arrows', 'The Blue Diamonds' had a difficult task on their hands, but they flew with aggression and panache and continued to thrill spectators with their daring manœuvres.

Below: A Hunter Mk 4 of No 98 Squadron, photographed in 1955. Unusually for this mark and for this period, no 'Sabrinas' are evident: WW658 is depicted here as the Squadron's solo aerobatic display aircraft, which probably explains the omission.

Unit		Principal location(s)	Equipment	Remarks
![crest]	No 111 (F) Squadron	North Weald, North Luffenham, Wattisham	F.4s (00/06/55–00/11/56), F.6s (00/11/56–00/00/61)	'The Black Arrows' aerobatic team, 1956–1961
![crest]	No 112 (F) Squadron	Brüggen	F.4s (00/04/56–00/05/57)	2TAF RAFG.
![crest]	No 118 Squadron	Jever	F.4s (00/00/56–00/00/57), F.6s 00/00/57–31/08/62)	2TAF RAFG.
![crest]	No 130 (Punjab) Squadron	Brüggen	F.4s (00/05/56–00/04/57)	2TAF RAFG.
![crest]	No 208 (AC) Squadron	Tangmere, Akrotiri, Eastleigh, Stradishall, Khormaksar,	F.6s (00/01/58–00/03/59), F.G.A.9s (00/03/60–10/09/71), T.7/8s (00/00/74–00/00/93)	Part of Aden Strike Wing 1961–1967. T.7/8s used for Buccaneer training.

continued p. 171

Right: Five of No 111 Squadron's 'Black Arrows' during the early days at RAF North Weald.
Below: Curtain call for the 'Black Arrows' at Wattisham in 1961, led at this time by CO Squadron Leader K. A. C. Wirdnam. Later that year the Squadron re-equipped with the English Electric Lightning and the team ceased to be.

COURTESY MICHAEL THURLEY

COURTESY WATTISHAM AIRFIELD MUSEUM

COURTESY NIGEL WALPOLE

Above: The No II (AC) Squadron flight line of Hunter F.R.10s, with serial numbers in both black and white.

Below: Its brake parachute doors open, a No IV (AC) Squadron F.R.10 returns from a flight; two Hunter F.6s of No 14 Squadron and a Lightning interceptor of No 56 Squadron form a backdrop, and a pair of Javelin all-weather fighters are to the left and right in the foreground, the latter two types equipped with Firestreak air-to-air missiles. From the photographs on this page alone it can be seen that no two Hunters carried identical camouflage patterns, the disruptive Dark Green following the official 'template' only in approximate terms.

COURTESY NIGEL WALPOLE/TONY BUTTLER

COURTESY ALASTAIR AKED

Left, upper: A Hunter Mk 6, seemingly anonymous but in fact being flown by No 66 Squadron prior to the application of unit markings.

Left, lower: *Not* an Iraqi Air Force Hunter! Following the delivery of fifteen export Hunter Mk 6s to the Royal Iraqi Air Force in May 1957 and a planned flypast by these aircraft before Arab dignitaries as part of a sales drive, it was decided by C-in-C Middle East Air Force that two No 66 Squadron aircraft, then based at Nicosia, would have their roundels replaced by Iraqi national markings and flown to Habbaniyah as standbys in the event of any unserviceability. XG236 (shown) and XG521, thus painted, were flown over Turkey to Habbaniyah on 7 May. In the event there were no problems and No 66's aircraft were not required. After the flypast the aircraft were flown back to Nicosia on 22 May, and the RAF roundels and fin flashes were reinstated.

COURTESY ALASTAIR AKED

165

Top: A No 43 (F) Squadron Hunter F.G.A.9 with its famous chequerboard marking carried on both fuselage and wing tips; the 'fighting cock' emblem is seen on the nose.

Above: A Mk 9 of No 208 Squadron in Aden, its gun ports heavily blackened by discharge gases. Notice the white-tipped drop tanks; for a period some of 208's Hunters carried a small triangular Squadron flash towards the front of the tanks—a device that was also embraced, for a period, for the fuselage squadron markings.

Bottom: Towards the end of their Hunter commissions in the Middle East, Nos 8 and 43 Squadrons shared not only aircraft but also a unique Squadron marking, as seen here. To the left, another Hunter sports a freshly painted nose cone.

Left: Hunter 4s of No 112 Squadron, their distinctive 'sharkmouths' recalling their forebears' days in the Western Desert during World War II, when the markings were first applied.

Below: A white-nosed and -tipped Hunter F.G.A.9 of No 208 Squadron—one of the last units to relinquish the Hunter in its rôle as a front-line fighter/strike aircraft. The tail cone has been stripped of paint.

Bottom: Personnel of No 234 Squadron at RAF Geilenkirchen in May 1957, with OC Squadron Leader E. C. Riseley seated centre. Unusually, the crew name—that of the 'Boss'—is carried on the canopy frame of the Hunter Mk 4 in the background, XF991.

COURTESY PHILIP JARRETT

COURTESY TONY BUTTLER

BILL TOOSZ HOBSON, COURTESY ROGER LINDSAY

Tiger Life *Flying Officer Ian Cadwallader*

Life on a fighter squadron in the 1950s for young men with an average age of 23 or 24 was almost unreal, and, looking back those fifty or so years, the most amazing thing about it is the freedom we had and the standard of living we enjoyed. My first introduction to this life was in April 1956, when I arrived by train and taxi at the Officer's Mess at RAF Horsham St Faith. There were not many people about on that Sunday afternoon, and the first person I met was the Orderly Officer—the station RAF Regiment Officer—who knew where to get the information as to what room I had been allocated and showed me to it.

I was very much the new boy on 74 Squadron, and although I had just completed the Hunter OCU, and thoroughly enjoyed it, I had volunteered to accept a posting to a Meteor 8 squadron. This turned out to be one of my better decisions, as my early months on the Meteor, learning the ropes, stood me in very good stead for when we re-equipped with the Hunter 4.

The lifestyle on any fighter squadron half a century ago was probably very similar to that which I experienced, although I understand that in 2 TAF in Germany there was even more freedom than we had and most luxuries were considerably cheaper! The team spirit on 74 was extremely

strong, both during working hours and in our leisure activities, and I think the main reason for this was that we all more or less lived together. A large percentage of the pilots were single, so we all lived in the Officers' Mess, and most of the married pilots lived in quarters very close to the Mess, so it was easy to get together for whatever reason (usually a party!). Quite a regular feature of the after-work hours for single pilots were visits to married pilots' homes for a meal, perhaps, and in the summer barbecues were very popular. Some of us did child-minding duties while our hosts went out to the cinema or for a meal.

Working hours were far from arduous, and, unless there was some sort of parade or exercise in the offing, we worked four and a half days a week 0800 to 1600. Wednesday afternoons were for sports, so unless you were in a Station team or helping to run one, you might have a game of squash or

Below: The writer (in the cockpit) and fellow members of the Squadron in 1958. Standing on the ladder is Flying Officer Pete Budd (sadly to lose his life in a mid-air collision the following year) and standing below, left to right, are Flying Officer Ian Sheppard, Flight Lieutenant Jack Atkinson, Pilot Officer Rock Hudson and Flying Officer Mike Ginn. The glossy finish of the paintwork was characteristic of RAF combat aircraft of the 1950s; this was later to change.

COURTESY IAN CADWALLADER

Above: The writer taxying in his F.6, XK141, his rank and name prominently displayed just beneath the windscreen as was common practice in Fighter Command—although this legend did not necessarily identify the occupant on every occasion! Ian was responsible for the design of the tiger's head emblem that No 74 Squadron Hunters carried at the time.
Below, left: Hunter with a tale: a former No 74 Squadron Mk 6 in the process of conversion by Hawker Aircraft into a Mk 9, early 1961. Above the nose emblem is the signature of 'Sailor' Malan, the Squadron's well-known South African fighter 'ace' of World War II; it is believed that he 'autographed' the aircraft during a visit to his old unit. The manufacturer has stencilled the aircraft's serial number above the tiger stripes in order to ensure that the aircraft's identity is retained when the rear fuselage is removed during the conversion process. The photograph also explains the function of the paired vertical stripes at various locations along the belly.

tennis and then go into Norwich for some recreation—usually in small groups, depending on who owned a car and how many seats it had.

The flying increased the trust we had in each other because we nearly always flew in pairs and trust in whoever was leading the pair had to be complete. If you were climbing through 20,000 feet or more of cloud in close formation, the leader concentrated on his instruments and you merely maintained your position on him—you had no idea whether you were flying straight or in a turn. I recall one occasion when I was Number Two to my Flight Commander on a trip from Aldergrove in Northern Ireland back to Horsham St Faith. The cloud base at Aldergrove was very low, as was the visibility. Lined up for take-off, we both increased power on the brakes, checked engine rpm and jpt, and when he got take-off clearance he gave me the 'Brake release' hand signal and we were rolling. After take-

BAE SYSTEMS

off I hit the gear button and after I heard the undercarriage 'clunk' into the 'up' position I probably took a very quick glance inside the cockpit to check that the undercarriage lights were out but from then on I did not look away from my leader until we broke cloud at about 30,000 feet. That's when you really have to trust the man leading you.

One aspect of squadron flying that created great enthusiasm and personal rivalry was the dogfight. As we flew in pairs most of the time on our training flights we would practise using the gun sight, ranging and tracking one another, or carry out practice interceptions for radar controllers, but after completing an exercise there was generally time for a quick dogfight. This involved the two Hunters flying away from each other for about thirty seconds, after which the leader would call 'Turn in' and we would approach each other virtually head-on. As we crossed, each pilot had to look behind him to see which way the other was turning, and then turn towards him to approach head-on again, now slowing down to get as tight a turn as possible, trying to move inside and behind him. These 'scissors movements' would often involve four or five cross-overs before one pilot could get behind the other—the pilot who could fly the tightest turns without stalling the aircraft. These manoeuvres required very smooth and accurate flying at low speed—not quite what one might be led to believe from Hollywood's depiction of aerial combats! Dogfights were hard work, involving as they did twisting and turning to look behind for most of the time, and got even more interesting when we flew one pair against another and the sky seemed to get rather crowded! Usually a shortage of fuel would dictate the termination of this fun, and of course it was always the leader's responsibility to make sure that everyone got back home with enough juice to do a circuit.

COURTESY PHILIP JARRETT

COURTESY PHILIP JARRETT

Top: Hunter Mk 6, XE689 in the colours of No 234 Squadron, photographed on display at Abbotsinch in 1961. The Aden cannon troughs have been spruced up with contrasting paintwork, and an intake guard can be seen in place. The tailplane has been clamped.

Above: One of No 257 Squadron's Hunter Mk 2s in early configuration without the link collector fairings.

Below: No 263 Squadron operated Sapphire-powered Hunters for most of its commission on type but took delivery of some F.6s shortly before its disbandment. XE584 was one of these, and is seen here at Wattisham, its forward fuselage blackened as a result of cannon discharge. The white wing tips are an anomaly in terms of No 263's Hunters: perhaps they were inherited from the previous user, the Central Flying Establishment.

COURTESY PHILIP JARRETT

Unit	Principal location(s)	Equipment	Remarks
No 222 (Natal) Squadron	Leuchars	F.1s (00/12/54–00/08/56), F.4s (00/08/56–00/11/57)	
No 234 (F) Squadron	Geilenkirchen	F.4s (00/06/56–00/07/57)	2TAF RAFG.
No 245 (F) Squadron	Stradishall	F.4s (00/04/57–00/07/57)	Shortest-lived front-line Hunter unit.
No 247 (Chino-British) Squadron	Odiham	F.1s (00/06/55–00/08/55), F.4s (00/07/55–00/03/57), F.6s (00/03/57–00/12/57)	
No 257 (Burma) Squadron	Wattisham	F.2s (00/11/54–00/03/57), F.5s (00/00/56–00/03/57)	
No 263 Squadron	Wattisham, Stradishall	F.2s (00/01/55–00/10/57), F.5s (00/00/56–00/10/57), F.6s (00/10/57–01/07/58)	Redesignated No 1 Sqn on final disbandment (q.v.)
No 1417 Flight	Khormaksar	F.R.10s (00/03/63–00/00/67)	Part of Aden Strike Wing.
No 229 OCU	Chivenor	F.1s (00/00/55–00/00/60), F.4s (00/00/59–00/00/00). F.6s (00/00/60–02/09/74), T.7s (00/00/58–02/09/74), F.G.A.9s (00/00/60–02/09/74), F.R.10s (00/00/62–00/00/73)	Primary Hunter training establishment. Included, at various times, 'shadow' units Nos 63, 79, 127, 131, 145 and 234 Sqns.
No 233 OCU	Pembrey	F.1s (00/00/56–01/09/57)	Absorbed by No 229 OCU on disbandment.

continued p.173

Below: No 229 OCU, based at RAF Chivenor in Devon, was the training establishment where, from 1955, all aspiring RAF Hunter fighter pilots learnt their trade. It operated the type for nearly twenty years, and its aircraft exhibited a very wide variety of markings, not least owing to the fact that it was allocated, successively, a variety of 'shadow squadron' designations (see table above) and the Hunters of the day bore the relevant squadron emblems as a result. This T.7, in silver finish with geometric orange 'dayglo' panelling forward, aft and across the wings, bears the emblem of No 234 Squadron (its dragon device, rather unusually, facing aft on the port side). Early Hunter trainers carried yellow fuselage and wing bands—see illustration on page 92.

COURTESY TONY BUTTLER

171

Above: XE608, an early Hunter F.6, had a twenty-year career in the RAF, having served with the Day Fighter Leaders' School and the Air Fighting Development Squadron at West Raynham before joining No 229 OCU. It is seen here while at Chivenor, carrying the markings of No 63 Squadron, one of No 229's 'shadow' designations. The 'low-visibility' national markings identify this aircraft as one of the very last Hunters serving in the RAF.

Below: A single-seat Hunter—also a Mk 6—of No 229 OCU and again marked with the emblem of No 234 Squadron, this time with the dragon the 'correct' way round (cf. photograph on the previous page). The OCU typically, though not invariably, coded its aircraft with numerals rather than letters, for the simple reason that the numbers on strength frequently exceeded the number of letters in the alphabet!

Below: A Mk 6 on the strength of No 4 Flying Training Squadron at Valley, with its call-sign unmistakably displayed forward and aft and neatly finished cannon ports complete with blast deflectors.
Right: The very last RAF units to fly single-seat Hunters were the Tactical

Weapons Units. This No 1 TWU F.G.A.9 was photographed at its home base of Brawdy in September 1984, just as the unit was re-equipping with Hawks. The 'shadow' markings are those of No 79 Squadron. Notice the very dull finish compared with that of the Hunter depicted below.

Unit	Principal location(s)	Equipment	Remarks
Tactical Weapons Unit	Brawdy	F.6s (00/00/74–00/00/78), T.7s (00/00/74–00/00/78), F.G.A.9s (00/00/74–00/00/78)	Split into Nos 1 and 2 TWUs (q.v.) 1978.
No 1 Tactical Weapons Unit	Brawdy	F.6s (00/00/78–00/00/84), T.7s (00/00/78–00/00/84), F.G.A.9s (00/00/78–00/00/84)	
No 2 Tactical Weapons Unit	Lossiemouth	F.6s (00/00/78–00/00/84), T.7s (00/00/78–00/00/84), F.G.A.9s (00/00/78–00/00/84)	
No 4 Flying Training School	Valley	F.6s (00/00/67–00/00/77), T.7s (00/00/67–00/00/77)	
Fighter Weapons School	Leconfield	F.1s (01/01/55–00/00/10/57), F.4s (00/00/56–00/10/57)	
Air Fighting Development Squadron	West Raynham	F.1s (00/07/54–00/00/56), F.4s (00/00/56–00/00/58), F.6s (00/00/56–00/00/62), T.7s (00/00/58–00/00/62), F.G.A.9s (00/00/60–00/00/62)	Component of Central Fighter Establishment.
Day Fighter Leaders' School	West Raynham	F.1s (00/07/54–00/00/56), F.4s (00/00/56–00/00/58), F.6s (00/00/56–00/00/62), F.G.A.9s (00/00/60–00/00/62)	Component of Central Fighter Establishment.

ROYAL AIR FORCE SQUADRONS AND OTHER UNITS FLYING HUNTERS AS PARTIAL EQUIPMENT

Unit	Principal location(s)	Equipment	Remarks
No 12 Squadron	Honington, Lossiemouth	F.6s, T.7/8s (00/00/74–00/00/94)	Used for Buccaneer conversion.
No XV Squadron	Laarbruch	T.7s (00/00/74–00/00/83)	Used for Buccaneer conversion.

continued p. 174

AD HOC PUBLICATIONS

WILFRIED ZETSCHE, COURTESY ROGER LINDSAY

Unit	Principal location(s)	Equipment	Remarks
No 16 Squadron	Laarbruch	T.7s (00/00/74–00/00/83)	Used for Buccaneer conversion.
No 216 Squadron	Honington, Lossiemouth	T.7s (01/07/79–00/00/80)	Used for Buccaneer conversion; absorbed into No 12 Sqn on disbandment.
No 237 OCU	Honington, Lossiemouth	T.7s, T.8s (00/00/71–00/00/94)	Buccaneer conversion.
Harrier Conversion Unit	Wittering	F.G.A.9s (01/01/69–00/00/71)	
Central Flying School	Scampton	F.1s, F.4s, F.6s.	
Notes		1. From the late 1950s it was general practice to include one or two Hunter T.7s on the strength of each of the front-line Hunter squadrons. 2. In addition to the foregoing, Hunters of various marks were from time to time employed by Station Flights on general duties (e.g., communications and liaison).	

FLEET AIR ARM SQUADRONS FLYING HUNTERS AS PRIMARY EQUIPMENT

Unit	Principal location(s)	Equipment	Remarks
738 Naval Air Squadron	Lossiemouth, Brawdy	G.A.11s (00/06/62–08/05/70), T.8s (00/06/62–00/08/70)	Advanced training.
759 Naval Air Squadron	Brawdy	T.8s, T.8Bs (00/07/63–04/12/69), T.8Cs (00/00/64–04/12/69)	Advanced flying training.
764 Naval Air Squadron	Brawdy	T.8s, T.8Bs, (00/12/58–27/07/72), G.A.11s, P.R.11s (00/07/63–27/02/72), T.8Cs (00/00/64–27/07/72)	Advanced training (inc. swept wing conversion).

continued p. 179

COURTESY DAVID HOBBS

Opposite: Two representatives of the Hunter T.7s that did duty with the RAF Buccaneer squadrons at Laarbruch in Germany as unarmed instrument trainers, seen in 1982. WV318, furthest, wears the markings of No XV Squadron; XL616, still in its red, white and blue 'Raspberry Ripple' scheme from its days with the RAE, was at this time assigned to the Station Flight. Above: A Hunter T.8C, XF991, assigned to 759 Naval Air Squadron at Brawdy (as indicated by the tail letters). In its original incarnation as an F.4,

this aircraft had served with No 234 Squadron RAF and No 229 OCU. Below: Another 759 NAS Hunter Mk 8. Like the aircraft depicted in the previous photograph, its 'silver' finish is broken by large 'dayglo' panels. Bottom: XL604 was another T.8 naval trainer—one of the ten examples built as such from the outset—and is here seen in the markings of 764 Squadron, based at Lossiemouth. This aircraft was later converted to T.8M standard and used in conjunction with Sea Harrier training.

COURTESY TONY BUTTLER

COURTESY PHILIP JARRETT

No Major Dramas *Group Captain Tom Eeles BA FRAeS GCVSA*

Throughout the Buccaneer's service in the Fleet Air Arm and the RAF the two-seat Hunter was always to be found alongside its much larger sister. The FAA could never afford the luxury of a two-stick version of any of its front-line combat aircraft, so the two-seat Hunter naturally became the aircraft of choice as the 'trainer' for Scimitar and Sea Vixen pilots.

With the advent of the Buccaneer, with its unique Integrated Flight Instrument System (IFIS), the standard Hunter T.8, the RN's version of the RAF's T.7 but equipped with an airfield-only arrester hook, was clearly unsuitable as a Buccaneer lead-in trainer. Five T.8s were therefore modified to become T.8Bs; this involved the installation of the IFIS display and standby flight instruments in front of the left-hand-seat pilot, the installation of the Airflow Direction Detector (ADD) and the provision of a new AC invertor system to provide 115-volt AC for the IFIS. The five aircraft modified were XF995, XF967, WV322, WW664 and XE664, all of which had originally been built as Hunter F.4s and had been converted to two-seaters later in their lives. WW664 and XE664 were again returned to the manufacturer in 1969–70, this time for conversion to Singaporean T.75s, and saw no further service with the RN or RAF. XF967 was for many years based at the Naval Aircraft Support Unit (NASU), Changi, where it

was occasionally used and abused by Sea Vixen and Buccaneer aircrew disembarked from carriers in the dockyard at Singapore.

I recall doing a night check in it with Lieutenant-Commander Alan Goodenough on 3 May 1967. The Hunter was never designed for night flying and it had no taxi or landing lamp, and I recall that we ended up ignominiously in a monsoon drain while attempting to taxi back to NASU. I often wonder how the aircraft got out to and back from Singapore. The other T.8Bs were looked after by 764 NAS at Lossiemouth and were used almost exclusively by the staff pilots of 736 NAS for pre-Buccaneer Fam 1 general handling and IFIS familiarisation sorties, instrument flying, bouncing strike progression and initial night checks. The other Hunter pilots on 764 NAS rarely flew them as they didn't understand either the IFIS or the electrical system. As I was a QFI on 736 NAS I clocked up many hours in these aircraft.

In 1971, when the RAF formed No 237 (Buccaneer) OCU, 736 NAS disbanded and the remaining T8Bs, '967, '995 and '322, were handed over to the RAF. Apart from a

Below: Personnel of No 237 OCU at Honington, with two of their charges, a Hunter trainer and a Buccaneer. Tom Eeles, Officer Commanding, stands in the foreground.

COURTESY TOM EELES

Above: Hunter T.7 XL613, bearing the later style of crossed cutlasses and mortar board emblem of the OCU on its forward fuselage, photographed up from RAF Honington.

repaint in RAF style camouflage they remained exactly as they had been in RN service. XF967 and '995 went to No 237 OCU and I believe that WV322 went to Laarbruch. However, in 1971 another source of IFIS-equipped Hunters was found. Back in the early 1960s there was no two-seat Lightning available to supplement the early Lightning F.1 and F.2, so the RAF converted some Hunter T.7s to what became known as T.7A standard to support the Lightning fleet until the advent of the Lightning T.4 and 5. These aircraft were identical to the T.8B but had no ADD, and were equipped with ILS. The airframes I can identify were XL568, '614 and '616 and WV318 . All these T.7As were handed over to the Buccaneer force, the majority being used at Honington by the OCU but also by Nos 12, 208 and, for a short while, 216 Squadrons. Eventually, as there was no Safeland Barrier at Honington, all these T.7As were equipped with the airfield-only arrester hook. In spite of being old and single-engined, and considered very much inferior to the Buccaneer, this mixed fleet remained remarkably serviceable and was rarely involved in any major in-flight emergency.

Another infusion of Hunters into the Buccaneer world occurred in 1980, when the Buccaneer fleet was grounded following the loss of Ken Tait's aircraft on 'Red Flag'. In order to keep the boys flying, a mixed fleet of single-seat F.6s and conventional T.7s—mainly aircraft recently retired from Valley—was provided to Honington and Laarbruch. These were flown with great style, even forming the infamous 'Green Marrows' display team (see pages 96–97), until the Buccaneer fleet was recovered to flying status again. However, quite a number of the T.7s stayed on to

provide a lead-in course for pilots trained on the Hawk, before they moved into Buccaneer-specific flying in the T.7As and 8Bs. In 1984, when I came back to the Buccaneer world after a four-year absence, some of these aircraft were still around: XL621 , XL601, WV372, XL573 and XL591 all feature in my log book in this period. With the OCU's departure from Honington to Lossiemouth in October 1984 all these T.7s ended up at Lossie, being used by mainly the OCU but also by Nos 12 and 208. In 1986 we put up a five-aircraft formation display for Lossie's Air Day using T.7s, 7As and 8Bs and I did a limited number of solo aeros displays, mainly using XL591. The Hunter carried on supporting the Buccaneer force to the end. As far as I am aware, none was ever lost in accidents, although I believe that there were a few close calls!

I rather lost contact with the Hunter T.7A/8B fleet after leaving No 237 OCU in 1987. I believe most of them became ground instructional airframes for a while after 1994 when the Buccaneer was withdrawn from service, being used at Scampton and Cranwell. Eventually they became surplus even to this mundane requirement and were disposed of to new civilian owners. One T.8B—XF967, I think—has crashed and been written off in the United States but I am fairly sure that WV318 is flying from Kemble to this day. XF995 may be in South Africa. It is interesting that the SAAF never felt the need for a surrogate Buccaneer trainer like the Hunter: did they ever use anything similar?

In summary, that small fleet of two-seat Hunters performed outstanding service within the Buccaneer force for very many years, without major dramas and with a high level of serviceability. I see from my log book that of my 1,300 hours on Hunters of various marks, nearly 900 were on T.7As and 8Bs, compared with just over 2,000 hours on the Buccaneer. I have fond memories of the Hunter.

COURTESY TOM EELES

Through the Mirrors *Captain John Myers FRAeS*

I was the lantern-jawed, steely-eyed leader of the illustrious 'Green Marrows', famous for their airborne prowess and daring and also their ability to dispose of large quantities of beer in a remarkably short time. This magnificent team was assembled in order to add excitement and lustre to the RAF Honington Open Day held on 7 June 1980. The team first of all led a flypast of fourteen Hunters prior to breaking away and thrilling the assembled multitudes to a stunning display of formation flying. We not only flew in 'Box' but also 'Swan' and 'Line Astern'. Oh, the versatility and diversity—sheer poetry!

I had always thought of the graceful Hunter as a jet-powered, swept-wing Spitfire, and not a bit like the Buccaneer! The reason behind this display was of course the sad grounding of the mighty Banana Bomber after the tragic wing-loss accident in Nevada. It was decided that a Station morale booster was required, and to help we were to fly the majority of our Hunters during the Open Day. The formation lead ship was WV322, a two-seat Hunter with a navigator in the right-hand seat. The Nav was none other than one of our tame Americans, Scott Bergren, at that time a mere Major but later to rise to exalted positions within the US Air Force—despite his exposure to the hooligan element within the Buccaneer force. Having a navigator on board had many benefits, not least of which was that there was someone to blame should it all go wrong. The Number Two ship was flown by yet another semi-tame American, Ken 'Alleycat' Alley, who went on to fly some great 'hot' aircraft and have a highly successful career in the USAF despite his involvement with the Buccaneer and its solo display crew for two years. The other wing was balanced in the Number Three slot by a great British gentleman (when he was sober), Keith 'Hargs' Hargreaves. He having had the distinction of trying to teach me how to fly a Gnat in 1971, it was, for me, 'get your own back' time! The Number Four slot was hung on to by the Boss, Wing Commander Phil Wilkinson, or 'Sir' to the rest of us. I have no idea why he wanted to fly the slot: maybe he thought it would keep him out of trouble

should the bird dirt hit the propeller! Not only did he hang on for grim death in there but I believe he also talked the Station Commander into authorising the whole shebang.

One thing that sticks in my memory was how we solved the problem of timing a mass engine start. That was done by having the huge stadium lights, facing us across the ramp, switched *off*. Prior to this our JEngO swept down the line of Hunters in the back of a Land Rover, rather like a demented dictator, getting a thumbs up from each of the pilots (and no doubt some other unofficial signals) that they were ready to go. He then went and switched the lights off. Why off and not on? Because the sodium lights came on *slowly*, and with lots of flickering, giving all the excuses in the world for a screwed-up and staggered start.

I must admit that, while flying in the lead ship, it was a fantastic sight to see all those aircraft in formation, even if it was through the mirrors. I remembered that moment and view again, when on 26 March 1994 Nigel Huckins led the final Diamond Nine-ship of Buccaneers at Lossiemouth.

Above: RAF Honington Hunter aircrew return from a sortie. The two aircraft at right have their unit markings set on a red background; the third aircraft in line is displaying the fox insignia of No 12 Squadron.
Below: Very few photographs of the illustrious 'Green Marrows' exist, but this is one of them. Sheer poetry!

COURTESY JOHN MYERS

FLEET AIR ARM SQUADRONS FLYING HUNTERS AS PARTIAL EQUIPMENT

Unit	Principal location(s)	Equipment	Remarks
899 Naval Air Squadron	Yeovilton	T.8Ms (00/00/81–00/00/82)	Sea Harrier training programme.
736 Naval Air Squadron	Lossiemouth	T.8s (00/07/58–00/11/58)	Naval Air Fighter and Strike School.
700B Flight	Lossiemouth	T.8s (09/04/65–00/05/65)	Buccaneer training unit.
700Y Flight	Yeovilton	T.8s (04/11/58–01/01/59)	Sea Vixen training unit.
700Z Flight	Lossiemouth	T.8s (07/05/61–00/07/61), T.8Bs (00/07/61–00/12/62)	Buccaneer training unit.

Notes

1. *In addition to the foregoing, Hunters were from time to time employed by Station Flights (Hal Far, Yeovilton) for general duties and by other Royal Navy establishments (for example, the Naval Flying Standards Flight).*

continued p.182

Below: A Hunter G.A.11 serving with the Fleet Requirements Unit. Though flying aircraft with military markings, the FRU and its successor organisations were manned by civilians.

Bottom: A G.A.11 from the Fleet Requirements and Air Direction Training Unit and based at RNAS Yeovilton. The FRADTU (later, more simply, FRADU) operated its Hunters well into the 1990s.

179

Standards! Standards! *Commander Keith Harris OBE*

As an 'A' Category flying instructor I flew with the Royal Navy's Naval Flying Standards Flight (NFSF, otherwise known as 'The Trappers'!), at RNAS Yeovilton, in the late 1960s and, after much time at sea, I returned in the 1970s as its Commanding Officer. During the early days at Yeovilton the Hunters—two-seat T.8Cs (with arrester hooks), single-seat GA.11s and, later, the T.8M (Sea Harrier avionics version)—were maintained by RN personnel (including many Wren mechanics). Later, in the early 1970s, Airwork Ltd took over this maintenance task as part of their contract to provide tracking and target practice for the Fleet in home waters as the Fleet Requirements and Air Development Unit. Six of the Hunter fleet at Yeovilton were specifically allocated to the RN Flying Standards Flight, NFSF being responsible for all RN fixed-wing pilot standards, including those for the civilian Airwork/FRADU personnel. Additionally, RN pilots occasionally flew fleet requirements sorties; and since no dual-control Buccaneer or Phantom was available, the Hunter was used as the test aircraft for the Standards Squadron and for instrument flying and rating testing for both the Buccaneer and Phantom, and for the Hunter itself.

Needless to say, the Hunter was a splendid aircraft to fly and the two-seat version provided a superb training platform—indeed, it was the 'workhorse' for Naval Flying and Instrument Flying Standards over many years. On one occasion RN Standards staff tested all the front-line RAF Hunter pilots of No 1 Squadron (UK Echelon) to assess their standards of flying with regard to the Squadron becoming the first unit to convert to the new Harrier aircraft. As another example of the work, the Standards squadron developed a special flight envelope that best simulated the characteristics of the Phantom, involving a 2,000-foot acceleration to 520 knots, followed by a 45-degree climb and push-over, etc. (This never fooled anyone!)

In the early 1970s, special rules were introduced to register Hunter Qualifications, laying down specific regular practice requirements for Hunter currency and captaincy. These rules were implemented to eliminate the tendency of disembarked pilots to sign for Hunters on training flights on their Phantom or Buccaneer 'ticket' whilst being significantly out of practice on the Hunter. A very real danger—and the cause of a number of accidents—was engine failure. However, while a single or double engine failure in a twin jet like the Buccaneer and Phantom dictated either a well-rehearsed single-engine landing or aircrew ejection, engine failure in a Hunter presented the pilot with the most demanding challenge—that of a 'dead stick' (and manual-control) forced landing. The level of skill required to guarantee success in such an event could best be ensured only by those with good practice on the type.

Occasionally, Hunters were borrowed from the Airwork allocation, and, likewise, Standards pilots might fly sorties to supplement FRADU tasking, while Standards pilots (and, latterly, those from FRADU), also conducted familiarisation flights for the Junior Officers' Air Course (JOAC). Standards instructors also flew the Hunters that participated in solo air displays. Hunters were used in the Portland Training Programme, and typically in the 'Thursday Wars', in which, following the introduction of the Falcon aircraft, Hunters would fly in close formation with the latter and 'launch' at a specified range from targets and descend to sea level in order to simulate Exocet missiles. Great fun! With the introduction of the Sea Harrier and Harrier T.4 into the Royal Navy, the need for the Hunters was virtually eliminated, although they continued in service with FRADU for a time afterwards.

I had one particularly 'hairy moment'. The sortie was in the two-seater WW661, and it was to introduce a young officer to the 'RN Air' world. I remember the short briefing I gave him just prior to taking off. I said that I was aware that his head would be buzzing with all the comprehensive instructions he had just received in the ejection-seat training session. I told him not to dwell on the detail but to pull the top handle without hesitation if I was to order him to eject—and that he would be left in no doubt in that regard. I then said, 'Now sit back and enjoy the ride.'

Below: Hunter T.8 trainer XL603, which served with the NFSF for a period in the late 1970s. The arrester hook and tail parachute housing can clearly be seen. This aircraft was also later converted to T.8M standard to serve as a trainer for the Sea Harrier programme.

COURTESY PHILIP JARRETT

Right: The T.8M conversion involved a number of changes in equipment and, outwardly, had a remodelled nose to accommodate the Blue Fox radar scanner that was fitted to the early Sea Harriers. In this form, XL603 re-entered service in 1980 with the Royal Aircraft Establishment at Bedford and was subsequently transferred to 899 (Sea Harrier) Squadron at RNAS Yeovilton.

Below right: Hunter Mk 11 WV381 being recovered from the water after overrunning the short runway at RNAS Lee-on-Solent; the aircraft was taking off on its delivery flight to Airwork on 1 November 1972 following an upgrade. The pilot, Lieutenant Mike Sharp, ejected safely.

COURTESY PHILIP JARRETT

The sortie had gone well and I finished up with a radar-controlled approach and roller landing. After lifting off at full power I selected 'Undercarriage up', but as the last wheel 'clunked' home there was a loud *whooompf* accompanied by heavy vibration and a complete loss of thrust. It was obvious to me that the aircraft had suffered catastrophic engine failure, and whilst I was in good practice at turning back to the runway, in this instance, with little height and speed, such an option was out of the question. I could only lower the nose to prevent an immediate stall and order my student to 'Eject! Eject!' Thankfully, he did so 'without hesitation'. The heavy canopy jettisoned and, one second later away, he went on his Type 4B Martin Baker seat. I then pulled my top handle and, again one (very long!) second later, I was gunned out of the aircraft. I just had time to see the aircraft dropping down, spewing fine smoke or flame, before I had to lift my legs over some power lines prior to somewhat inelegantly hitting a ploughed field. The student was already up and running towards me as I untangled my parachute.

Later I was only too pleased to visit the ejection-seat servicing bay to thank the riggers for their excellent and conscientious work in keeping the equipment in first class working order. In due course I was also able to personally thank Sir James Martin for his invention!

COURTESY TONY BUTTLER

Below: 'Thursday Wars': two Airwork Hunter Mk 11s about to masquerade as Exocet missiles, accompanied by a Dassault Falcon 20 electronic warfare training aircraft operated by FR Aviation.

COURTESY PHILIP JARRETT

GOVERNMENT AND CIVILIAN ESTABLISHMENTS FLYING HUNTERS

Unit	Principal location(s)	Equipment	Remarks
Aeroplane & Armament Experimental Establishment	Boscombe Down	Various marks 1953–1980s	Tests and trials.
Royal Aircraft Establishment	Farnborough, Bedford	Various marks 1953–1980s.	Tests and trials.
Empire Test Pilots' School	Farnborough	F.1s, F.4s, F.6s, T.7s at various times	Test-flying.
Air Direction Training Unit	Yeovilton	G.A.11s (00/09/72–30/11/72), T.8s (00/06/70–30/11/72)	Absorbed into Fleet Requirements and Air Direction Unit 01/12/72. Managed by Airwork Services.
Fleet Requirements Unit	Hurn, Yeovilton	G.A.11s (00/09/72–30/11/72), T.8s (00/06/70–30/11/72)	Absorbed into Fleet Requirements and Air Direction Unit 01/12/72. Managed by Airwork Services.
Fleet Requirements and Air Direction	Yeovilton	G.A.11s (01/12/72–00/05/95), T.8s (01/12/72–00/05/95)	Formed 01/12/72 by amalgamation of ADTU and FRU. Managed by Airwork Services and latterly by FR Aviation.

COURTESY TONY BUTTLER

Opposite, upper: Hunter T.7 XL621 while serving with the Royal Aircraft Establishment. This aircraft is now on permanent display at Dunsfold.
Opposite, lower: One particularly unusual Hunter was F.6 XE601, which was used for a variety of tasks by the Aeroplane & Armament Experimental Establishment. As depicted it is equipped with 'Porton tanks' and spraying equipment in conjunction with investigations into biological warfare.
Above: F. Mk 6 XE656 in service with No 229 OCU. This Hunter has also been preserved, and now resides in Germany.

Below: Another of the Hunter T.7 trainers that served in the Buccaneer squadrons in an auxiliary capacity, this is WV318 with its squadron number clearly proclaimed on the tailfin.
Bottom: Fresh from No 4 Flying Training School and retaining the standard training scheme of the day, T.7 XL600 is seen serving with No 16 Squadron (notice the 'Saint' emblem on the fin) in an emergency capacity during the temporary grounding of the Buccaneer fleet that was brought about by a flying accident in the United States in February 1980.

GÜNTHER KIPP, COURTESY ROGER LINDSAY

WILFRIED ZETSCHE, COURTESY ROGER LINDSAY

Above: A Fleet Air Arm Hunter T.8 carrying, unusually, the station code for RNAS Hal Far, Malta, on its fin while operating as a component of the Fleet Requirements Unit based there.

Below: The immaculately presented 'Admiral's Barge' XE665, the second of three T.8s to be so finished (successively, not simultaneously), based at Yeovilton and utilised by Flag Officer Flying Training in the mid-1960s in the course of his duties.

Bottom: Another handsomely painted Hunter trainer, this time a T.7, XL563, used for a period in this finish by the Institute of Aviation Medicine, a world-renowned RAF facility based at Farnborough.

184

HUNTER COLOURS

Royal Air Force, Royal Navy and British Government Establishments

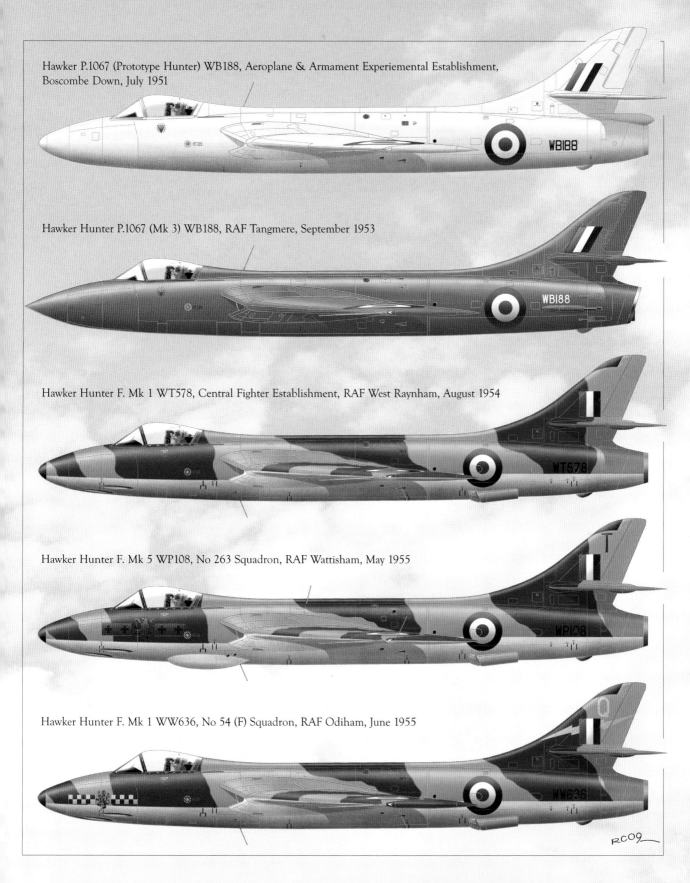

Hawker P.1067 (Prototype Hunter) WB188, Aeroplane & Armament Experiemental Establishment, Boscombe Down, July 1951

Hawker Hunter P.1067 (Mk 3) WB188, RAF Tangmere, September 1953

Hawker Hunter F. Mk 1 WT578, Central Fighter Establishment, RAF West Raynham, August 1954

Hawker Hunter F. Mk 5 WP108, No 263 Squadron, RAF Wattisham, May 1955

Hawker Hunter F. Mk 1 WW636, No 54 (F) Squadron, RAF Odiham, June 1955

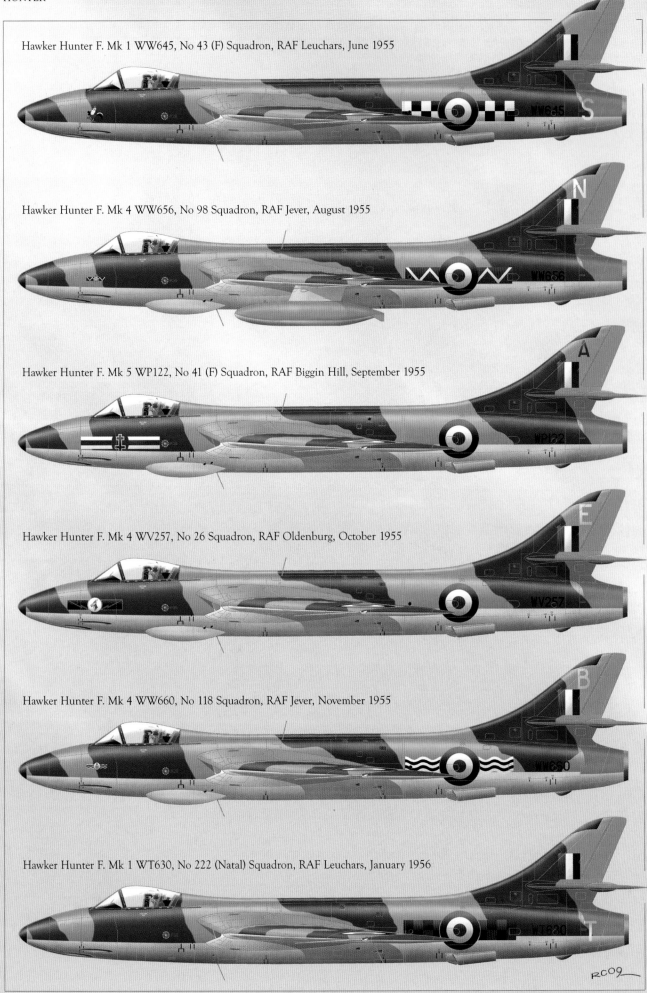

Hawker Hunter F. Mk 1 WW645, No 43 (F) Squadron, RAF Leuchars, June 1955

Hawker Hunter F. Mk 4 WW656, No 98 Squadron, RAF Jever, August 1955

Hawker Hunter F. Mk 5 WP122, No 41 (F) Squadron, RAF Biggin Hill, September 1955

Hawker Hunter F. Mk 4 WV257, No 26 Squadron, RAF Oldenburg, October 1955

Hawker Hunter F. Mk 4 WW660, No 118 Squadron, RAF Jever, November 1955

Hawker Hunter F. Mk 1 WT630, No 222 (Natal) Squadron, RAF Leuchars, January 1956

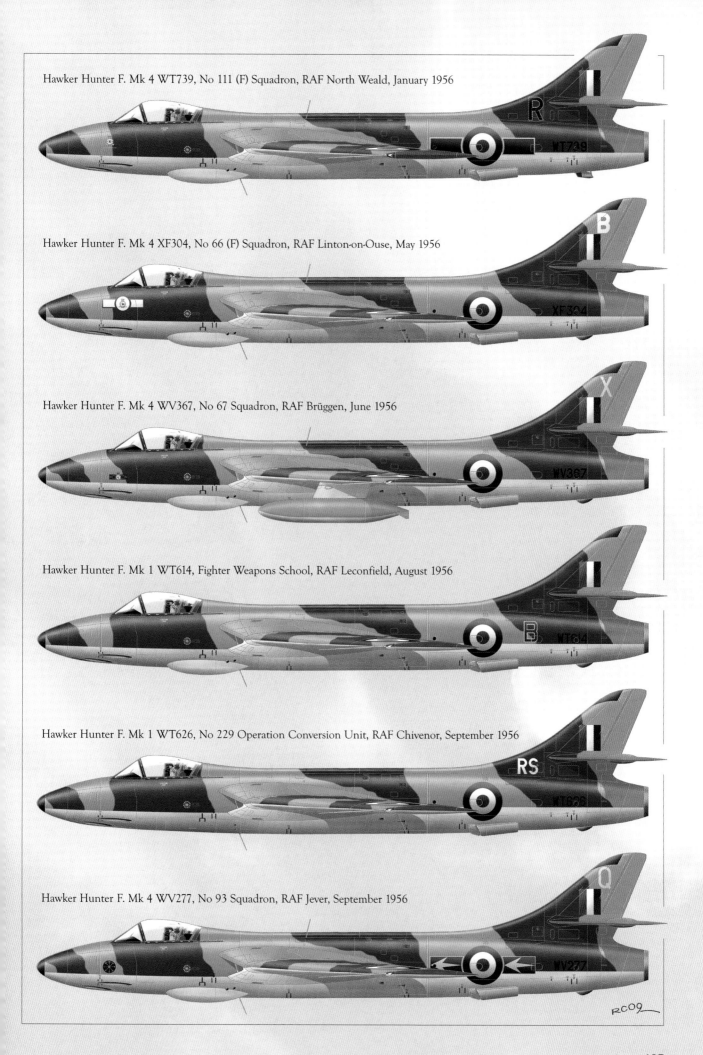

Hawker Hunter F. Mk 4 WT739, No 111 (F) Squadron, RAF North Weald, January 1956

Hawker Hunter F. Mk 4 XF304, No 66 (F) Squadron, RAF Linton-on-Ouse, May 1956

Hawker Hunter F. Mk 4 WV367, No 67 Squadron, RAF Brüggen, June 1956

Hawker Hunter F. Mk 1 WT614, Fighter Weapons School, RAF Leconfield, August 1956

Hawker Hunter F. Mk 1 WT626, No 229 Operation Conversion Unit, RAF Chivenor, September 1956

Hawker Hunter F. Mk 4 WV277, No 93 Squadron, RAF Jever, September 1956

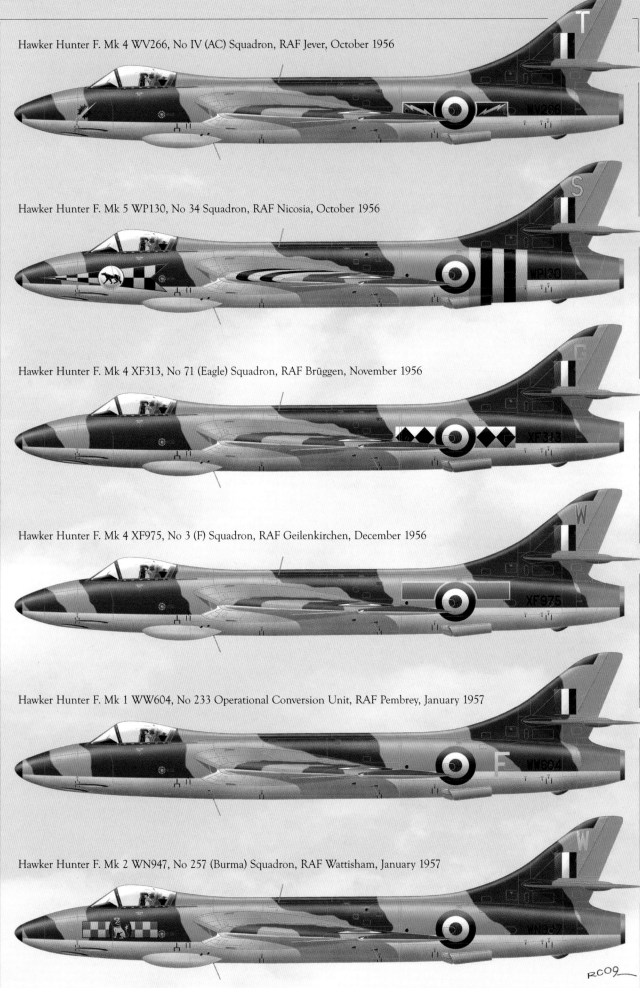

Hawker Hunter F. Mk 4 WV266, No IV (AC) Squadron, RAF Jever, October 1956

Hawker Hunter F. Mk 5 WP130, No 34 Squadron, RAF Nicosia, October 1956

Hawker Hunter F. Mk 4 XF313, No 71 (Eagle) Squadron, RAF Brüggen, November 1956

Hawker Hunter F. Mk 4 XF975, No 3 (F) Squadron, RAF Geilenkirchen, December 1956

Hawker Hunter F. Mk 1 WW604, No 233 Operational Conversion Unit, RAF Pembrey, January 1957

Hawker Hunter F. Mk 2 WN947, No 257 (Burma) Squadron, RAF Wattisham, January 1957

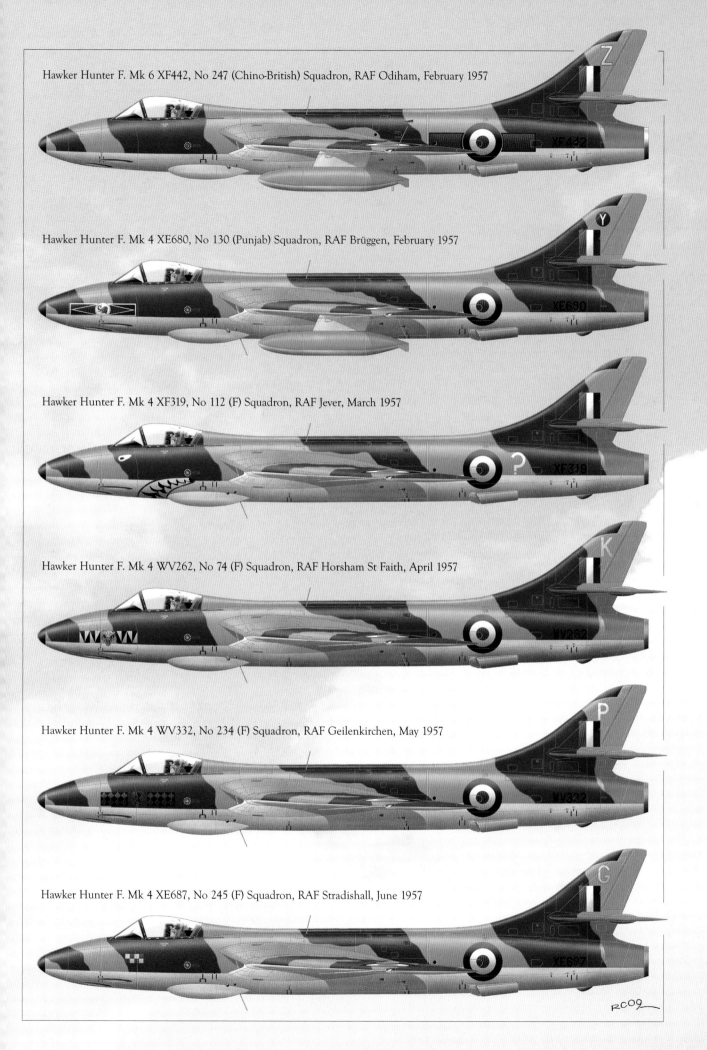

Hawker Hunter F. Mk 6 XF442, No 247 (Chino-British) Squadron, RAF Odiham, February 1957

Hawker Hunter F. Mk 4 XE680, No 130 (Punjab) Squadron, RAF Brüggen, February 1957

Hawker Hunter F. Mk 4 XF319, No 112 (F) Squadron, RAF Jever, March 1957

Hawker Hunter F. Mk 4 WV262, No 74 (F) Squadron, RAF Horsham St Faith, April 1957

Hawker Hunter F. Mk 4 WV332, No 234 (F) Squadron, RAF Geilenkirchen, May 1957

Hawker Hunter F. Mk 4 XE687, No 245 (F) Squadron, RAF Stradishall, June 1957

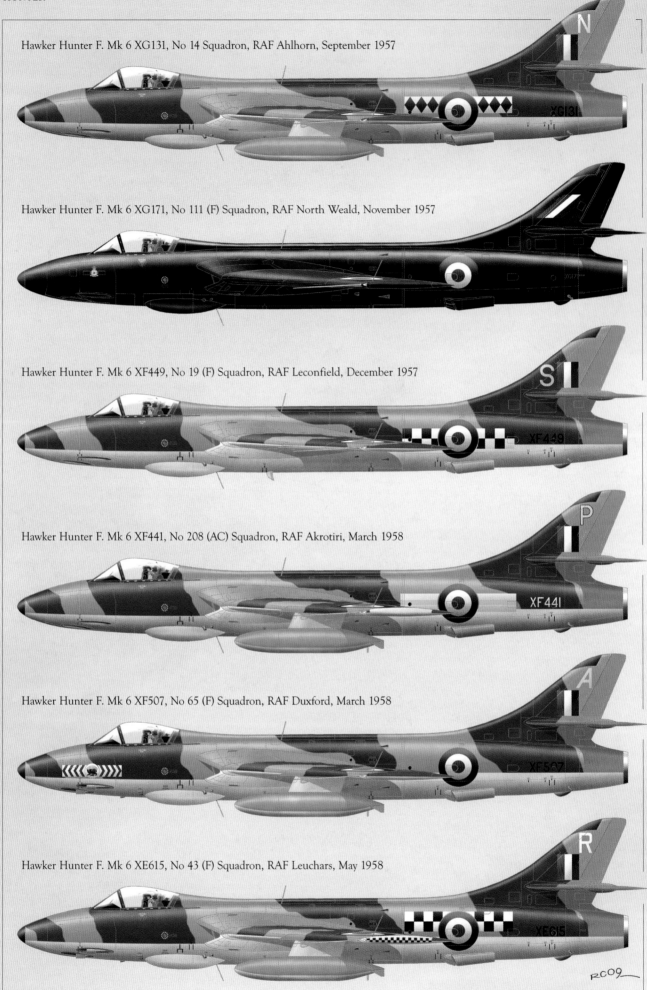

Hawker Hunter F. Mk 6 XG131, No 14 Squadron, RAF Ahlhorn, September 1957

Hawker Hunter F. Mk 6 XG171, No 111 (F) Squadron, RAF North Weald, November 1957

Hawker Hunter F. Mk 6 XF449, No 19 (F) Squadron, RAF Leconfield, December 1957

Hawker Hunter F. Mk 6 XF441, No 208 (AC) Squadron, RAF Akrotiri, March 1958

Hawker Hunter F. Mk 6 XF507, No 65 (F) Squadron, RAF Duxford, March 1958

Hawker Hunter F. Mk 6 XE615, No 43 (F) Squadron, RAF Leuchars, May 1958

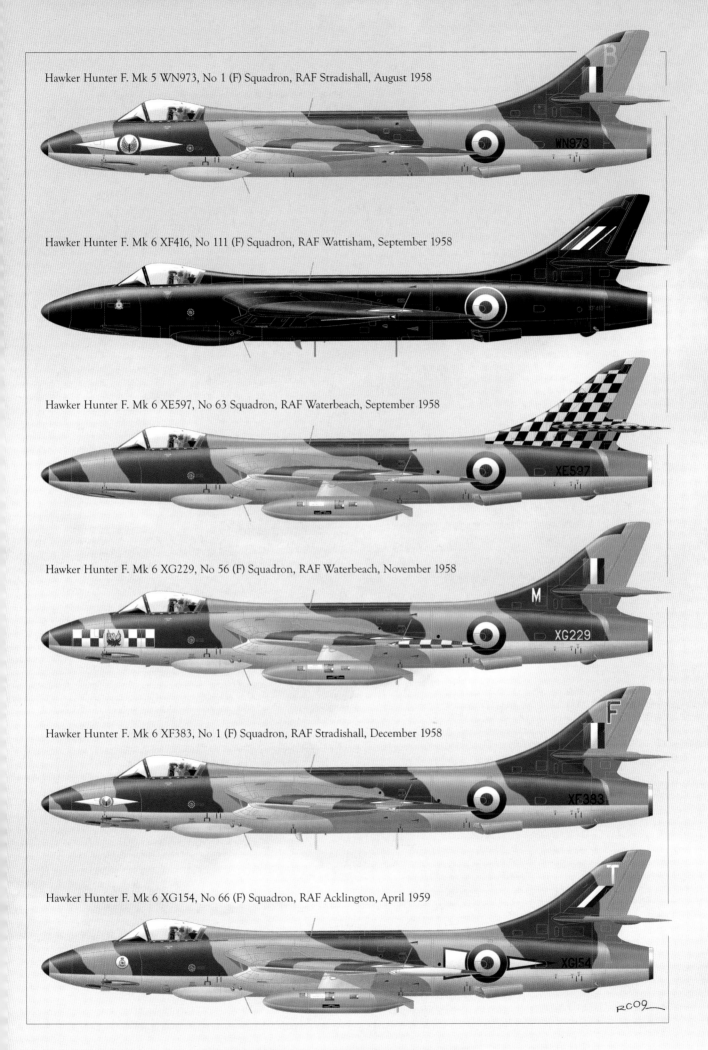

Hawker Hunter F. Mk 5 WN973, No 1 (F) Squadron, RAF Stradishall, August 1958

Hawker Hunter F. Mk 6 XF416, No 111 (F) Squadron, RAF Wattisham, September 1958

Hawker Hunter F. Mk 6 XE597, No 63 Squadron, RAF Waterbeach, September 1958

Hawker Hunter F. Mk 6 XG229, No 56 (F) Squadron, RAF Waterbeach, November 1958

Hawker Hunter F. Mk 6 XF383, No 1 (F) Squadron, RAF Stradishall, December 1958

Hawker Hunter F. Mk 6 XG154, No 66 (F) Squadron, RAF Acklington, April 1959

FLOWN BY THE AUTHOR

HAWKER HUNTER F. Mk 2

WN898, No 257 (Burma) Squadron, RAF Wattisham, October 1956

RC09

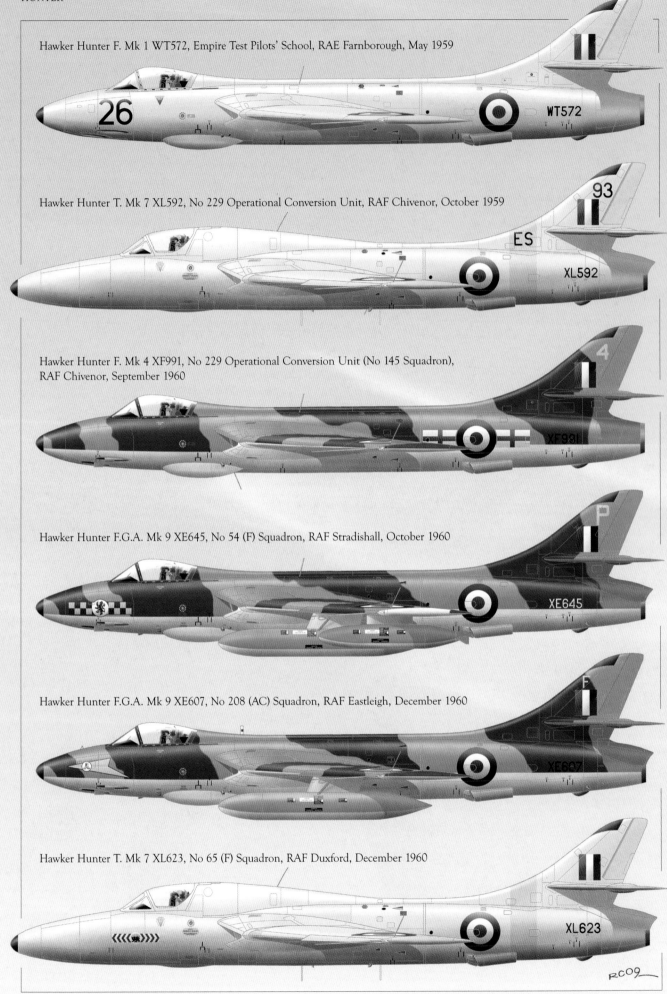

Hawker Hunter F. Mk 1 WT572, Empire Test Pilots' School, RAE Farnborough, May 1959

Hawker Hunter T. Mk 7 XL592, No 229 Operational Conversion Unit, RAF Chivenor, October 1959

Hawker Hunter F. Mk 4 XF991, No 229 Operational Conversion Unit (No 145 Squadron), RAF Chivenor, September 1960

Hawker Hunter F.G.A. Mk 9 XE645, No 54 (F) Squadron, RAF Stradishall, October 1960

Hawker Hunter F.G.A. Mk 9 XE607, No 208 (AC) Squadron, RAF Eastleigh, December 1960

Hawker Hunter T. Mk 7 XL623, No 65 (F) Squadron, RAF Duxford, December 1960

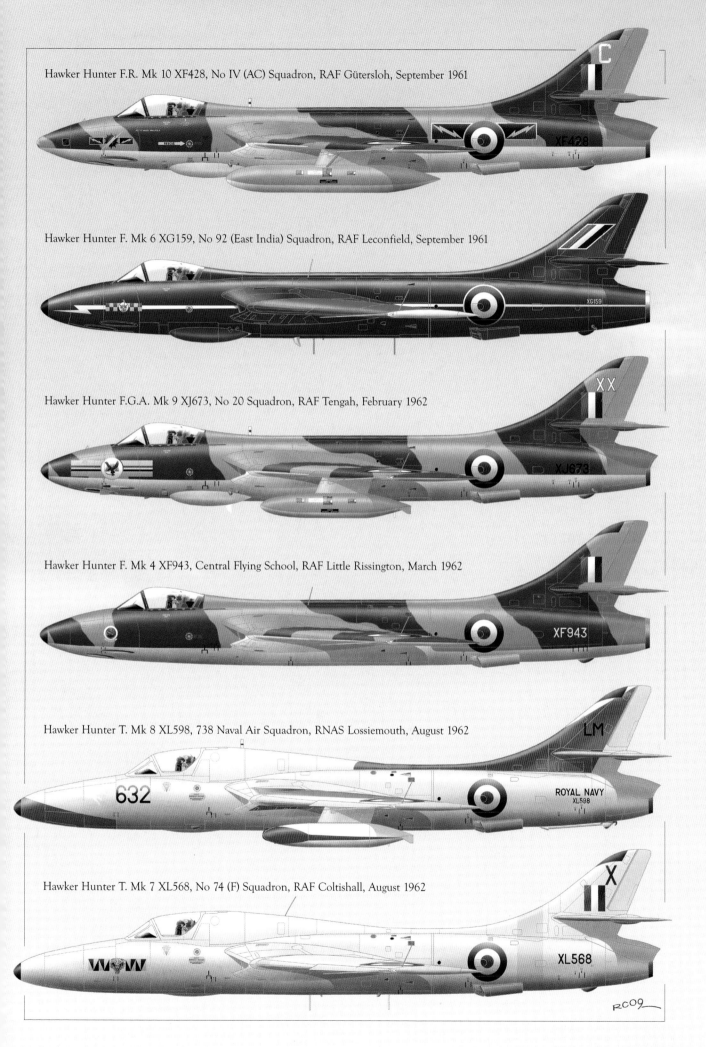

Hawker Hunter F.R. Mk 10 XF428, No IV (AC) Squadron, RAF Gütersloh, September 1961

Hawker Hunter F. Mk 6 XG159, No 92 (East India) Squadron, RAF Leconfield, September 1961

Hawker Hunter F.G.A. Mk 9 XJ673, No 20 Squadron, RAF Tengah, February 1962

Hawker Hunter F. Mk 4 XF943, Central Flying School, RAF Little Rissington, March 1962

Hawker Hunter T. Mk 8 XL598, 738 Naval Air Squadron, RNAS Lossiemouth, August 1962

Hawker Hunter T. Mk 7 XL568, No 74 (F) Squadron, RAF Coltishall, August 1962

RC09

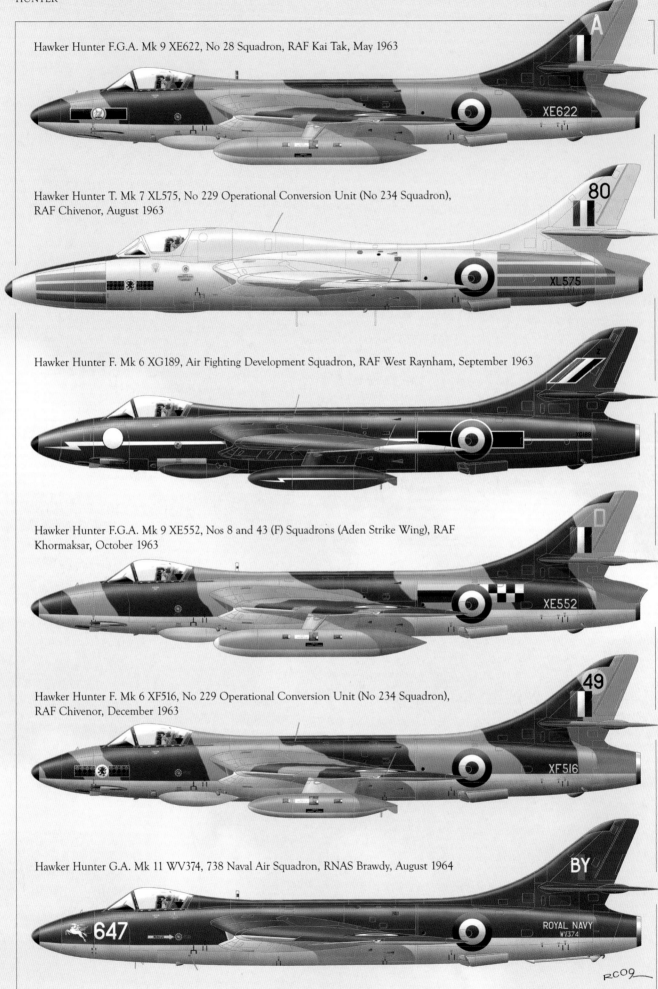

Hawker Hunter F.G.A. Mk 9 XE622, No 28 Squadron, RAF Kai Tak, May 1963

Hawker Hunter T. Mk 7 XL575, No 229 Operational Conversion Unit (No 234 Squadron),
RAF Chivenor, August 1963

Hawker Hunter F. Mk 6 XG189, Air Fighting Development Squadron, RAF West Raynham, September 1963

Hawker Hunter F.G.A. Mk 9 XE552, Nos 8 and 43 (F) Squadrons (Aden Strike Wing), RAF
Khormaksar, October 1963

Hawker Hunter F. Mk 6 XF516, No 229 Operational Conversion Unit (No 234 Squadron),
RAF Chivenor, December 1963

Hawker Hunter G.A. Mk 11 WV374, 738 Naval Air Squadron, RNAS Brawdy, August 1964

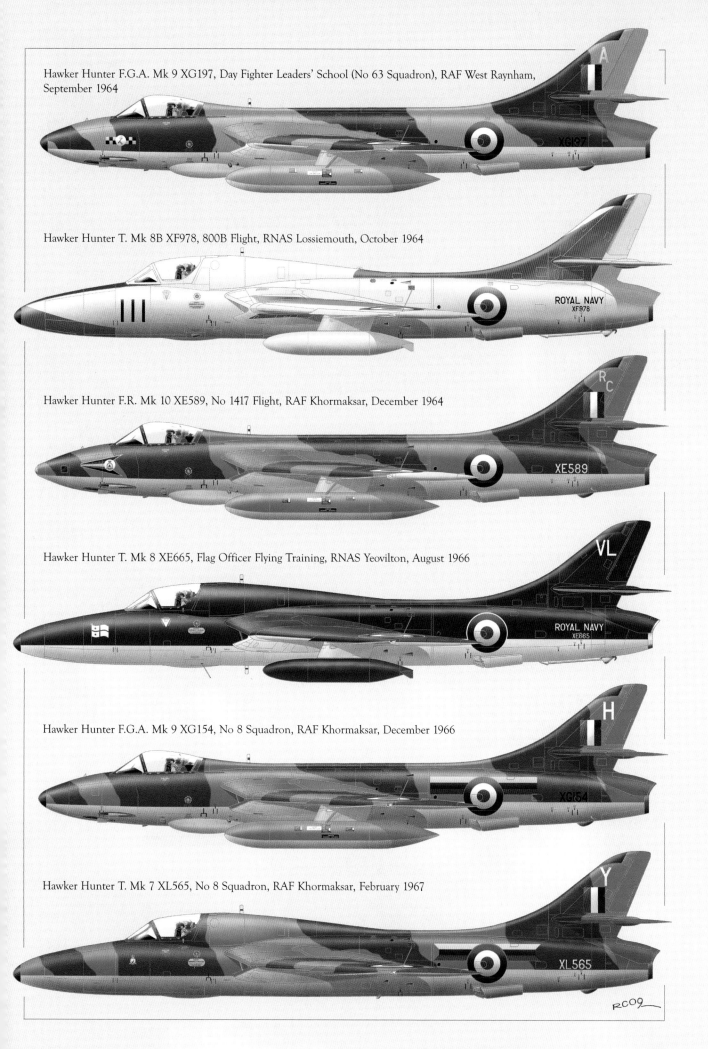

Hawker Hunter F.G.A. Mk 9 XG197, Day Fighter Leaders' School (No 63 Squadron), RAF West Raynham,
September 1964

Hawker Hunter T. Mk 8B XF978, 800B Flight, RNAS Lossiemouth, October 1964

Hawker Hunter F.R. Mk 10 XE589, No 1417 Flight, RAF Khormaksar, December 1964

Hawker Hunter T. Mk 8 XE665, Flag Officer Flying Training, RNAS Yeovilton, August 1966

Hawker Hunter F.G.A. Mk 9 XG154, No 8 Squadron, RAF Khormaksar, December 1966

Hawker Hunter T. Mk 7 XL565, No 8 Squadron, RAF Khormaksar, February 1967

Hawker Hunter T. Mk 7 WV372, No II (AC) Squadron, RAF Brüggen, January 1970

Hawker Hunter P.R. Mk 11 XE689, 764 Naval Air Squadron, RNAS Lossiemouth, May 1970

Hawker Hunter F.R. Mk 10 XE585, No II (AC) Squadron, RAF Brüggen, July 1970

Hawker Hunter T. Mk 8C WV396, Station Flight, RNAS Yeovilton, June 1971

Hawker Hunter T. Mk 8 WT799, Fleet Requirements Unit, RNAS Yeovilton, July 1973

Hawker Hunter F.G.A. Mk 9 XK137, No 45 Squadron, RAF Wittering, May 1974

RC09

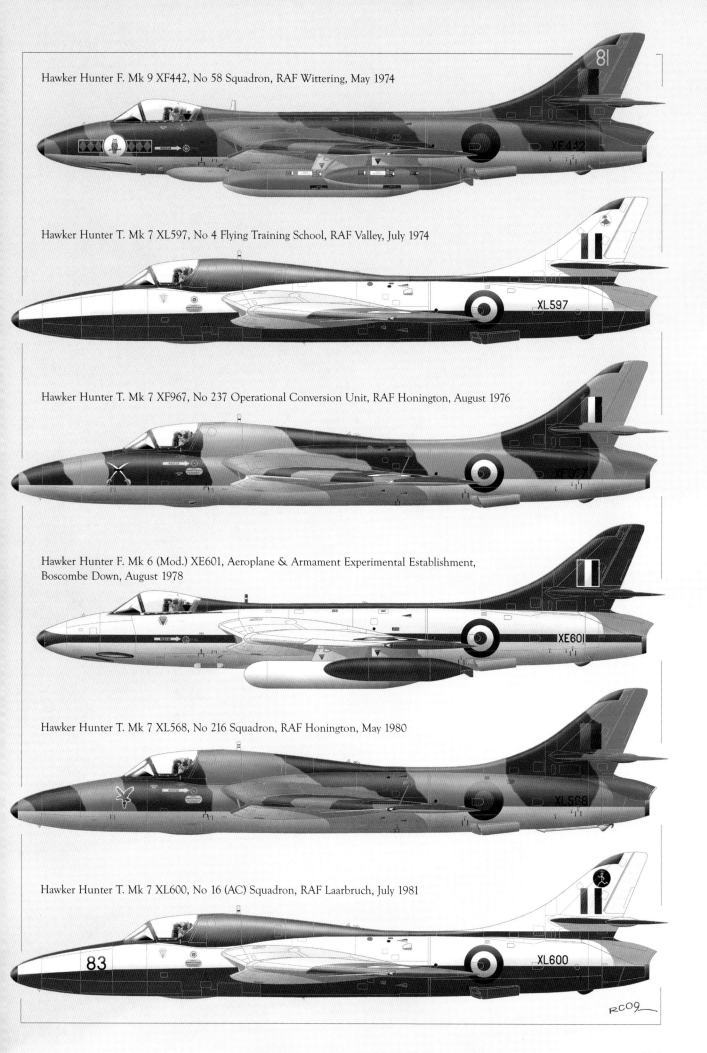

Hawker Hunter F. Mk 9 XF442, No 58 Squadron, RAF Wittering, May 1974

Hawker Hunter T. Mk 7 XL597, No 4 Flying Training School, RAF Valley, July 1974

Hawker Hunter T. Mk 7 XF967, No 237 Operational Conversion Unit, RAF Honington, August 1976

Hawker Hunter F. Mk 6 (Mod.) XE601, Aeroplane & Armament Experimental Establishment, Boscombe Down, August 1978

Hawker Hunter T. Mk 7 XL568, No 216 Squadron, RAF Honington, May 1980

Hawker Hunter T. Mk 7 XL600, No 16 (AC) Squadron, RAF Laarbruch, July 1981

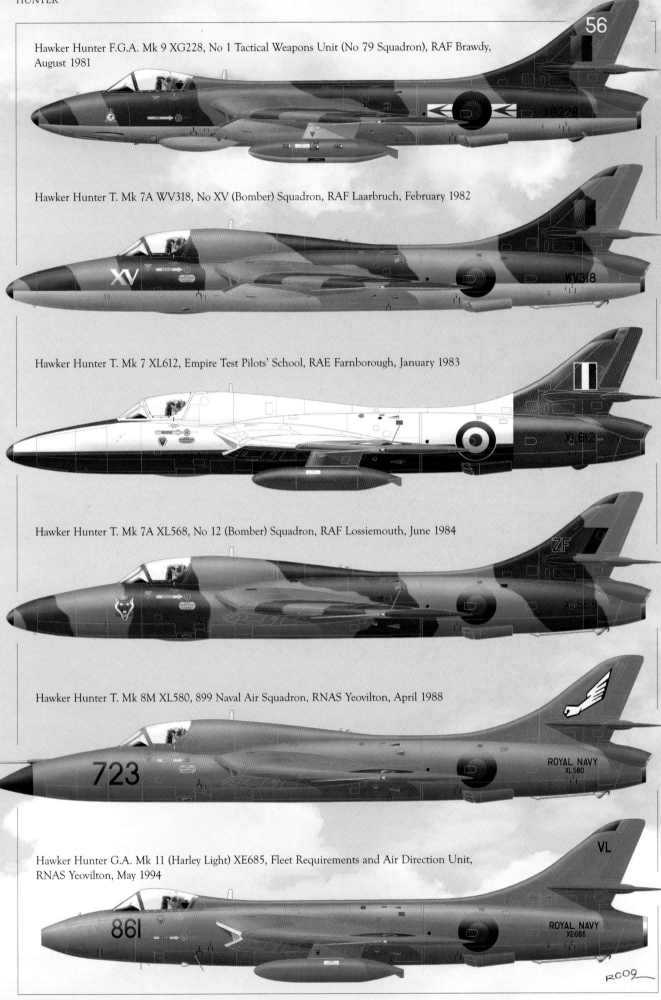

Hawker Hunter F.G.A. Mk 9 XG228, No 1 Tactical Weapons Unit (No 79 Squadron), RAF Brawdy, August 1981

Hawker Hunter T. Mk 7A WV318, No XV (Bomber) Squadron, RAF Laarbruch, February 1982

Hawker Hunter T. Mk 7 XL612, Empire Test Pilots' School, RAE Farnborough, January 1983

Hawker Hunter T. Mk 7A XL568, No 12 (Bomber) Squadron, RAF Lossiemouth, June 1984

Hawker Hunter T. Mk 8M XL580, 899 Naval Air Squadron, RNAS Yeovilton, April 1988

Hawker Hunter G.A. Mk 11 (Harley Light) XE685, Fleet Requirements and Air Direction Unit, RNAS Yeovilton, May 1994